The Children of God

There is Life after the Cult

Faye Thomas, M.Div.

Strategic Book Publishing and Rights Co.

Book Design/Layout by Kalpart. Visit www.kalpart.com

Strategic Book Publishing and Rights Co.
12620 FM 1960, Suite A4-507
Houston, TX 77065
www.sbpra.com

ISBN: 978-1-60860-528-6

Dedication

I dedicate this book to my beloved mother, the late Carrie Johnson, and to her sister Silvia. My aunt and my eldest sister, Josephine, raised me when my mother died. I was only thirteen years old. Aunt Silvia taught me that though my mother's death was an emotionally traumatic experience, I still had my full life ahead of me. It was imperative that I learn to love the life that God had called me to live.

Aunt Silvia often said, "If you are one minute late, you might as well be one hour late." She insisted that I live my life with discipline and order. These concepts became vitally important as I grew to spiritual maturity.

I trust that through reading this book my family, whom I hold dear, would understand the extent to which I was deceived into believing the doctrines of the Children of God. Through confronting my mistakes, I received God's forgiveness. Now, I am compelled to bestow my life to helping others to be set free from all that binds them.

Table of Contents

Acknowledgements

I am most grateful to the late Dr. Margaret Pittman, who provided the seed money (one million dollars) to Wesley Theological Seminary, Washington, DC, around 1990, for the Urban Ministry program. Her gift enabled me to obtain a two-year scholarship to attend the seminary. I participated in the Master of Divinity three-year program in the Urban Ministry track at the school. Dr. Pittman was responsible for making the flu vaccine available to Americans.

Dr. Pittman was a trusted friend and a great encouragement to me whenever we had lunch at the student lounge at Wesley Seminary. At the time, I was a candidate for Ordained Ministry in the United Methodist Church.

Dr. Pittman's tenacity about changing the direction of the Seminary by offering a curriculum in spiritual gifts was the driving force that encouraged me to work (1992-1994) with the Academic Dean, Dr. Henry Kilmore, and the Rev. Dr. Art Thomas, as well as other notable faculty members. We labored tenaciously to institute three major courses in spiritual gifts at the Wesley Theological Seminary: 1) Holiness and Pentecostal Movements; 2) Spiritual Gifts for Congregational Ministry; and 3) The Healing Ministry of the Church.

I am obliged to the Rev. Dawn Burrell, Senior Pastor of New Creations Church and Ministries, Lanham, MD. She has been a sounding board during the years that we have supported one another in ministry. Also, Pastor Burrell introduced me to the Full Gospel Baptist Church Fellowship (FGBCF) in July 2004, when I became an individual member. I remained a member of the Fellowship until December 2009. During that time, Bishop Michael V. Kelsey, Sr. was the State Bishop. Also, during that time, Bishop Paul S. Morton, Sr. was the reigning International Bishop for the FGBCF.

I give special thanks to Bishop Kelsey for the pastoral training classes conducted at the New Samaritan Baptist Church, Washington, D.C. The FGBCF was a strong support system to augment the growth of the Church on the Hill and the National Network of Christian Men & Women (NNCMW).

The Rev. Dr. James E. Jordan of Refreshing Spring C.O.G.I.C., Riverdale, MD, is a buttress of support. A trusted friend, his vision and perseverance in the ministry continues to inspire me. I stand confident that I should continue to pursue my calling as Senior Pastor of the Church on the Hill and National President of the National Network (NNCMW).

Special thanks to Mr. Scott Lawrence at the Adventist Community Services of Greater Washington in Silver Spring, MD, for his expert Information Technology services. He was our Church on the Hill IT specialist while I was completing the initial editing process of this book.

I offer my sincere gratitude to my grown son, Rafael, who has been a strong spiritual influence in my life.

Rafael's leadership when the Church on the Hill was launched in November 1995 is unprecedented! To date, his remarkable support and sound insights, particularly in the most difficult of circumstances, is deeply appreciated. His intuitive suggestions provided the church with a solid foundation during the early years. He currently lives in North Carolina with his beloved wife Joanna. They are the proud parents of Theresa Ann, a new baby girl.

Mrs. Gene Allison, my former mother-in-law, inspired me to write this book. I am grateful to her that she had the vision for its successful publication. She was adamant in her stance that I needed to tell my story in order to help other current cult members (and ex-cult members) seek God's forgiveness as they repent and submit to spiritual leadership in the traditional church. Her first born was my former husband, the late Andy Allison. Mrs. Gene Allison has two other grown children, Betsy and Wanda. They are both married and have children of their own.

My appreciation goes out to Bishop Shirley Jenkins, who has been a dynamic spiritual support system during the last fourteen years. She leads a pastoral support group for female clergy every other month (on the first Saturday of the month). Also, the co-founder of the group, Pastor Susie Jackson, makes an effort to stay in contact with me. I am grateful for their consistent reminders about the importance of participating in regular fellowship meetings with other clergy women.

I am most thankful to Evangelist Goode, who still provides strong spiritual advice. She is indeed my right hand in the most problematical situations. She has been at the forefront of providing prayer, counseling, and spiritual guidance to members of the Church on the Hill-National Network (NNCMW) as we flourish around the nation. Currently, we have National Network (NNCMW) membership in the Washington,

DC. metropolitan area, New York, N.Y. and Atlanta, Georgia. We look forward to launching another Chapter in the Atlanta, Georgia area in September 2013.

My sincere gratitude to the late Bishop John Meares, Evangel Cathedral, Upper Marlboro, Maryland, who was an encouragement to me during the early years of the development of the Network of Christian Women (now National Network of Christian Men & Women). His Tribute Service was conducted on Friday June 3, 2011, at Evangel Cathedral.

Former staff member, Delia Stanford, was the founder. I was elected as the first recording secretary of the organization. Ms. Stanford eventually moved to the Atlanta, GA metropolitan area and invited me to become the next president. Upon my graduation from Wesley Theological Seminary an adhoc committee (of two people) confirmed Ms. Standford's invitation and named me as its new president. I have held this position since 1994.

The organization admitted men in November 1995, after our first National Convention at the Washington Convention Center, Washington, DC. Dr. Corinthia Boone (National Day of Prayer chairperson) was the keynote speaker. Thereafter we officially changed the name of the organization to the Network of Christian Men & Women (NNCMW) at an official meeting at the Rayburn House Office Building.

Ms. Michelle Gibson has been a strong support as the NNCMW expands into the Atlanta, GA metropolitan area. We have been friends since my high school days in Brooklyn, N.Y. I am appreciative of her continued support.

Ms. Pamela Presley, who has been a strong intercessor for Church on the Hill, remains a trusted friend. I am appreciative of the support she provided during the early years of establishing Church on the Hill.

Deacon Angela Long, who has been a trusted friend for about twenty-five years, has provided special prayer support during the years of growing the Church on the Hill/National Network. She was the first person at Evangel Temple (now Evangel Cathedral, Upper Marlboro, MD) whom I informed that I had a call to the ministry. I participated in her former KLF (Kingdom Life Fellowship) group at Evangel. Over the years Deacon Long has been our intercessor when I became president of the NNCMW and pastor of Church on the Hill (November 1994-November 1995). Also, she attended the first Church on the Hill worship service in November, 1995. Furthermore, Deacon Long has been a stalwart support system in the most difficult of circumstances.

Council Member Walter Ficklin, Bladensburg, MD, continues (since August 2009) to extend his support of the Church on the Hill/National Network as we grow around the nation. We remain deeply grateful for his spiritual insights.

Foreword

Have you ever been lost with no earthly idea where you are? If you're like me, when you finally realize your predicament, you become anxious and frustrated. It's not unlike pulling into a gas station and asking a stranger for directions. But here is the dilemma: can you trust the veracity of the person giving you the directions? Being lost, uncertain about which direction to turn and unsure of the intentions of strangers, can be an existentially bewildering condition. Perhaps the best advice to give to a traveler, whether in life or as to some geographical situation, is to take a road map. Faye Thomas has experienced the terrible feeling of being lost. She spent two years traveling around the world as a member of the Children of God (COG) cult.

The COG is the perverse brainchild of the late David B. Berg. It had its origins in the late 1960's Jesus movement. Berg rejects most of the orthodox Christian faith. His infamous Mo Letters, which advocates polygamy, adultery, and incest, elevates them to the status of holy rights. John Sparks has correctly said, "David Berg has managed to transform a gigantic personal temper tantrum against authority into a worldwide movement."

Faye Thomas uncovers for the reader an inside view of cult life and how they target young people who are lonely or disenchanted. You will marvel at the experiences she has had and wonder how she's still alive. For example, she reveals how as a lonely foreign exchange student in Madrid, Spain, she was introduced to and hooked by the cult. It is an eye opening account of brainwashing and intimidation. Throughout the book, Faye reveals how she struggled with some of the practices and doctrines of the cult and always seemed to be at odds with the leadership. She shares the truth that destructive cults have a sinister way of obfuscating the truth so as to keep its members in the dark.

Faye Thomas' story reads like a Danielle Steel novel. It is a remarkable story of deception, struggle for freedom, intrigue, and sexual exploitation. Faye was indeed lost with no idea of which direction to go. She couldn't trust the advice of those around her because they were lost as well. There is nothing more damaging to the human psyche than a feeling of being lost with no directions. Again, the best advice to someone who is lost is to locate a map.

It was the unalloyed Word of God, the Bible, which she finally rediscovered, that gave her clear direction out of the COG cult. Her advice to young people is that they locate this map and tenaciously cling to its words.

Today, thank God, Faye is not lost! She is, in fact, a minister of the good news of Jesus Christ. Therefore, I recommend this book to young and old, who might think that cult life is harmless. Faye's response is not to kid yourself; life in a destructive cult is like traveling without a map--you will end up lost!

The Rev. Dr. James R. Love

Senior Pastor

Love the Gospel Church, Temple Hills, MD

Author of Get Over Yourself: Purposeful Kingdom Living in a Me-Centered World

Introduction

Founded by the late David Berg (1919-1994), the Children of God movement started in Huntington Beach, California, around 1968. It was the offshoot of the Jesus movement of the late 1960's with many of its converts drawn from the hippie movement. The movement was conceived around the activities of the Huntington Beach Light Club (a small mission/coffee house). When the son of Ted Patrick, a famous deprogrammer, tried to join the group around 1971, the first organized anticult group was formed (FREECOG).

Originally, the group was known as "Teens for Christ" or the "Revolution for Jesus." Eventually, the name of the group was changed to the "Children of God," the "Family of Love," and by 2004, "The Family International" (TFI). Recent statistics by TFI puts full-time and fellow members at just over 11,200 in over 100 countries (around 4,000 adult full-time members and 4,000 children). At the beginning of 2005, there were 1,238 TFI homes.

* * *

In 1972, there were approximately 130 communes or "colonies" in fifteen countries. In 1993, 7,000 of the 10,000 members were under eighteen years of age. Some estimates have placed the total number of people that have passed through the group at 35,000. Also, in the late 1970's the popular singing group Les Enfants de Dieu in France (or Los Niños de Dios in Spain) sold thousands of albums to the public. At the end of 1983, the popular radio show "Music with Meaning" had audiences that had grown to approximately 20,000 members.

In 1974, David Berg introduced a new method of proselytization--Flirty-Fishing ("FFing"). In addition to the growing controversy surrounding "FFing" (going to bed, if necessary to win converts), the practice was compared to religious prostitution. Therefore, the media and periodicals deemed the group the "Sex Cult of the Eighties." In 1987, because of the internal and external controversy surrounding "FFing," the organization discontinued the practice for fear of contracting AIDS.

When David Berg died in October, 1994, Karen E. Zerby (formerly known as Maria Berg or Queen Maria) took leadership of the group. She later married her longtime partner, Steven Douglas Kelly (also known as Christopher Smith or Peter Amsterdam). He became her traveling representative due to Zerby's reclusive separation from most of her followers.

Under new management, the organization is divided into World Services, Creations, and Family Care Foundation. In addition, TFI has numerous programs, local foundations, and projects through which it operates around the world, including Aurora Production AG and Activated Ministries.

In February 1995, the group introduced the "Love Charter," which defined the rights and responsibilities of Charter members and Homes. The Charter also included the "Fundamental Family Rules," a summary of the rules and guidelines from past "Family" publications, which were still in effect with the enactment of the Charter.

Under new management by Karen Zerby and Steven Kelly since 2004, members now fall into the following categories: Family Disciples (FD), Missionary Members (MM), Fellow Members (FM), Active Members (AM), and General Members (GM).

For more information, you may visit the "current activities" at The Family International's website: www.thefamilyinternational.org.

To learn more about "The Family International" from the perspective of former members of the group, you may visit: www.exfamily.org.

* * *

The famous evangelist, Richard Roberts, says, "The God I serve is the GOD OF A SECOND CHANCE! He specializes in mending broken dreams, in healing wounded hearts, and in making something beautiful out of our lives, because when you turn your life over to the GOD OF A SECOND CHANCE, He'll take the broken pieces of your dream. He'll give you back a plan for your life more wonderful than you ever dreamed possible."1

It is with this truth in mind that I write this book. This famous evangelist failed God on many occasions in his life. But when he repented, God turned his life around. Today, he has a successful healing ministry!

Many years ago, I entered a very dark moment of my life: I joined a cult. The place was Paris, France. The cult was The Children of God. I was a victim of mind control and self-degradation for a period of two years.

These many years later, I too can proclaim that our God is "the God of a Second Chance." Although many books have been written about cults, my story reveals my personal experience of why I joined the Children of God and why I left the sect. Most importantly, the book explains my personal decision to rejoin society and live a productive Christian life!

Though I'd failed God miserably and lived for two years with sin dominating my life (even though I was a Christian), God looked down one day and enlightened my path. It was His enlightenment that led me out of the Children of God and the stain of cultist living. After leaving the Children of God, I was faced with the many problems that all ex-cult victims are faced with. How does one forget the pain and heartache of such an experience? What events in the victims' past caused them to join a cult?

Upon reflection of my experience (1977-1979) with the COG, I confess:

I was brainwashed.

It started as a missionary group, but was eventually tainted by the unnatural sexual passions of its leader, the late David Berg.

I was enticed by Daniel, who was one of the COG leaders in Madrid, Spain. Upon acceptance of his invitation to visit with the "Paris Show Group" (December 1977) in Paris, France, I was coerced by the COG leaders to the group to join.

Though these reflections are valid, who has to take the responsibility when we backslide? Ultimately, we do. In exposing myself, I free others. In taking responsibility for my spiritual state even when I was off track, I recognize my continuous need for God's forgiveness and direction in my life.

Now, as senior pastor of the Church on the Hill, Prince George's County, MD, I continue to proclaim the good news of the gospel. We serve a wonderful God, and He will forgive our sins when we call out to Him.

* * *

Since 2003, I had an extraordinary change in my spiritual direction. The Church on the Hill made the decision to utilize the A.D. Headen Chapel of the Refreshing Spring Church C.O.G.I.C., Riverdale, MD, for worship services (two Sundays a month). The Rev. Dr. James E. Jordan, Jr., is the senior pastor. Dr. Jordan, with the loving support of his wife, has served as senior pastor of the church since September, 1995.

The astounding popularity of the Refreshing Spring Church has been confirmed by the visits of a number of political leaders. The church has been pleased to host former States Attorney Glenn F. Ivey, Prince Georges County, MD, at the A.D. Headen Chapel (of the Refreshing Spring Church) in 2004 for our Church on the Hill 9th anniversary celebration. He was proud to deliver a "healing testimony" of how God cured him of a cancerous tumor on his kidney.

In addition, Gov. Martin O'Malley of Maryland, former County Executive Jack B. Johnson, along with Mr. Raymond Skinner of the Department of Housing and Community (DHC), signed a "Memorandum of Understanding" (MOU) on July 29, 2008, at the Refreshing Spring Church. A formal press conference was conducted, establishing the new program called HOPE (Homeowners Preserving Equity Program). This program encourages local banks to refinance loans for those individuals subject to foreclosure who might require special underwriting criteria.

To follow-up with the church's commitment to empower the economically challenged, on Monday, Jan. 16, 2012, The Collective Empowerment Group conducted a dynamic worship service in honor of the late Dr. Martin Luther King, Jr. The vision of the group is: "Collectively empowering underserved communities." Pastor James Jordan is a proud board member of the organization.

In the text of this book, some conversational Spanish is used to enhance my experiences. An Appendix has been included to translate Spanish expressions into English.

Scripture quotations are from the Holy Bible (King James Version or Amplified Version).

Endnotes can be found after the Appendix.

Faye Thomas, M.Div.

To request the author to speak, contact information is as follows:

Website: www.revfayetkoroma.org

Email: info@revfayetkoroma.org

Phone: 240-764-6514

Part One: Europe and the U.S.A.

Chapter 1
Madrid

Winning a scholarship to study Spanish in Madrid, Spain, was the dream of a lifetime. I applied to several "study abroad" programs not really expecting to be accepted. Tenaciously, my sister Jessica supported me as I completed my application for the Study Abroad program at Loyola Marymount University in California. Since I had selected business marketing as my major course of study at Fairfield University in Connecticut, I would have to transfer to Loyola Marymount for the year that I would study abroad.

When the letter came that I would be a student at Schiller College (now Schiller International University) in Madrid, Spain, I was as jubilant as a hummingbird. Schiller College is an American university in Europe. My professors would teach all of my business courses in English. A native from Madrid, Spain, would teach my Spanish literature course.

With my bags all packed, my sisters, Josephine and Jessica, drove me to the airport where I registered my luggage at the check-in counter. Upon reaching Gate 27, the most difficult task was loading an emerald green trunk onto the conveyer belt. The airline attendant frowned as I loaded the other pieces of luggage.

Josephine and Jessica kissed me on the cheek before I boarded the plane. Tears swelled up in Jessica's oval shaped face. Josephine's slim frame stood firmly at the gate. They waved good-bye as the flight departed. The captain made an announcement that it would take approximately seven and one-half hours for the plane to fly across the Atlantic Ocean to Madrid, Spain!

* * *

When the plane was hovering over the airport, waiting to land in Madrid, I had jet lag. I had hardly slept during the long trip. I was excited, yet anxious, about my journey across the ocean to Europe. The plane eventually landed and excitedly I walked down through the exit walkway. As I left the airplane, the warm summer breeze was blowing briskly in my face. It was August, 1977, and I just knew a fantastic year was ahead of me!

* * *

I thought I'd never get a taxi as I pulled my luggage, including the huge emerald green trunk filled with clothes, onto the cart. I was exhilarated, yet apprehensive. Had I made the right choice by coming to Madrid? After all, it was a long way from home; and surprisingly, I was feeling a little homesick already. Just as I was thinking these depressive thoughts, a man stepped out of a yellow cab and asked, "Buenos Dias, Señorita, a donde vas?"

Pleasantly surprised, I told him I was looking for a hotel.

"A que precio?" he asked.

"Barato," I replied in Spanish.

I'd taken Spanish from my junior high school years and through my senior year at high school. Since I had developed an aptitude for the Spanish language, I continued taking advanced and conversational Spanish during my first two years of college at Fairfield University. To my benefit, I had memorized all of the appropriate Spanish grammar, but quite frankly, speaking the language was still a struggle.

Quickly, I told the yellow cab driver that I wanted to stay in a hotel only for the weekend. Also, I explained I would be calling Schiller College on Monday morning to find out about my living arrangements while I spent my time in Madrid. After loading all of my belongings into the car, the taxi driver speedily drove off.

"Como se llama?" he asked.

"Me llamo Faye," I replied.

"Is this your first time in Madrid?" he asked.

"Si Señor," I replied smiling. Then I told him I was enchanted with Madrid!

"Espero que te pasas un buen tiempo a Madrid," he replied.

"Gracias!"

By this time we had arrived at the hotel; and with a quick wave of his hand, the yellow cab driver beckoned the bellboy. Then, he helped unload my bags and graciously said good-bye. I paid the fare and thanked him. The bellboy continued to assist me as I slowly walked to the hotel door. I was exhausted, yet being in Madrid was more exhilarating than I had expected.

* * *

After I checked in, the bellboy helped me to bring my luggage to my room. I fell on the bed, where I rested for fifteen minutes. I was so thrilled to finally be in Madrid that I suddenly jumped up and changed my clothes. Although my body was tired, I was too restless to sleep and I just couldn't wait to see the city.

I walked around the small hotel room and glanced out the window. It was strange seeing only Spaniards walking around the streets. Some of those who passed the window were speaking quickly in their native language. I wondered if I would ever be that fluent in Spanish. I looked at the clock and noticed that it was already one p.m.

Then suddenly, I felt as if I should get back on the plane and go home. It was like being on a roller coaster. I was happy, but at the same time I felt somewhat apprehensive about the fact that I would be such a long way from home for the next year. Perplexed by these feelings, I decided to brush my unhappy emotions away, rushing out of the hotel and running down the stairs like a little child anticipating her first ride on her new bicycle. I was so confident that Madrid was going to be the most promising part of my entire life.

* * *

Rushing toward the street corner, I saw a Metro sign. This must be the subway, I thought. I wanted to do some sightseeing before dark! As I boarded the train, I noticed many people staring at me. I didn't realize it that day, but later found out that there were very few African Americans in Madrid, although there were some Africans living there from Morocco and other African countries.

The train ride was delightful. I didn't stay on past too many stops for fear of getting lost and decided to exit the train in a shopping area. As I walked about the streets, which were bustling with people looking at the shops, I noticed that the shoes and the clothing styles were unusual to me. They were nothing like I had seen at home in the U.S.

After my sightseeing it was almost dark, so I boarded the train to return to the hotel.

* * *

Monday morning came and with it my heightened excitement as I began the first full day of my new life in a foreign city. Expectation and curiosity accompanied me that day as I rushed out of the hotel to catch a blue cab to take me to Schiller College.

I knew that I was in a city whose importance as a center of government, culture, and commerce had grown steadily. Not only were all of the ministries of the Spanish government located in Madrid, but also scores of multinational business firms, such as Univac, IBM, and General Electric, had subsidiaries there.

Upon arriving at the school, I was surprised to see that it was such a small building. Expecting to see a huge edifice with a campus, I later learned that the Schiller College Center in Madrid was a small, quaint facility where study abroad students took their courses. There were only about ten classrooms in the entire building. Mr. Jenkins, the guidance counselor, had an office, but the teachers did not have their own offices.

To be certain that I was in the right place, I found Mr. Jenkins' office and knocked on his door. When he opened it, I questioned him about the study abroad program to make sure I had the right building.

Mr. Jenkins immediately pulled out my school records room a stack of papers that he had neatly piled on his small black desk. I found out that I indeed was at Schiller College. Although the school was small, I was about to discover that the courses were excellent.

* * *

After registering, picking up my curriculum, and talking to a few new classmates, I asked Mr. Jenkins about lodging arrangements on my own. I was shocked to learn that although Schiller College had a number of Spanish families who received study abroad students into their homes, everything was filled. Then, Mr. Jenkins pointed toward a bulletin board where there were advertisements placed for people seeking housing (or for others who needed roommates). I walked over to the bulletin board. As I gazed at the assortment of material on the board, two American girls approached me.

"Hi, I'm Diana," the heavyset girl said.

"Yo soy Faye," I replied.

"Are you looking for a place to stay?" she asked.

"Yes, do you know of anything?"

The slim girl replied, "We have a four bedroom apartment not far from the school, and we're looking for two roommates. Would you be interested?" Continuing to hold onto my hand, she introduced herself: "My name is Margie."

We sat down and discussed rent, utilities, and food. "Your rent would only be one hundred dollars a month," Margie said. "We will be splitting it four ways since the total cost for rent is four hundred dollars a month." I was not sure that I was interested, so I told Margie and Diana that I would think about their offer and would give them an answer the following day.

I walked out of the Center thinking about lodging. I sure did need a place to stay, right away. The hotel rates would be too expensive. I was very disappointed, since I had really expected to find housing with a Spanish family. However, I reasoned that living with Diana and Margie would be temporary until I could find a Spanish family to live with.

* * *

So far, I was impressed by the academics. The Schiller College Madrid Center emphasized course work in international business, economics, international relations, psychology, and Spanish. This gave me an opportunity to study my business courses (since I was a marketing major) in English. I had read in their catalog before I left for Madrid that Schiller College also had centers in Heidelberg, Germany; London, England; Paris and Strasbourg, France. Although Mr. Jenkins had explained everything about my business courses, I still did not know the name of my Spanish professor and I was looking forward to the next day's classes.

Upon returning to school the following day, I saw Diana and Margie again right after lunch. They asked me if I had thought about their offer. I had made up my mind to move in with them, but I still wanted to see the apartment first.

"Can I see the room at your apartment?" I asked.

"Sure," Diana replied. "We'll take you there."

As we left the Center, I asked them a few questions about where they came from and why they had come to Madrid to study. I wanted to make sure our goals were similar. As they told me about their backgrounds, academic achievements, and expectations of the Spanish program at Schiller College, I felt comfortable with them. I thought they were decent people and discovered they were both strongly interested in developing a fluency in Spanish. Although Diana, whose father was a physician, was somewhat fluent in Spanish, it appeared that Margie had been taking Spanish in school for a longer period of time. Therefore, she had a stronger grasp of the grammar and conversational aspect of learning the language.

As we approached their building, I felt as if I were dreaming. Could this be true? I thought. It appeared that everything was working out despite my periodic feelings of apprehension.

"Buenos tardes, señoritas," said the landlord who greeted us at the stairs.

"Buenos tardes, señora," we replied.

Diana and Margie introduced me to her: “Her name is Faye,” they said.

”We hope that she will be living with us,” Diana and Margie continued.

“Nice meeting you. My name is Señora Gomez,” she replied, as she extended her hand toward me. “Con mucho gusto,” I said as I gripped her hand.

“Hasta luego,” she shouted as she dashed down the stairs. “Tengo que ir al bano.”

We looked at one another and chuckled as she left.

After we had climbed about four flights of stairs, Diana said, “Here’s the apartment.”

“Doesn't this building have an elevator?” I asked.

“Yes,” Diana replied. “But it doesn’t work right now. They’re repairing it.”

When we entered the apartment, I was amazed at how large it was.

“Go ahead and look around,” Diana said. As I walked through the apartment, Diana followed me. I noticed it had four bedrooms, and the view of the street from the living room was astounding.

There were two larger bedrooms. “This is my bedroom,” Diana said as she pointed toward one of them. “And that one is Margie's,” she said as we looked into the other large bedroom.

As we headed down a long hallway, I noticed the two small bedrooms right next to each other.

“These are the two we want to rent out,” Diana said. “You can choose whichever room you want.”

I examined the two small rooms and decided on the one that had a window with a view of the neighborhood. “I'll take this one,” I said.

“Fine,” Diana replied. “Let me show you the bathroom, the kitchen, and the dining room.”

I was impressed with the apartment; everything was clean and well taken care of. As we roamed through the kitchen and dining room, I noticed that Margie had sat down at the dining room table and was eating a sandwich. “Have a seat,” she said, with her mouth full of food. “How do you like the apartment?” she asked.

“I love it,” I replied.

“Good, then let's talk business. We would like one month’s rent and one month's security deposit," Margie said, as she was writing figures on a piece of paper. "That will be two hundred dollars."

"Our rent is four hundred a month," Diana reiterated. "However, we are expecting another roommate to move in. With the extra person, we can split the rent four ways. Also, we will split the utilities among all of us," Margie continued.

"Would you like to install your own phone? Or, you can use our phone," Margie said.

"Good, when can I move in?" I asked. "I'll let you know my decision about phone installation later."

"You can move in immediately," Diana and Margie confirmed in unison.

I grabbed my jacket and said, "I have a two o'clock class."

"Hasta luego," Diana and Margie shouted joyfully, waving good-bye.

"I'll see you all tomorrow night with all of my belongings," I shouted as I closed the door behind me. I ran down the four flights of stairs like an eager child racing to grab a new toy. Yes, living in Madrid was going to be the most fun-filled year of my life, I thought as I headed back toward the Schiller College Center.

* * *

That evening I went back to my hotel and packed all my suitcases. The most difficult thing to handle was my gigantic, green trunk. I wasn't quite sure why I did not listen to my Aunt Silvia about leaving it in the U.S. I vividly remember her relentless probing as she questioned me about why I felt it necessary to bring the oversized trunk with me. I believe that my decision to study abroad provided assurance for me that I was finally moving out on my own. I sincerely felt that packing a hefty trunk and taking the majority of my clothes assured me that I would not have to come back to live in her home in Brooklyn, New York.

I felt that I would find my sense of purpose by living in Madrid. Also, I felt confident that I would probably finish school at Fairfield University upon my return to the U.S. Thereafter, I planned to find secure employment in the business world beyond New York. I was certain that I would not have to return to Brooklyn except for a brief visit with my family.

When Margie and Diana offered me a room in their apartment, I was glad to be moving out of the hotel room and finally getting myself settled into a whole new lifestyle. As I packed my things, I opened the shutters of the hotel room and thoughtfully gazed at the neighborhood. Madrid had a special aura about it. I watched the people talking as they hurried down the streets. There weren't too many people out just then, as everyone was resting after a long day at work.

I noticed during the time I stayed at the hotel that from six o'clock to eight o'clock in the evening, the streets were almost empty. Then at ten o'clock, the streets were bustling with people. I asked a Spanish native at the Center, whose name was Herberto, about this strange schedule, and he explained that the Spanish people have a work day of 10:00 a.m. to 2:00 p.m. Then, they take siesta from two o'clock until about five o'clock in the evening, when they eat a big luncheon meal (dinner for Americans) and rest. Thereafter, they go back to their place of employment at about six o'clock until eight o'clock in the evening. After work they go home and rest. At about ten o'clock in the evening, the Spanish eat a light meal, drink at local cafés, and visit with friends. Everyone returns home around midnight.

This all seemed so foreign to me, but I had noticed this routine during the three days I spent at the hotel. The people kept on the schedule that Herberto had told me about. Closing the shutters, I sat down on the bed to pray. I wanted to make sure that I was doing the right thing. I wasn't sure if it would work out. I wondered about the other roommate that Diana and Margie intended to find. They insisted that they still wanted to rent out the other small bedroom and I was apprehensive about whether or not the new person and I would be compatible. So many doubts swarmed through my head. But, I thought, if it didn't work out, I could always find another place to stay. I felt assured that the room in the apartment with Diana and Margie would be suitable until I could find a Spanish family to live with.

Despite my apprehension about the living arrangements with Diana and Margie, I felt confident I would learn the Spanish language. Margie was very fluent in Spanish, and I felt positive that she would help me to speak the language fluently while I lived there. After packing all my belongings, I went to sleep. I was sure that by morning I would have a clear answer.

* * *

After waking and dressing, I went to school still quite enchanted with Madrid. I had made a decision. I would move in with Margie and Diana, but later I would find a Spanish family to live with.

When I entered the school, I headed toward my Spanish class. This was my first Spanish class since starting at the school. It was already Thursday, and I still hadn't met my Spanish teacher.

As I entered the class, my Spanish professor met me at the door. "Buenos Dios," he said. "Me llamo Señor Gonzalez."

"Buenos Dios," I replied.

As I sat down in my seat, he started speaking to us. "Good morning, class, my name is Señor Gonzalez. I don't speak English, but I will speak very slowly."

Oh my, I thought, I'm going to fail this class. I looked at the other students, and it appeared from the looks on their faces that they were thinking the same thing. Mr. Gonzalez was not speaking slowly. As a matter of fact, he was speaking very fast.

This was a Spanish literature course where we were to read books in Spanish and discuss them in class. All of the students in my class were American except Carletta, the Spanish native, whom I had met earlier that week. Although she lived in Madrid, she was also fluent in English. I was glad to have her in the class. She promised to help us interpret the lessons when the class couldn't understand Señor Gonzalez. Amazingly, he never spoke slowly; we always had to ask him to repeat himself. During our first classroom session, however, he made me feel comfortable since he had emphasized the importance of the school's intensive Spanish immersion program.

When the bell rang, I jumped up to leave. The first day of Spanish class was exhilarating! Yet, I felt challenged. Although I knew I would enjoy the course, I also knew that I was going to have to learn Spanish or else I'd have to contend with Señor Gonzalez. Therefore, I was more determined than ever to speak Spanish daily so that I could develop a fluency in the language.

* * *

Upon arriving at the new apartment building the following morning, I dragged my green oversized trunk and the rest of my luggage onto the elevator. I pushed the buzzer on the door and used the intercom to ask Diana and Margie to meet me in the hallway. They were standing at the elevator as soon as it arrived on the fourth floor. They opened their arms, hugged me, and assured me that they were certain I had made the right decision.

When I got inside, Diana beckoned me to sit down at the dining room table. She had prepared tea for me. As we sat down, I gave her the money for the rent and deposit, but informed them that I was going to bed. I was too tired to do any socializing. So, even though Diana wanted to engage in a conversation with me, I excused myself and told her that we could continue our discussion the next morning. I also informed her that I would get my receipt from her at that time. Hurriedly, I went into my room, undressed, and fell on the bed. Exhausted by the move, I drifted off to sleep.

* * *

When I awoke, it was eight o'clock the next morning. Diana was knocking at my door telling me to get up or I was going to be late for my class. I thanked her and went to the bathroom, washed up, and dressed. In amazement, I looked at all my scattered belongings. Everything was spread all across the small room. I knew I was going to have to do a lot of sorting. I decided to go to school and return later that afternoon to take on the task of unpacking.

When I entered the kitchen, Margie had cooked a good American breakfast. It was nice to have scrambled eggs, toast, and juice for breakfast. It was a lot better than the typical hard roll and coffee that I ate during my short stay at the hotel. Diana and Margie both explained to me that surprisingly, this was a traditional Spanish breakfast.

After our delicious meal, we walked the five blocks together to the Schiller Center. It was a bright, sunny summer morning, and Madrid was astounding. As we continued walking toward the Center, Diana asked, “Faye, did you sleep well last night?”

”Yes,” I replied. “Thanks for the American breakfast,” I said, turning toward Margie.

“De nada,” she replied.

We talked a lot about the city and the culture shock that Diana and I were experiencing. Diana explained that her father had died just before she came to Madrid and that studying abroad was helping her to take her mind off her father’s death.

Margie, I discovered, had often boasted about being in Madrid the year before. She was thrilled about taking classes at Schiller College. Also, she was elated to inform Diana and me that her fluency in speaking the Spanish language was the result of making an effort to practice speaking Spanish on a daily basis. I was amazed at her great command of the language. I asked Margie repeatedly if she would accept money, should she decide to be my Spanish tutor.

“That won’t be necessary,” she stated. “You'll catch on to learning the language soon,” she assured me.

We entered the Schiller Center and walked briskly to our prospective classes.

* * *

Despite all the excitement of learning Spanish, I didn't realize that going to college to study Spanish in Madrid would also be lonesome. I felt a bit homesick, but I was determined to have a good time. The moderately priced bus trips on the weekends to El Escorial, which is a breath taking province right outside of Madrid, were delightful. There, I saw lots of old Spanish cathedrals decorated lavishly inside. The aged Spanish architecture was beautiful as the majestic buildings were built in medieval times and had a unique style.

I also visited Valle de los Caidos, which is a memorial to the departed Spanish soldiers who lost their lives in the Spanish wars. These trips were awesome and helped me to understand the Spanish culture and their history as a nation. I looked forward to getting up on a bright, sunlit Saturday morning to board the bus for these exciting tours.

* * *

After about six weeks in Madrid, I was beginning to speak quite well. Margie was right. With some practice and tenacity, I was developing a fluency in the Spanish language. Yet, it was still tricky when I went to the bank to make a deposit or went "a correos" to mail a postcard. I had to make sure that I spoke the proper Castillan Spanish, which the natives of Madrid spoke. Otherwise, the Spaniards would not understand what I was saying.

Unfortunately, living with Diana and Margie was becoming problematic. I began to find their somewhat bossy and intrusive attitudes very disturbing, I also felt like I was living with two jail mates in a high security prison. They wanted me to ask their approval to go out, especially at night. I'm not sure if their consistent probing about my personal affairs was because they were concerned about my safety or just insistence on prying into my private life. Just the same, in only a few shorts weeks, I realized that we didn't have much in common. Moreover, several incidents, including morning bathroom conflicts and different eating habits, began to take their toll on our living arrangements.

However, I loved the apartment since it was large and roomy, and I'd spent lots of afternoons in my bedroom reading my Spanish books for my literature class. The room was small, but it did have a window with a great view of the neighborhood. Also, the furniture was modest.

After my seventh week at the apartment, the living situation with

Margie and Diana worsened. Priscilla moved into the room right next to mine. Priscilla was the type of person who did anything you told her to do. Margie and Diana bossed her around and tried to treat me the same way. Yet, the more they pressed to control my life, the more defensive I became about my independence, especially since I was away from my family. I was adamant that my time in Madrid would help me to mature and to find happiness. I was twenty years old, idealistic, and very positive about my career prospects once I finished college.

Despite my doubts about my ability to make my living arrangements with Margie, Diana, and Priscilla work, Madrid was still a delightful place to be. I was enjoying my classes, even though keeping up with Professor Gonzalez's swift speaking pace was still challenging.

The afternoons were especially peaceful. Just down the street from the school was a pasteleria, where they sold all kinds of Spanish pastries. It was so exciting to walk in and ask for a pastel chocolate, which was a chocolate pastry filled with cream and absolutely scrumptious. Or on other days, I would ask for an apple pastry, which was my favorite.

However, there were days in Madrid that I felt really displaced. Being so far from home was beginning to take its toll on me. I would sometimes walk to a nearby café at around ten o'clock at night and drink hot milk just so that I could sleep at night. Part of the reason that I had sleepless nights was the anxiety caused by my not getting along with my roommates.

One particular night was especially difficult, so I decided to go to a Spanish café near the University of Madrid for a glass of sangria!

Chapter 2
The Encounter

When I arrived at the café, I met some friends from the Schiller Center. We all sat down at one of the tables and ordered Spanish sangria. Although I was feeling depressed, I tried to keep a smile on my face so that my classmates would not notice how distraught I was.

Soon a strange group of singers came into the café. They had guitars and were singing in English. They must be Americans, I thought, especially with that accent. The music was delightful and cheered my heart. I looked toward my associates, who seemed to be enjoying the music too. One of the musicians in the group abruptly pushed a cup in front of me and asked for a donation. I was surprised, but he was handsome and had a heavy mustache and blondish-brown hair. His eyes were hazel brown. I was enticed by his friendly smile into dropping a few pesetas into his cup. Also, I was anxious to hear this intriguing group sing another song.

"Hi, I'm Daniel," the man with the friendly smile said.

"Como estas?" I replied.

"Muy bueno," he said.

I turned my attention toward my friends, who were talking about how good the Spanish sangria was.

Daniel persisted, "I've never seen you here at the café before," he said. "You must be a new student."

"Yes," I replied. "I just started a program at Schiller College."

"Can I have your phone number?" he asked. "I'd like to call you sometime."

I looked at him hesitantly. Gee, I thought, he is Caucasian and I am African American. I wasn't sure if I was interested. But he was so charming. As these thoughts ran through my mind, Daniel shoved a piece of paper in my hands with his name and phone number on it.

"Okay," I said and without thinking, I snatched the paper.

"Please give me your number," he insisted.

I wrote my name and number on a piece of paper; he quickly grabbed it, smiled, and beckoned his friends that it was time to go on to the next café. They dashed out the door. As they departed, I thought about his name - Daniel; that was a strange name. Wasn't that a name found in the Bible? My curiosity peaked as I wondered why he was singing and asking for money.

After spending another hour at the café, I finished my sangria and said good night to my colleagues. I returned home and thought a lot about Daniel, who seemed like a nice person. I made the decision to call him the next day.

* * *

When I phoned him, someone other than Daniel answered. "Hola, mi nombre es Brian," he said in a casual voice. "Quien es?"

"Soy Faye. Esta Daniel?" I asked.

"Si, espera un momentito."

When Daniel came to the phone, he said, "Hola, soy Daniel."

"Remember me? I'm Faye. We met last night at the café."

"Si," he replied. "It's good to hear from you."

I asked him why was he singing and asking for money. He explained to me that he was a member of a group called the COG who were full-time missionaries. His "ministry" was to bring others to Christ through music. They solicited donations to raise money for their work in Madrid and for "the children."

"Oh, that is great," I said. "What do you do at the missionary home?" I asked.

"We live in a colony and work together as a team, having all things in common like the early apostles," he answered.

"What is the purpose of your group?"

"We give one hundred percent of our lives to serving God," he continued. "We pass out literature daily; we sing at cafés at night to spread the gospel; we witness to people to tell them about Jesus."

"I'm intrigued with your dedication," I said; "but I have to go now."

"Wait a moment," Daniel said. "Would you like to visit our colony?" he asked.

"Yes, I would like to visit your colony," I replied.

"How about tomorrow?" he asked.

"That would be fine," I answered.

* * *

The next day I visited the colony and was really impressed. It was a short walk from the Schiller Center. When I entered the apartment, there was music, happy faces, laughter, and guitar playing; it was all so hypnotic.

"Forsake all, and come follow Jesus," someone said to me as I walked into the living room.

I wasn't quite sure what that meant, but they seemed to be a happy group of people. Daniel finally appeared from the kitchen.

"Hola, Faye," he said. "I'm glad you could make it."

"Hi, Daniel," I said.

As we sat, I asked him more about his group. "Who was the fellow who said 'forsake all,' and what did that mean?" I asked.

As we sat down, Daniel explained that they had forsaken all to join the group. For example, Daniel noted that every COG member who joined the group was required to give up all of their worldly possessions. This included leaving their jobs and their families to be full-time missionaries. They called themselves the Children of God. Daniel explained that they had a leader, Moses David, who was an end-time prophet. They received their missionary orders from him through the Mo Letters. These were letters written by David Moses to his COG disciples. He said that he would love to sponsor me as a new member and asked if I wanted to join.

I told him that I would think about it. Daniel and I chatted for about twenty minutes, and then he beckoned me to mingle with the group members. He introduced me to some other musicians, who usually sang with him at the student cafés and local hotels.

Looking toward the door, I noticed that there were other visitors entering the apartment. The group members surrounded the visitors with hugs, kisses, and the expression "Jesus loves you."

After meeting some of the newcomers, who seemed just as happy as Daniel, I decided it was time to go. After all, I had been at the colony about an hour. All of the singing was beginning to hypnotize me. Turning to Daniel, I thanked him for inviting me and asked him to walk with me to the front door. "Thanks for inviting me," I said.

"I'll call you tomorrow," Daniel promised.

Waving good-bye, I left. A certain excitement and apprehensiveness washed over me as I rushed down the street towards the Metro.

While riding the train, I reflected on my visit with the COG. I was somewhat interested in the possibility of forsaking all to serve the Lord full time. They definitely seemed like happy people, I thought. Perhaps if I served as a full-time missionary and gave my life in service to God, my feelings of homesickness would ease, I thought. I left the train and walked two short blocks to the apartment.

* * *

The next day I called Daniel. When he answered the phone, I was so excited to speak to him again. "I'd like to know more about your group," I said.

"Sure, we can talk more tomorrow," he replied. "Where can we meet so that I can explain more about the COG?"

I suggested that we meet at the Schiller Center, but Daniel thought it would be best to meet at the park near the school.

* * *

The following day, after school, Daniel was sitting on the bench at a large recreational area about one-half mile from the Schiller Center. I noticed that he had two sandwiches with him. He told me that he had made two chicken salad sandwiches and offered me one.

"Yes, thank you," I said grabbing the sandwich. "My, it's a lovely day," I said.

Daniel asked how I was I adjusting in Madrid. I explained to him that I had been in Spain for about seven weeks, but I still had culture shock. I confessed to him that even though I was speaking Spanish with greater ease, I was still feeling quite homesick.

I told him that I was feeling very uncomfortable with my roommates and that the new student, Priscilla, who had just moved into the room next to mine appeared to have an uneasy feeling about me. I wondered if she really liked me, or if she was pretending. I confessed to Daniel that Diana and Margie often complained about how much I ate. Since I bought my own groceries, I thought that it was inappropriate for them to question me about my personal lifestyle.

Finally, I told Daniel that I was seriously thinking of moving out of the apartment. I had already taken the initiative to ask Mr. Jenkins, the student counselor, about the possibility of living with a Spanish family. "After all," I suggested, isn't this the best way to learn a foreign language?"

Daniel looked at me seriously and said, “Whatever decision you make about your home life, I will be here to support you.”

I quickly changed the subject. “Tell me about the Children of God,” I said.

With his eyes glistening like the clear blue sky, Daniel explained that in the COG there were no exchanges of wedding vows, so couples lived together and became partners. Daniel explained that Moses David felt that COG disciples should only be married to God's work: the Children of God. Daniel was convinced that seeking marriage in the COG would hinder the Lord’s divine purpose for our lives.

Daniel confessed that the prophet Moses David had mandated that the Children of God were a new nation. Therefore, they were God's end-time prophets. He explained how God had special rules for the COG. “Would you like to be a member of our group?” he asked abruptly.

“I don't know,” I said. “I have been feeling very lonely and unhappy about my living situation,” I explained. “I want to have a closer relationship with God,” I continued.

“God is trying to tell you to forsake all, come with us, and serve Him fulltime,” Daniel continued. “Maybe your feelings of unhappiness are a confirmation that God is leading you to join our group. You would be answering the call to be a missionary,” he continued.

“I don't know,” I said, interrupting him. Despite my desire to continue learning more about the Children of God on another day, Daniel insisted on asking me if I had made a decision to join the group. Just like the apostles of the early church, Daniel informed me I would have to forsake all to serve God. This included dropping out of school. Also, he made it clear that I would have to forsake my family and old friends.

I wasn't sure I was ready to make such a commitment, but I did want to travel like most of my school friends. I reasoned that missionary work would be a good way to see new places, since Daniel said the Children of God traveled to different colonies throughout Europe. I was also anxious to learn what it meant to become a missionary. I thought this meant that if I had faith, God would supply all of my needs. However, before I made a decision to join, I needed to know more about the COG.

I wanted to change the subject since Daniel’s conversation about forsaking all scared me. Relentlessly Daniel went on; he insisted on telling me that whenever a Children of God member traveled to another colony, he or she usually only carried one suitcase. It was evident that I would have to give away most of my clothes and that seemed devastating at the time.

* * *

Because I thought they would be very angry if I dropped out of school, I did not tell my family back in the U.S.A. about my "encounter" with the Children of God. Whenever I wrote home, I only conveyed the good things about Madrid: the sightseeing, the restaurants, and the trips to El Escorial. Most impressive was the famous Museo del Prado, which had the most complete collection of the works of Titian, Velázquez, El Greco, Goya, and Bosch.

I never revealed in any of my letters to my folks that I was feeling torn about my service to God. However, I made a point to let them know that I was steadfastly seeking to know more about God and that I was determined to find His perfect will for my life.

I knew that my friends at school, my roommates, and my guidance counselor, Mr. Jenkins, would also discourage me from joining the Children of God. However, I felt isolated in Madrid and missed my friends in the U.S. I told Daniel how I felt and also that my current roommates would not understand. Inwardly I was certain that because I desperately wanted my independence, I did not want to ask anyone's opinion about the Children of God. I wanted to make a personal decision about what I wanted to do with the next year of my life.

As these thoughts were running through my mind, Daniel said, "You know, Faye, you can come to one of our gigs at La Concha hotel tomorrow. You can see how you like being with the group before you decide if you want to join," he suggested.

Daniel clarified that some of the people he was with at the student café the night we met were part of a larger group called Les Enfants de Dieu or the "Paris Show Group". He explained that the singing group was only visiting in Madrid to sing in a few cafés and perform at the hotels. This was an effort to raise money for the Spanish colony in Madrid that I had visited.

In Paris, France, he explained that Les Enfants de Dieu were very popular and had produced two albums. One of them, The Bible, was selling exceptionally well in Paris. Daniel boasted that the group was very popular throughout France. Daniel's enthusiasm was greatest when he spoke of the famous French artist, Monique Mayson, who had discovered them.

Daniel insisted that I visit Paris so that he could introduce Monique to me. He insisted that we go during the Christmas holiday to meet her and Les Enfants de Dieu. I was impressed and really curious about his group. It appeared that God's blessings were upon them.

"Daniel, I must get back to school," I interrupted. My greatest joy came as I looked down at my black patent-leather shoes. They were perfect for walking back to the Schiller Center.

All the talk about Paris, France, was electrifying. Most of my classmates at Schiller College often spoke about taking a trip to Paris. For many, it was just a dream. Others, more determined, took advantage of the low cost student fare and traveled by train to experience the famous city.

"Okay, let's go," he exclaimed. We walked back to Schiller Center, where Daniel kissed me on the cheek and said, "See you tomorrow at La Concha; our show is at eight o'clock in the evening." Then, he shoved the directions in my hands and waved good-bye. What a guy, I thought, as I took the directions to La Concha hotel.

* * *

Arriving back at the Schiller College Center, I walked briskly into the building. It was vital that I make an effort to attend my evening International Business Marketing class. After all, Schiller College was my rock, as well as my connection to God. I was grateful for the opportunity He had granted me; therefore, it was imperative that I be successful in Madrid. This was the only way that I could keep my Junior Year Abroad scholarship.

Upon walking into the classroom, I looked at my watch and noticed that I was ten minutes late.

I rushed to an empty desk, sat down in the chair, and opened my textbook. Gazing at the teacher, I was determined to be a good student at Schiller!

* * *

The next morning before class, I asked Diana if we could chat for a moment. As we sat down at the kitchen table, I explained to her that I was unhappy with my living arrangements. As we continued speaking, Margie and Priscilla came into the kitchen. It appeared that they also wanted to have a group discussion about our living situation. With frowns on their faces, Margie and Priscilla sat down at the table and spilled out fictitious complaints about me. It seemed that they had all teamed up against me. I had been at the apartment over six weeks, and I was fed up with their poor attitudes about our living arrangement.

Margie and Diana insisted that I ate too much, and I used their phone too much. Most disturbing was that they insisted that I discontinue being secretive about my private life. They continued to probe me about Daniel. They wanted to know where he lived, what was his faith, and if I was serious about him. Unable to convince them that my relationship with Daniel was private, I reluctantly explained that Daniel was a new friend of mine who was a missionary. I also explained that he was a member of the Children of God.

As far as my eating too much, I revealed to my roommates that I was not on a diet. I had gained a few pounds, but I explained that I was still only 120 lbs. Therefore, I did not make any apologies about how I enjoyed the Spanish cuisine and the pasteleria shops throughout Madrid. Since they were all on strict diets, it was difficult for the girls to fathom my passion for Spanish cuisine!

I decided to share some details about the COG with them. Margie and Diana seemed interested in learning more about my experiences. My roommates seemed to be generally concerned about me. However, at times it was difficult to fathom their sincerity because of their mean attitudes.

As we continued our conversation, I confessed to my roommates that I had already talked to the guidance counselor, Mr. Jenkins, at Schiller. He had informed me that there was a room available at the home of a Spanish family. For the first time, I was very bold in telling Margie and Diana that I felt it was in our best interest for me to move out. They continued to be critical of me, which made my mind up once and for all about leaving.

Angrily, I left the kitchen and gathered my schoolbooks, which were on the living room table. Briskly, I walked toward the front door. Although I was furious about our conversation, I opened the door, and closed it gently behind me. I ran to the elevator and pushed the button for the first floor. I needed to get some fresh air.

* * *

As I walked the five blocks to the Schiller Center, I was fuming. Mumbling under my breath, I felt betrayed by my roommates. I had paid the rent and made an effort to make Priscilla feel comfortable. Yet, Margie and Diana continued to make a point that it was their business to pry into my private life. They told me that they felt that I was purposely not telling them everything about the Children of God. On the contrary, I did not feel that any of the young ladies with whom I lived had a right to delve into my personal life. Also, I did not feel obligated to answer any of their questions about the Children of God. Frankly, I felt it was none of their business.

Approaching Schiller College, I started to calm down. What did it matter? I was sure that I had made a mistake by moving in with Margie and Diana in the first place.

* * *

After entering the Schiller Center, I rushed down the long hallway and went straight to Mr. Jenkins's office. Unfortunately, he was not in the office, so I headed toward the main office and asked if he was expected to return to the Center later in the afternoon. The secretary, Mrs. Lancer, told me that Mr. Jenkins would be returning in fifteen minutes. I was in total distress, so I thanked Mrs. Lancer and then walked down the corridor back to Mr. Jenkins's room. I had decided to sit on the bench just outside his cozy office. Deep inside, I knew that I would have to move out of the apartment with Diana and Margie as soon as possible.

* * *

When Mr. Jenkins arrived at his office, I asked him about the Spanish family that had a room for rent. He informed me that indeed he knew of a family who lived about one block from the school. The couple was asking $160 a month for rent, which included three meals a day and laundry facilities. Their names were Señor and Señora Martinez. Mr. Jenkins gave me a piece of paper with their names and address on it. I took the information, smiled, and thanked him. Then, I walked cheerfully out of his office.

* * *

At lunchtime, I walked down the street looking for the Martinez residence. As I crossed the street, just one block from the school, I saw their building. As I entered the big iron gate, which was gracefully opened by a doorman, I walked into the building and looked for their apartment number. When I located Apt. 3B, I rang the buzzer and a sweet soft voice answered. "Quien es?"

"Buenos tardes, Señora Martinez. My name is Faye, and I'm a student from Schiller College. I'd like to see your room for rent," I said.

"Si, entre," she said as she rang the buzzer.

I rode the elevator to the third floor. As I stepped off, I hastily walked down a long hallway. Staring steadily ahead, I could see a woman waving at me.

* * *

When I reached her door, she confirmed that she indeed was Señora Martinez and beckoned me to come into the apartment. She had a pleasant demeanor. Her round, jubilant face glowed like the sun on a hot summer day. Anxiously, I asked her about the room she had for rent.

"Esta por alla," she said as she pointed toward the dining room.

"Tu eres un estudiante a Schiller College?" she asked.

"Si, señora," I replied.

"A quanto tiempo vas a pasar en Madrid?" she asked.

"Un ano," I replied.

"Bueno," she said as she rose and headed toward the room.

When Señora Martinez opened the door, I noticed the room was small, but adequate. It didn't have much of a view, but I was so eager to move in with a Spanish family that I didn't care. The room had a single bed, a tiny sink, and a medium-sized closet to hang my clothes.

"Te gusta el cuarto?" Señora Martinez asked, as she closed the door.

"Si, señora. When can I move in?" I asked.

Just as she was about to answer, the door opened and a short man with a medium frame about five feet, seven inches tall walked briskly into the gigantic living room. He had a clean shaven, square-shaped face. His gray-blue eyes were sparkling like ginger ale bubbling over a clear glass. His snow white teeth were gleaming as his radiant smile warmed the atmosphere. Reaching for my hand, he shouted, "Buenos tardes," as he moved toward the couch and sat down. "Quien es ella?" he asked Señora Martinez, pointing towards me.

"Ella se llama Faye. Quiere alquilar el cuarto," Señora Martinez replied.

"Oh, bueno," he said as he beckoned me to sit down next to him.

Señora Martinez formally introduced Señor Martinez to me. Señora Martinez was a pleasant lady. She had a plump frame and a sweet smile. She asked me a few questions about my future plans and why I was in Madrid. She also asked about my family at home in the U.S. and then about my present living situation.

I explained to her that I was living about five blocks from the school with three American girls. Without revealing any major details, I carefully explained to her that I was not getting along with my roommates. I went on to tell her that from the first time that I visited the Schiller Center and viewed the bulletin board that displayed housing opportunities, I had been seeking to live with a Spanish family.

I was elated that Señora Martinez agreed with me that I would benefit from my living with them. She politely explained that neither Senor Martinez nor her maid, Marie, spoke any English. Therefore, although she was fluent in English, it was the apartment rule that only Spanish could be spoken. I heartily agreed. Señora Martinez then provided me with a form to complete.

Attached was a list of rules and regulations, which I had to sign. Señor Martinez was quiet the whole time we talked. He didn't ask me any questions; he just smiled as he crossed his legs. I found it comical that he asked his wife about their "siesta". Señora Martinez simply smiled at him and beckoned Maria to begin preparing the paella, a popular Spanish dish with various meats, such as beef, pork, fish, and chicken, with rice and vegetables and a tomato sauce. After talking with Señora Martinez for about one half-hour, I apologized for interrupting their mealtime. I almost forgot that lunchtime for me was "siesta" for them.

As I was about to leave, Señora Martinez said she would be glad to host me as a Study Abroad student. Señor Martinez nodded his head, which I assumed meant that he was in agreement with his wife. Señora Martinez asked me when I could move into the room. I explained to her that I would return that evening with my luggage. As she opened the door to let me out, I smiled and shook her hand. I thanked her as I ran down the flights of stairs to the main floor of the building. I shouted with joy that I had finally found a Spanish family to live with. I had been in Madrid almost two months waiting for the opportunity to move in with a Spanish family. Finally, I knew that God had answered my prayers.

With these thoughts running through my mind, I charged out of the front door of the apartment building, crossed the street, and hurried to La Pasteleria to buy a pastel de manzana. Finding a new place to live was cause for celebration.

* * *

That evening, I told my roommates that I'd found another place to live. I apologized for being upset with them that morning and asked their forgiveness. I also apologized for any inconvenience that I may have caused them. I explained that I would still like to remain friends. Diana, Margie and Priscilla accepted my apology. They asked if I needed any assistance to move my belongings. Then, they all shook my hand and wished me well.

I went to my room and packed my belongings. After packing my entire luggage and loading my trunk and suitcases into the elevator, I asked Diana to call a taxi. She agreed and asked Margie to assist me with taking my luggage to the lobby of the building. Margie and I waited about fifteen minutes in the lobby for a cab. When it arrived, Margie helped me to load all of my suitcases and my trunk into the back seat of the taxi. I kissed Margie on the cheek and hugged her. I told her that I looked forward to seeing her and Diana at the Schiller Center in the morning.

* * *

As I rode in the yellow cab to the Martinez residence, I thought of Daniel. I vaguely remembered that I had agreed to have a date with him at eight o'clock in the evening. We had discussed a few days ago that I would meet him at La Concha hotel, where his group "Los Ninos de Dios" was performing. Oh my, I thought, I'd better get settled in fast.

* * *

When I arrived at the Martinez residence, I rang the buzzer and asked Señor Martinez to please come down and help me with my luggage. The taxi driver pulled the heavy green trunk and the rest of my suitcases into the lobby of the building. I paid the taxi fare and he left. Señor Martinez joyfully grabbed my trunk and pulled it onto the elevator.

"Let me help you," he said in Spanish. After I beckoned Señor Martinez to assist me with my luggage, he collected the rest of the suitcases and pushed himself into the elevator. There were so many suitcases that I thought the two of us would not be able to ride upstairs to the apartment together.

"Venga," Señor Martinez shouted. "Nos vamos a subir!"

I was excited, but at the same time apprehensive about the move into the apartment of Señor and Señora Martinez. When we arrived at the third floor of the apartment building, surprisingly I saw four young American girls running to help us. Also, Señora Martinez came running out of the apartment to my aide.

I asked Señor Martinez who the young women were. He heartily explained that the four students were his other boarders. Furthermore, he explained that he and Señora Martinez rented rooms yearly to students in cooperation with the Junior Year Abroad program at Schiller College.

Then a beautiful woman, who Señor Martinez introduced as his maid, Maria, appeared at the apartment door. She beckoned me to come in. Her milky white skin was glowing, and her eyes were gleaming as she smiled. "Tu tienes hambre?" she asked.

My goodness, I thought, who are all these people?

As we sat down, Señora Martinez further explained to me that they had three other bedrooms that they rented to students. However, my room was the only single room for students.

Then, Señora Martinez introduced me to Kathy and Debra, who shared a room. I thanked them for helping with the luggage. Then, after Marie asked me again if I was hungry, we all sat down to have a light meal.

Señora Martinez explained that the heavy meal in Spain was eaten at "siesta." She introduced me to "tortilla Espanola," a popular Spanish dish made with potatoes and eggs. Two other young American women emerged from a bedroom at the far end of the huge apartment. Señora Martinez introduced them as Barbara and Louellen, who shared the other room. They were also Study Abroad students, who had come to Spain for the school year. Marie formally explained that she would be cooking the meals and washing our clothes. Each of us was given a day to deliver our laundry to her. Also, she informed us what hour of the day to pick up our laundry from the large utility room at the back of the apartment.

Welcoming all who sat at the large oval-shaped dining room table, Señora Martinez explained that only Spanish could be spoken while we ate. She reiterated that the Spanish speaking only rule was a requirement of the Study Abroad program at Schiller College. She particularly emphasized that the Study Abroad program at the Universidad de Madrid, where the other students studied, also had this rule.

I formally introduced myself and said that I was very glad to meet them all. All of the American girls appeared to be my age.

* * *

The tortilla Espanola was covered with a rich tomato sauce. It looked delicious. They invited me to sit with them to eat. After just a few bites, although I found it scrumptious, I politely asked to be excused. I apologized to everyone, explaining that I needed to put all my belongings in my room, since I had a date at eight o'clock.

* * *

I went to my room and hung up a few of my clothes in the small closet. After putting away some of the suitcases in the closet, I sat down on my bed for a moment. I just needed to take a brief moment to rest and reflect on the day's events. I'd been hustling and bustling all day long. Suddenly, I looked at my watch and noticed that it was 7:15 p.m.

Startled, I jumped up and finished dressing. I only had forty-five minutes to get to La Concha hotel to meet Daniel. I remembered that he had told me a few days ago that Los Ninos de Dios were performing at the hotel at eight o'clock sharp!

On my way out of the door, I could see that there was still some tortilla Espanola left on the exquisitely decorated table. It looked and smelled great! Señora Martinez and the other students were still finishing their meal. Yet, even though the food looked mouth-watering, I was full and decided to wait until the next evening to ask for another slice! "Save me a piece for tomorrow," I blurted out to Marie, in Spanish, as I hurriedly ran out the door. I'm going to be late for my date," I said closing the door behind me.

* * *

Once I exited the front door of the apartment building, I flagged down a taxi and gave him the written directions to La Concha hotel. By politely stating that he knew exactly where La Concha hotel was, he insisted that the ride would only be fifteen minutes.

When I entered the hotel, I asked the doorman where Los Ninos de Dios were performing. He pointed toward the ballroom. Just as I approached the beautifully decorated room, Daniel came toward me with his guitar in his hand.

"Hi Faye, I'm glad you made it. Did you get lost?" he asked.

"No," I answered. I explained to Daniel that I was running late because I had moved in with the Martinez family.

"Good, I'm glad. Congratulations," Daniel said happily!

"Come in. I saved you a seat in the front row," he said as he escorted me into the ballroom.

I was elated to see that the room was bustling with people. After I was comfortably seated, Daniel rushed to the stage and introduced his group as "Los Ninos de Dios." The crowd cheered with joy!

The group sang wonderfully, and I was impressed with the way they played their instruments! I was so impressed with Los Ninos de Dios that I began to think how much fun it might be to be a part of their group. They seemed so happy, and the songs really touched my heart. Since I was seeking to know God in a more personal way, I thought that being a missionary with the Children of God would be a perfect way to learn about developing my faith. Perhaps by making a commitment to join one of their colonies, I would find friendship and peace during my search for God's will for my life, I thought.

After their last song, the crowd cheered as Los Ninos de Dios bowed their heads. Daniel came over and kissed me on the cheek. I was beginning to really like him, and the feelings appeared to be mutual. "How did you like it?" he asked.

"Oh, Daniel, you all were wonderful," I replied. "So professional," I added.

"Good," he said. "I'm glad you enjoyed the concert."

"Do you sing here regularly?" I asked.

"From time to time," he replied. "We like to sing in various places, so that we can witness to a variety of people," he added.

"Oh, that's great," I said, as I gazed at Daniel. I was beginning to fall in love with him, and I knew that I wanted to please him. I also reasoned that he wanted me to be a part of their group. I reasoned within myself that if I joined, I'd win his heart. Daniel grasped my hand, kissed me on the cheek again and said, "We're going over to the café to have fondue. Are you hungry?"

"Yes, I'd love to join you for fondue," I replied.

As we left the hotel, Daniel introduced me to his group members. They were Abashai and Jacob (the other two guitarists) and Rachel and Donna. I congratulated them on their concert. Their singing blended so well together. When I told them that they had beautiful voices, they smiled. Their eyes glistened as I continued to thank them for the gospel message I heard through their music. They all seemed like nice people. Everyone explained in detail about how many souls they were winning to the Lord through their music. Although they did not go into all of the details, it was obvious that they were thrilled about their other missionary work. They informed me that they would be overjoyed if I joined their group.

* * *

When we arrived at the restaurant, Daniel asked for a table for six. The waiter brought menus, and we sat down gazing at the varieties of fondue. Daniel and I ordered a cheese one, and the girls ordered a beef fondue, and the two guys, Jacob and Abashai, ordered a vegetable one. Lastly, we ordered Spanish sangria to drink while we waited for our meal.

Los Ninos de Dios were not shy. Jacob and Abashai boasted about their success in Paris. They also proclaimed that they felt confident that they would have the same success in Madrid! When the waiter brought the food, we all shared each other's dishes, and we were having a great time! “The crowd really loved you,” I said as Daniel poured more sangria into our glasses. Everyone laughed and toasted to their successful show!

Abashai and Jacob explained that they were both from Paris and spoke heartily about going back for Christmas. Although they were part of the Paris Show Group, they also felt it was necessary to visit Madrid to help raise money for the Spanish colony that I visited. Rachel and Donna told me that they were American and had been in Europe with the Children of God for three years. They confessed that they actually lived at the Spanish colony that I visited.

Daniel looked toward me, held my hand and said, “Faye, would you like to come to Paris with me for Christmas? You can stay with the ‘Family’ there,” he continued. “Don't worry about getting a hotel,” he said.

I looked at Daniel in disbelief.

“Yes, that would be great, you can meet the Family in Paris and maybe you'll join our group,” Abashai shouted!

I hesitantly glanced at Abashai. Then, I looked sternly at Daniel since I did not believe that the invitation was valid. The only thing that came to my mind was that they were inviting me to Paris to be polite, especially since they explained that Daniel was very fond of me.

“You guys are joking,” I shouted! Then I said, “Let me think about it,” realizing that the pressure was on. I was convinced that Los Ninos de Dios were determined to win me as a disciple, and I still had not made up my mind to join.

It was early November. I had been dating Daniel for about two and one-half months by then. Christmas was fast approaching. Paris, I thought, my goodness - I was dreaming of traveling there. Their invitation appeared to be an opportunity of a lifetime.

“I'll keep it in prayer,” I said politely, as I smiled at Daniel. On the surface I was groaning about my failed relationship with Diana and Margie. But deep inside, my heart was bursting with the excitement of a possible excursion to a most treasured place - Paris, France. By the time we had finished our various selections of fondue, the waiter brought the menus again. Everyone agreed that we wanted to order chocolate fondue for dessert. Our evening meal was really delicious, and the chocolate fondue was absolutely magnificent.

I thanked Daniel for the meal and told his friends that it was good meeting them. With all of them surrounding me and talking about Paris,

I felt that I had to leave. The pressure was too great. As I finished my last piece of chocolate fondue, I kissed Daniel on the cheek and told him to call me the next day. I jumped up and suddenly left the table. I went outside, flagged down a taxi, and gave him directions to the apartment. I wondered why I had turned down Daniel's invitation to escort me back to the Martinez residence.

* * *

When the taxi arrived at my building, I ran up the long driveway that led to the entrance of the building. I took the elevator up to the third floor and rang the buzzer. Señora Martinez answered the door. It was about eleven o'clock in the evening, and I was completely exhausted. After she opened the door, I sauntered into the apartment and Señora Martinez asked me in Spanish how my date was. I told her that I had a great time with a friend at La Concha hotel. I kissed her on the cheek and said goodnight. I was careful not to release prematurely any information to her about the Children of God.

As I went into my bedroom, I undressed and pulled my lavender and gold-trimmed gown from one of my suitcases. I plopped on the bed and drifted magically to sleep.

Chapter 3
Los Ninos de Dios

When I awoke the next morning, I put on my pink robe and went to the bathroom to shower. As I entered the restroom, I noticed that there wasn't any soap. Therefore, I hurried into the dining room where everyone was sitting and eating breakfast. I turned to Señora Martinez and asked, "Puedo tener sopa para el bano?" Everyone at the table laughed. *Why are they laughing?* I thought. I just want soap to take a shower.

"Oh, tu quieres jabon para el bano," Señora Martinez answered.

I was too embarrassed to laugh. I was trying to follow the rule in the house that only Spanish could be spoken while we were in the apartment. Unfortunately, I meant to ask for "soap, while I had actually asked for "soup." Ignoring their laughter, I proceeded to go into the bathroom. My hand was trembling slightly. Then, I reached for the knob and turned on the shower. The lukewarm water that splashed in my face was exhilarating. Ah, the shower was relaxing and calmed my nerves.

After showering for about ten minutes, I dried myself off and put on my housecoat. I walked briskly to my bedroom to get dressed. Then, I dashed into the dining room to sit down and eat. I was famished.

Marie brought hard rolls and coffee and rested them on the large, oak dining room table. As I ate my breakfast, my apartment mates, Kathy, Debra, Barbara, and Louellen, were still laughing at me. Still, I felt assured that my ability to speak Spanish would improve over time; therefore, I ignored them and continued to eat breakfast.

* * *

Later on that day, I chuckled when I thought about the error I had made when asking for "soup" for the bathroom. After all, I reasoned, I had been innocent of my ignorance. My lack of ability to speak Spanish fluently was normal, especially since I had only been in Madrid for about three months. Only with practice would I develop a fluency in the Spanish language, I thought.

* * *

Kathy and Debra told me about their intensive educational programs at the University of Madrid. Kathy was a business major with a minor in Spanish. She was a small, slim girl with curly, black hair. She continually reiterated that she was very homesick and wanted her parents to visit her in Spain. She was hopeful because she was expecting them to take a flight to Madrid at the end of October.

Debra was tall with long, blonde hair. She had a boyfriend back in Denver, Colorado, where she lived. She said he was consistently writing her and demanding that she return home to the U.S. She confessed that she was in love with him. Debra said that she also was very homesick.

Barbara was medium height and had short, brown hair. She was the only one of my roommates who was having a good time. Barbara had dates lined up for almost every evening that week. Like me, she really loved being a student in Madrid. Barbara was fascinated with the Spanish men. Also, she loved the Spanish paella.

Louellen had short, black hair. She was very quiet and introverted. As a result, her Spanish conversation at the dining room table was very limited. Yet, her dark black eyes glistened whenever she heard me speak. She informed me that she was impressed at my command of the language. At the same time, Louellen's ivory white face looked discouraged when she articulated her inability to keep up with my progress. She confessed that her poor ability to speak Spanish was becoming more obvious to her Spanish teacher.

"Do you think you will pass your Spanish course?" I asked.

"Yo no se," she replied bashfully. However, she made it clear that she was elated about her enrollment at the University of Madrid. In addition to her excitement about her Spanish course, Louellen was studying International Marketing.

* * *

After chatting with the girls, I finished dressing and told Marie and Señora Martinez, "Adios," as I dashed out of the door. Señor Martinez left the apartment with me, and we rode down together on the elevator. "I think you'll learn Spanish here," he said gleefully as we reached the first floor.

"Espero que si," I said as we walked briskly out of the front door of the apartment building.

Señor Martinez was a delightful man, and I really liked him. I was overjoyed that I was finally living with a native Spanish family. He waved good-bye as he ran across the street to catch the bus. I walked down past La Pasteleria; and I peeked in, but I didn't buy any desserts. Since overeating there was becoming habitual, I decided to skip a day from binging on the desserts. Yet, the fresh Spanish pastries were hard to resist. Besides, there were so many pastry shops throughout the city. As I went up the stairs to the Schiller Center, I could smell fresh bread baking at La Pasteleria. Oh, that aroma is nearly irresistible, I thought. I continued to walk down the hall to my International Psychology class.

* * *

By the middle of December, I had been living with the Martinez family for about six weeks. Christmas was fast approaching, and I thought seriously of Daniel's offer to go to Paris, France. Since I had never visited the city, I was anxious about the possibility of finally getting a chance to experience the French culture. I had always wanted to visit the museums, eat the French cuisine, and learn to speak French.

About a week before Christmas, Kathy's parents, Mr. And Mrs. Holtz, finally came to visit her for the holidays. They invited my roommates and me out to a very fine restaurant. We ate paella and saw a beautiful flamenco show. This is a popular form of Spanish dancing, done at various restaurants and clubs throughout Spain. We were having a wonderful evening. I had never seen Kathy so elated. It was obvious that she was very happy to visit with her parents. They were wonderful people and had planned on spending two weeks in Madrid with her.

Mr. and Mrs. Holtz asked us about our studies, as well as about our progress with learning Spanish. By that time, my Spanish had really improved, and I told them that I had a very strong "B" in my Spanish class. I'd come a long way since the beginning of the course; I had thought for sure I was going to have a difficult time with my Spanish literature course. The semester, however, was easy; and I related that I had all "A's"and "B's" in my other courses. I informed them about my economics, international psychology, and marketing classes. Also, I told them that I had enrolled in a social studies and an art class. I was proud of my grades and knew that my family would be proud that I was having a good semester at Schiller College.

The other girls said they were doing equally well. We all loved Señor and Señora Martinez. We told the Holtz's about how great Marie's cooking was and how much weight we were gaining. We agreed during dinner that we would talk to Señora Martinez about having more salads for our evening meals.

We all spoke about Señora Martinez, who was fluent in Spanish, English, and French, but would never speak a word of English to us in the apartment. There was a general consensus that Señora Martinez had a warm, friendly personality. Most impressive was her insistence that we speak only Spanish at home. She wanted to be sure that we developed a fluency in the language. Outside the apartment, she would be kind enough to explain in English something that we didn't understand. Her support, as well as the assistance of a young woman in my Spanish literature class at school, who was fluent in English and Spanish, was truly a blessing. It was their continued support during my first few months in Madrid that proved to be beneficial as I developed a good command of the language.

We also told the Holtz's that Señor Martinez didn't speak any English. Therefore, we were forced to speak Spanish at the dinner table. Unfortunately, he spoke so fast that all the girls agreed with me that we could hardly understand him. We conveyed to the Holtz's that we loved living with the Martinez family. We were one big happy family and everyone got along well. We informed them that we were truly becoming more accustomed to living in Madrid and we were certainly learning Spanish.

The Holtz's were delighted to hear our joys and concerns. They assured us that as time progressed, we would become even more comfortable and that the siesta was certainly enough time in the day to reflect and become more familiar with Spanish culture. Our dinner with the Holtz's was indeed a memorable experience. I was elated that the girls and I made an effort to get together outside the apartment. It was helpful that we had all made an effort to be candid about our experiences in Madrid.

After dining and the flamenco show, the Holtz's dropped us off at home. We thanked them for a wonderful night out. They left and went to their hotel.

* * *

The next day Daniel called to wish me happy holidays. He said he was coming over to visit me that evening. He wanted to know if I had decided to travel to Paris with him for Christmas. I told him I would give him an answer that evening once he arrived at the apartment.

I asked Señora Martinez if I could invite Daniel up to the apartment when he came. She gently informed me that there was a large salon on the ground floor of the apartment building where guests were received.

"Okay," I said; but I was questioning inwardly. Why did Señora Martinez refuse to let Daniel come into the apartment?

I asked Louellen later why I couldn't invite my friend Daniel upstairs. She said it was Spanish custom that men who visited young women would always wait downstairs in the salon. The parents of Spanish girls insisted that these rules be followed. She admitted that adapting to Spanish culture was difficult at times. She told me that Spain's population is ninety percent Catholic and that they are very religious people.

I admitted that I was having a big problem with siesta. Sometimes on a Saturday, I'd awake at eleven o'clock, have breakfast, get dressed, and go shopping. By the time I arrived at the mall, all the stores were closing for siesta. My goodness, I would think, is siesta also at one o'clock in the afternoon on Saturday?

I was told that siesta on the weekends was earlier than during the week. Therefore, I'd find a restaurant, eat lunch, and reluctantly wait until four o'clock in the afternoon, when the stores reopened, to shop. I found this so alien. Yet, I also found it difficult to shop on Saturday morning. So, I continued to struggle with getting accustomed to this tradition. The Spanish clothing, however, was beautiful and well worth the effort in adjusting my shopping schedule. I particularly adored a beautiful brown silk blouse that I bought one day at a Madrid boutique.

During this time, I learned that Spain is known for excellent leather items. I noticed that the Spanish girls sometimes wore tight leather pants. Other times they wore close-fitting, denim jeans. My goodness, I thought, for being so religious these girls certainly wear tight fitting clothes.

* * *

When Daniel arrived that evening, he rang the buzzer and La Señora said, "Quien es?"

"Soy Daniel," he answered.

"Faye, su amigo esta aqui," Señora Martinez said.

"Gracias," I replied as I went down to meet him.

Daniel was dressed so handsomely that evening. He had on a brown designer suit, which matched his blondish-brown hair. His face, with its hazel-brown eyes, was set off by a bright white smile accented by his heavy mustache. Leaning in, he gazed at me and said, "You look beautiful."

"Gracias," I replied.

We went to one of the more expensive cafés that night where we had dinner and drank sangria. We had Spanish flan for dessert and espresso. I knew Daniel had his mind fixed on my accepting his invitation to Paris, since he had a sparkle in his eyes. Soon he started pressuring me about becoming a member of Los Ninos de Dios.

"Faye, will you be coming to Paris with me? I'm leaving in four days," he said.

"My goodness," I responded, " is it only a few days until Christmas?"

Daniel held my hand and smiled. I looked at him hesitantly and started to say no, but then, he reached over and put his hand on my cheek and said sweetly, "Por favor."

How could I deny his invitation? The dimmed lights in the café, the soft, melodious Spanish music, and the pleasant grin on his face were hypnotic. "Si," I said without thinking.

"Great," he replied. Then he grabbed me around my waist and pulled me onto the dance floor. We danced the rest of the evening to the smooth, mesmerizing sound of Spanish music.

* * *

The next day, I told Señora Martinez and the girls at the apartment that I was going to Paris for Christmas. It seemed like perfect timing. Kathy was spending Christmas with her parents in Madrid. Barbara and Debra were going home to the U.S. to visit their families for the holidays. Barbara was returning to the U.S. for only a few days; she planned on returning to Madrid, she explained, to spend New Year's Eve with her new boyfriend. Louellen was staying in Madrid for the holidays. We had become good friends. She was the only one of the girls that I could confide in about the Children of God.

* * *

Over the next few days before my departure to Paris, Louellen and I had a chance to discuss my involvement with the COG. I explained to her that I was going to Paris to spend a week with the COG to see if I wanted to become part of their group. She said she had never heard of them.

"They're missionaries," I said happily.

"Faye, to be a missionary, you'd have to quit school," she said sternly. "Are you prepared for this? What would your family say if you dropped out of school?"

"Louellen, I just want to know God in a way that I've never experienced Him before," I answered. "Being on the mission field will help me to grow in commitment to serve God."

"Think about what benefits the group would offer you," Louellen said.

"I'm sincerely seeking the Lord," I explained. "I've been feeling an emptiness in my walk with God," I continued. "Maybe through the COG I can fill the emptiness in my heart," I said. "Besides, I'm only going to take leave from school for six months. After serving as a missionary, I'll go back to school," I assured Louellen. "Besides, I'm very fond of Daniel," I added.

"Oh no, that's the real reason you want to join," she said. "I knew there was an underlying reason for you joining the COG."

Interrupting Louellen, I said, "No, I'm sincerely looking for a way to strengthen my Christian walk, and I believe the Children of God mission is my answer. Forsaking all to serve God is a wonderful idea. I'll be able to serve God one hundred percent of the time."

However, I hadn't made a decision yet to join the COG. I was still weighing the odds. In spite of all of the benefits I had outlined to Louellen, I still had great reservations. What if it doesn't work out? What would my family think if I dropped out of school? How would I explain this decision to Loyola Marymount University in California? They had awarded me a Study Abroad scholarship. These thoughts permeated my mind and overwhelmed me.

It seemed that Louellen could read my mind. "You're having doubts though, aren't you?" she asked.

"Yes," I admitted.

"Then pray about it some more," she said.

I kissed her on the cheek and thanked her for having a listening ear. "Goodnight," I said.

I walked slowly to my room and sat on the bed and prayed. I wrestled with the idea of joining the COG that night. I didn't sleep that well.

* * *

A few days before Christmas, surprisingly Daniel called me and said that he'd have to take an earlier train to Paris. However, I informed him that I couldn't leave until I had finished making preparations for the trip.

"I'll see you in Paris on Christmas Eve," Daniel romantically whispered, as he hung up the phone.

* * *

When I awoke the next morning, I was still not sure about joining the COG. It all seemed like a dream. I was in Madrid and getting ready to travel to Paris. The thought of being a member of a group of happy people like the COG seemed too good to be true. They appeared to be dedicated people, who loved God. Most impressive was their desire to forsake all to serve Him one hundred percent as missionaries.

I packed enough clothes to stay in Paris for seven days. I was so excited about going to visit with the COG; throughout the day, I could hardly eat. By dinnertime, I was famished. I nervously sat down with Señor and Señora Martinez, Maria, and Louellen. The traditional Spanish dinner was usually very light. That evening, we had a bowl of soup. Also, there was a scrumptious tortilla espanola in the center of the table. Spanish dinner rolls completed the meal.

While seated at the table, I explained to everyone that I was taking a train to Paris the next morning for the holidays. All of the other students happily boasted about their individual plans. Señor and Señora Martinez each cautioned us to be careful during the holidays.

After chatting with everyone for about an hour, I excused myself from the dining room table, and walked to my bedroom.

"Buenos Noches," everyone said in unison.

* * *

The next morning at breakfast, I asked Señor and Señora Martinez to pray that I have a safe journey to Paris. Then, I went back to my bedroom to get my luggage. Struggling with my large suitcase, I pulled it near the front door. Gasping for breath, I waved good-bye as I left the apartment.

"Hasta Luego," Señora Martinez said as she hugged me and said good-bye.

Chapter 4
Paris

I gazed at the shops and theaters in the city as I rode in the taxicab to the train station. As we passed by my favorite pasteleria, I could smell fresh pasteles de manzanas baking. Tears came to my eyes as I thought about how much I was going to miss Madrid. Upon arriving at the station, I bought my ticket to Paris at one of the windows. Student fares were about thirty dollars round trip. I looked at the schedule and noticed that my train would be leaving in fifteen minutes. I quickly gathered my bags and headed toward Track Two.

As I boarded the train, I thought of Daniel and how excited I was to be going to Paris and to be meeting the Paris Show Group. I walked through four coaches looking for a seat in the front of the train. When I found one, I put my bags in the overhead compartment and sat down next to a young woman with short, jet black hair. Suddenly, I heard the doors closing; the train was leaving, and I was on my way to Paris, France.

* * *

The express train ride to Paris would take about twelve hours, so I decided to read a book. It was about ten o'clock in the evening, and I was exhausted from all of the packing for the trip. Still, I couldn't seem to get Daniel out of my mind. I was impressed with him ever since I met him at the Spanish café. I wondered if his friends were just as inspiring.

I turned my attention toward the passengers who were riding the train. I assumed that most of the people were Spaniards since they were conversing in Spanish. The train was full to capacity, which I imagined was not unusual for the holiday season.

After about two hours of reading, I walked into one of the coaches that had several rows of small beds. Exhausted, I pulled out the cot, plopped down, and fell asleep.

* * *

I was awakened by a voice shouting, "Nous sommes arrivé!" I sat up immediately, gathered my belongings, and headed toward the door.

As soon as I left the train and walked into the station, I could smell coffee and fresh croissants. Yes, I had definitely arrived. Walking through the station, I reached the exit where the taxicabs were waiting. Pulling out my directions, I flagged down a taxi. When the cab, which was a blue station wagon, suddenly stopped in front of me, I jumped in the back seat and began conversing in Spanish with the tall, good-looking taxicab driver. He had a glossy, brown mustache and his eyes were sky blue. His smile was broad and sincere. I had heard that the Parisians spoke both French and Spanish. This was expected since the countries were so close together.

"Como estas?" I asked.

"Estoy bien," he answered.

"Me encanta con Paris," I said.

I explained to him that I wanted to go to Colombes, a suburb just outside of Paris. I also told him that it was refreshing that he understood Spanish, especially since I was still struggling with learning French.

The driver told me that most Europeans spoke two languages. He explained that it was not uncommon for the French to also speak Spanish. He said that some of his friends even spoke perfect English. He then told me that the ride to Colombes would be about one half-hour.

"Esta bien," I said as we took off.

As we drove through Paris, I looked at the shops. The fashions were exquisite. I saw lots of people walking briskly in the streets. I noticed that many of the couples were dressed alike. It was fascinating to see why people called Paris the fashion capital of the world.

* * *

When we arrived at the Colombes home, I thanked the taxicab driver for the wonderful ride. I was awestruck at the huge, white house, which was nestled on about an acre of land. I expressed my opinion to the driver that Paris was really picturesque. He helped me to carry my luggage through the big, white gate in front of the house. After I rang the buzzer three times, a young woman came running out to meet me and introduced herself as Judy. She hugged me around my neck, kissed me on the left cheek, and welcomed me to Paris.

Judy was tall and looked about six months pregnant. She appeared to be in her late twenties. She had wiry, blonde hair and brownish blue eyes. Cheerfully, she helped me bring my luggage into the house. As I gazed at the furniture and the pictures on the walls, I noticed that everything looked expensive.

Another attractive young woman came running down the steps. Reaching for my hand, she kissed me warmly on my right check and introduced herself as Becky. "Oh, you must be Faye. Daniel told me that you would be arriving from Madrid," she said. "Let me take your coat."

Becky was short and had long, brown hair. She had a wide, closed-mouth smile, which lifted her cheeks and accented her cute dimples. She appeared to be in her early twenties. As I handed her my coat, Judy beckoned me to take a seat at the dining room table. Glancing at the charming view of the garden outside the house, I nervously sat down with my hands folded across my lap.

"Do you all own this house?" I asked.

"No," Judy said. "We are renting it from a friend."

"Do you all have a Paris Show Group here in Paris?" I asked.

Judy's eyebrows peaked at the mention of the group. "Yes we do," she answered. "We call ourselves Les enfants de Dieu. Becky and I sing for the group."

"I also play guitar and the violin," Becky said excitedly. Then, they told me that they were both Americans and were thrilled with their work as COG missionaries.

"How long have you been disciples in the COG?" I asked.

"Five years," Judy said.

"Three years," Becky added.

"Are you planning to join our group?" Judy asked.

"I don't know," I replied abruptly.

Suddenly, Daniel came running down the steps, hugged me, and kissed me on the forehead. "You made it," he said happily. He then whisked me from my seat, grabbed me around my slim waist, and pulled me to my feet.

Pleasantly surprised, I clutched Daniel's right hand. "Yes, I made it. It was a beautiful trip, and the taxi ride to the house was truly scenic!" I exclaimed.

By this time, Daniel had walked with me to the window and opened it, so that I was able to take a panoramic glimpse of the Colombes property. The emerald green lawn of the Colombes mansion glistened. Daniel provided some historical information about the construction of the mansion and told me that the owners were allowing The Paris Show

Group to rent the property at a significant discount. As we closed the window, the fading daylight intermittently seeped through the blinds.

"How do you like our colony?" Daniel asked.

While I was astonished at the beauty of the neatly trimmed landscape around the home, I was equally amazed at the carefully chosen furniture. Astoundingly, the paintings that dressed the walls of the mansion were mostly French impressionistic artwork. I was certain that the Paris Show Group had an interior decorator that had assisted them in making the Colombes mansion a magnificent site.

"It's a great colony," I answered, as I stared directly into Daniel's glowing, hazel brown eyes.

Suddenly, several people burst through the door with guitars. I turned my attention toward the front door. Daniel introduced the singing group as Les enfants de Dieu. I was jealous of the attention that he was now giving them. This was my first time meeting with Les enfants de Dieu, and I thought their demeanor was aggressive, and their appearance somewhat awry.

Daniel turned toward the group and gleefully announced that they were members of the Paris Show Group. He also boasted that they had just released a new album called "The Bible". Unexpectedly, Daniel shoved the album into my hands as he exclaimed how happy they were about producing it. As Daniel introduced me to the members of the Paris Show Group, each joyfully shook my hand and welcomed me to Paris.

"We will play for you at dinner tonight!" one of the group members exclaimed.

"Great!" I said. I was impressed with Daniel's friends, and I looked forward to hearing them sing at dinner. Becky and Judy thanked me for coming and then excused themselves. As they ran up the stairs, the rest of the crowd followed them. Daniel and I walked out the front door of the mansion into the garden.

Daniel asked sternly, "Faye, have you made up your mind to join?"

"No, not yet," I answered.

Daniel told me that he had to leave later that evening for Madrid. He said that he had business to take care of. However, he assured me that I was welcome to stay at the Colombes home for a week.

"My friends will make you feel at home. They'll take good care of you," he said.

"I'm going to miss you," I replied. "Will you be back?" I asked quietly.

"I don't know if I'll be able to come back right away," he said. "It's getting chilly out here," Daniel said, changing the subject. "Let's go inside for tea."

After re-entering the house, Daniel walked into the kitchen and turned on the stove to make a pot of tea. The smell of fresh croissants filled the room, which was large and exquisitely decorated with stylish art pieces. Sitting at the authentic redwood dining room table, I noticed several photos on the walls of the Paris Show Group.

I turned to Daniel and told him that I was really upset that he was leaving. He insisted, however, that he had to go back to Madrid. He told me that after he took care of some personal business he had to perform with Los Ninos de Dios in Madrid on the day after Christmas.

"Monique Mayson is coming over for our Christmas Eve party," Daniel exclaimed.

"Who's she?" I asked.

"She's a very popular singer here in Paris," Daniel answered. "She helped us produce our album."

"Oh, I'd love to meet her," I said. I kissed Daniel on the cheek and told him that I was weary from my travel. Understanding my fatigue, he graciously walked with me outside to the guesthouse. It was a small, picturesque abode with a bedroom, kitchenette, and bathroom. I thanked Daniel and told him how exhausted I was from the twelve hour train ride from Madrid to Paris.

Daniel said, "Take a nap. I will be sure to wake you up before dinner. You'll be comfortable here," he assured me. Then, he embraced me, wished me a Merry Christmas, and closed the door behind him.

Glancing out of the window as Daniel left, I watched his medium sized frame steal back into the dusk. Suddenly, I saw his ivory white hand firmly grab the front doorknob of the Colombes mansion. Daniel briskly opened the door, walked quickly into the house, and closed the door tightly behind him.

Not able to get control of my romantic feelings for Daniel, I walked over to the bed, plopped down on the side closest to the window, and fell asleep.

* * *

When I awoke, I jumped out of bed, changed clothes, and walked toward the main house to check if dinner was ready to be served. As I approached the large, white house, I could hear music, singing, and laughter. I was amazed at the mansion's size and speculated that it must have at least eight bedrooms.

As one of the COG members opened the door to the main house for me, I heard Daniel yelling, "Faye, is that you? Come on in."

Rushing to the door, he pulled me into the living room and welcomed me as a member of the COG. He proceeded to introduce me to Theo, whom he said had been a singer with the Paris Show Group for only a year. Surprised, but elated by his enthusiasm, I smiled and laid my head on Daniel's right shoulder.

"Did you have a good nap?" he asked.

"Si," I replied.

"Please come and meet our other guests," Daniel said. Without answering, I looked at my watch and noticed that it was about seven o'clock in the evening. I had been sleeping for about two hours.

In amazement, I gazed again at the exquisite architecture of the Colombes home. Captivated with the French portraits that hung royally on the walls, I was sure that I had made the right decision about coming to Paris. As I followed Daniel into the huge kitchen, I noticed all of the food that had been prepared for the Christmas Eve party. Then, I peeked into the beautifully adorned dining room, and noticed the exquisitely decorated table.

I looked up and saw a tall, handsome African American man leaning on the banister of the stairwell. Adjacent to him was a large group of people gathering in the living room. I wondered why the house was so full of people. Then, I remembered Daniel had told me earlier that they were having a big Christmas Eve party that evening.

Walking over to the tall, handsome African American guy, I said, "Hi."

"Hello," he said. "My name is Eli. What's yours?"

"My name is Faye," I said casually.

He told me that he was the COG provisioner. Eli had jet black hair and a copper colored complexion. Gazing at me intently with his dark brown eyes, he explained that his job was to go to the meat and vegetable markets to solicit donations for all the colonies in Paris. "Are you thinking about joining the COG?" he asked.

"Yes, I'm thinking about becoming a member," I answered.

Daniel was standing on the other side of the banister. Grabbing my hand he said, "Come, let me introduce you to some of our other guests."

We walked across the living room, and he introduced me to a medium height, attractive woman with red hair. "This is Monique Mayson," he said. "She's a famous Christian singer here in Paris."

Monique introduced me to her agent, Pierre. She explained to me that she had developed a very successful singing career in Paris with Pierre's help. Daniel said that although Monique was American, she had become very famous in Paris. Because her success as an artist grew rapidly, she promoted Les enfants de Dieu. Therefore, the popularity of their new album, "The Bible," also grew rapidly throughout the Parisian metropolitan area.

Daniel and I chatted with Monique and Pierre for about a half-hour. Then, he beckoned me to come into the dining room. The Paris Show Group members had gathered around the table and were singing Christmas carols. After we sang about five songs, Judy announced that the dinner was ready and asked everyone to take his or her place at the dining room table.

Although the dinner was buffet style, Daniel insisted that he wanted to serve me. As he walked to the sideboard, I glanced at Eli, who seemed to be mixing in with the crowd. He was very handsome and slim. It appeared that he was really enjoying himself. Daniel passed a plate to me, which was dressed with a variety of French dishes, including pommes frites. As he sat down, I confessed to him that I was having a great time at the party.

* * *

After a few hours of celebration, people were starting to leave. Eli said goodnight to me as he walked towards the front door. "We'll see you around; I really have to get back to my colony," he said. "Welcome to the Family." Waving goodbye, I wondered if I'd have a chance to meet him again.

Suddenly, I heard Daniel telling me that there was plenty of food left, including French desserts. Pointing toward a large table, he explained that there were several bottles of French wine still chilling in the big silver bucket. We walked over to the big table and opened a bottle of red wine. He could have chugged the fizzy, red wine right out of the bottle, but he decided to use his manners and grabbed two wine glasses. Filling my glass first, he then poured himself a glassful and asked me to have a toast with him. Excitedly, he kissed me on the cheek and said, "Merry Christmas!" He had a wonderful smile on his face. I could tell he was enjoying the party as much as I was.

We walked to the stairwell that led upstairs to the bedrooms. I asked Daniel to give me a tour of the house, and he agreed.

* * *

We climbed the majestic stairs to the third floor, after which he proceeded to show me the rooms. On the top floor, there were three nicely decorated bedrooms and a small bathroom. Each room was exquisitely furnished with French antiques. We walked down to the second floor, which also had three bedrooms, larger than the bedrooms on the third floor.

"These rooms are for the leaders of the group," Daniel explained.

"They are simply gorgeous," I said with excitement.

I confessed to Daniel that I was impressed with how beautifully furnished and exquisite the house was. Daniel held my hand as we walked back down to the main level. I could hear the sound of laughter as we entered the kitchen. With the tall ceiling and beautiful white walls, the kitchen was my favorite part of the whole house. It was decorated with modern, ivory colored furniture and was very spacious.

As we went back into the living room, Daniel snatched his guitar and began singing to me in French. The song was "Mon Amor, Je Taime." Blushing, I told him that it was the prettiest song that I'd ever heard. The other Paris Show Group members gathered as they joined in with Daniel.

After they finished singing, the applause from the guests was thunderous, and the atmosphere was euphoric. Grabbing me, the Paris Show Group said in unison, "Merry Christmas, Faye. Welcome to the Children of God."

The pressure to join the group was too much to bear. To relieve the stress, I asked Daniel to take me outside. I needed to get away to think. The cool December air refreshed me. Daniel and I crossed over to the other side of the garden. I asked him to give me more time to think about joining the COG. Though I was impressed with his friends, I wasn't sure if I was ready to become a member.

Daniel said that he hoped that I would join the COG; but if I wanted to think about it overnight, I could sleep in the small guesthouse where he had taken me earlier.

Excusing myself, I asked Daniel if he would help me carry the rest of my luggage to the guesthouse. He had placed my bags in a large closet right outside the kitchen. Holding hands, we walked to the closet and Daniel pulled out my luggage. He placed my bags on the right of the closet and closed the door. “I'll be leaving late tonight. I'll call you from Madrid,” he said.

Fatigued from the activities of the day, I simply said, “Okay, I'll be waiting for your call.” Overwhelmed, I did not want to argue with Daniel, but I insisted that he tell me why he had invited me to Paris and now was leaving for Madrid so soon. Daniel was determined not to provide me with any further details about his trip. Since he was insistent about returning to Madrid that evening, I resolved to spend Christmas day with the members of the Paris Show Group.

With the rest of my luggage in his hand, Daniel walked with me back outside to the guesthouse. Embracing my shoulders, he said goodnight. I thanked him for his hospitality, kissed him on his left cheek, and said good-bye. Perplexed, I entered the modest guesthouse and sat on the bed. I thought of running after Daniel to tell him how much I resented his leaving for Madrid; but I braced myself and decided to stay the week in Paris as I had promised.

I knew what it would cost me to join the COG. I had to drop out of school. I knew my family would be angry. How could I tell my counselor back at Schiller College that I had decided to quit school and join the COG? What would the Spanish family with whom I was living think? I undressed, lay on the bed, and cried myself to sleep.

* * *

The next morning, I woke up and looked for my luggage, which had been neatly placed near the large dresser. Grabbing a pair of slacks and a blouse from my bag, I went into the bathroom to wash up. I joyfully looked down at my black patent leather miracles! I had bought the shoes as a Christmas present for myself just before leaving Madrid.

After dressing, I combed my hair and added a little copper blush to my cheeks. Putting on my red winter coat, I walked back to the main house. It was a cold winter morning, but for some reason it didn't bother me. After all, it was Christmas day!

Approaching the Colombes mansion, I knocked on the door and then turned the doorknob. The door was unlocked, so I walked in and headed toward the dining room. Four of the Paris Show Group members were sitting at the kitchen table enjoying coffee and fresh croissants. I glanced at my watch and noticed that it was about nine o'clock in the morning.

Suddenly, a couple walked up to me and introduced themselves as Joe and Marie. They proudly confessed that they were the leaders of the

Paris Show Group and the "shepherds" (COG leaders who were in charge of a colony) of the Colombes home. Looking directly into my eyes, Joe asked me if I had made a decision about joining the COG.

Avoiding Joe's question about joining the COG, I excused myself and walked over to the table to sit down for breakfast. Two other members of the Paris Show Group were standing by the table, playing the guitar, and singing. Then, Becky also asked if I had decided to become a COG member?

Almost hypnotized by the music, I explained to her that I wanted to wait until the spring semester of school to make a decision. Joe, Marie, and Becky surrounded me and began quoting Bible verses. They insisted that now was the time to make the decision. I felt pressured by their insistence that I join the COG. The number of Paris Show Group members who had gathered in the dining room was beginning to frighten me.

"How can you pass up the moment to join the COG?" the group members asked.

"Turn your life over one hundred per cent to the Lord," they continued.

Judy, who was sitting at the head of the table, opened the Bible to Matthew 9:37-38. She read: "The harvest truly is plenteous, but the laborers are few; Pray ye therefore the Lord of the harvest, that he will send forth laborers into his harvest."

I felt guilty when Judy said that now was the time to give my entire life to serving God one hundred percent. How could I refuse? I thought. I burst into tears and fell into a state of confusion. Breaking under the pressure, I agreed to join the COG!

Joe and Marie and the rest of the Paris Show Group who were in the dining room laughed, sang, and surrounded me. They kissed and hugged me and shouted, "Jesus loves you. Welcome to the Family!"

Chapter 5
The Indoctrination

The time I spent during the first few weeks after joining the COG and living in that stunning white house was sobering. It appeared that I had certainly found my place in God's kingdom. Daily, music and laughter filled the Colombes colony.

Monique Mason was a frequent visitor at the alluring mansion. The COG leaders heartily tried to convince her to become a member of the group, but she never made the commitment. Yet, she strongly supported the Paris Show Group and the cause of the COG.

Les enfants de Dieu had daily personal interviews with the media. Also, TV news reporters and radio show hosts had various appointments with the Paris Show Group members throughout the week. In addition, there were reporters who visited and wrote magazine articles about us.

Edward, an Italian duke, was also a frequent visitor at the Colombes home and a fan of Les enfants de Dieu. He was very tall, of medium weight, and had dark hair. He joined the COG when he met Brigitte in Italy. They were married there and had a lavish wedding. It wasn't every day that anyone in the COG married a wealthy nobleman, so that their union caused a big stir.

* * *

I was assigned to work with Richard during the day. Although he was a COG member, he was visiting from another colony. Richard was a singer and a guitar player. Singing on the Metro with Richard was lots of fun. I was told to pass out the offering receptacle and ask for donations for the COG while Richard sang. Parisian people loved the music and asked us if we were members of Les enfants de Dieu.

"Yes," we replied boldly. Then, they smiled and gave generous donations.

At other times, I went out to sing with Judy. She had a beautiful soprano voice, and she also sang a solo on "The Bible" album. Many people recognized her when we rode the Metro and often asked if she was a member of Les enfants de Dieu. After confirming that she was a COG member, some of them would thrust the album in front of her and demand her autograph. Judy smiled bashfully, but she would graciously sign her name on their albums.

I asked the COG leaders if I could go out alone to visit some of the monuments or museums of Paris. I was particularly interested in the Louvre museum. I was told that it was forbidden to do anything alone during my indoctrination as a new COG disciple, which would take from six to eight weeks.

It was not against the rules, however, for me to go out sightseeing (or witnessing) with other COG members. Therefore, occasionally on Sundays, we were allowed to visit the cafés, eat at the bistros, or walk down the Champs Élysée. The Arc de Triomphe electrified me. It was one of the popular tourist attractions in Paris.

* * *

Over the next few weeks, Eli was asked to move into the Colombes home to help me become acclimated to the COG rules and regulations. He was assigned to be my "buddy" (COG member who was in charge of indoctrinating a new member). His job was to train me to successfully become a COG disciple.

Daily, Eli and I read Mo Letters about Moses David, the COG founder. Eli insisted on my daily training sessions with him. He was with me for most of the day, cautiously watching everything that I did. He informed me it was essential that I complete my indoctrination period before I could return to Madrid to retrieve my belongings.

Eli emphatically told me that Moses David was considered to be an end-time prophet for the last days. He was our King, and we were the end-time missionaries, called by God for the commission of bringing lost souls into the kingdom. Eli said that we were a new nation. The people in the world were systemites and did not understand our doctrine or our purpose.

Eli explained to me that I would be getting a lot of pressure from my family at home. He encouraged me to ignore their comments and criticism about the COG. Those who were not members of the COG could not understand us, he cautioned. Eli emphasized that the Mo Letters were now my new handbook for truth. Therefore, the Bible was a supplement to the Mo Letters.

For the COG members, their staunch doctrines were their rock -

their connection to God. Many of their practices were centered on the Mo Letters. The COG even took the liberty of binding the letters in a hard cover book. The leaders provided each "colony" with an edition that was used for their guidance in daily living.

The Mo Letters were written to COG disciples on a monthly basis (sometimes more often) to inform the colonies of what God was saying to us through our prophet, Moses David. It was the prophet's way of keeping in contact with his flock. Eli informed me that the Mo Letters, which were supposedly "revelations from God," had special importance. We were expected to obey them without question. Otherwise, we could be ex-communicated from the Family.

Even though I needed time to internalize some of their more bizarre beliefs, I accepted the Mo Letters and agreed that I would be a faithful follower of the COG. I had one-hour study periods every day with Eli so that I could learn more about the COG rules and regulations. I agreed to "litness" (pass out COG literature in the streets) daily and to sing on the Metros with one of the Les enfants de Dieu group members. Through "litnessing" and singing, I would be bringing in my share of income as a COG member.

* * *

One day I decided I should call home to tell my Aunt Silvia that I had joined the COG. When she answered the phone, I said, "Bonjour, this is Faye."

"Hi, this is Aunt Silvia," she replied.

"I've decided to leave school and join a missionary group called the Children of God," I said softly.

Silence.

"Aunt Silvia, are you still there?" It sounded as if she had dropped the phone.

"You have what?" she asked.

"Remember, I told you in my last letter about the wonderful group of missionaries I met."

"Yes," she replied.

"Well, I've decided to quit school and give my life to the Lord as a missionary," I continued. Suddenly, I heard the voice of my oldest sister, Josephine, on the phone. She must have been listening on an extension.

"Faye, how could you leave school? What about your scholarship?" Josephine asked.

“I'll have to go back and finish another time,” I answered.

“You must be crazy,” she snapped.

Then Eli, who was standing in the hallway while I was making the call whispered, “Faye, remember, I told you systemites don’t understand our calling.”

Immediately, I said to my sister, “I really have to go. I'll write you a letter.”

Then I hung up the phone. I was very upset, but Eli tried to comfort me. He explained to me that when we join the COG, we have to forsake all. He emphasized that unfortunately, sometimes we would have to renounce even our families. Then he quoted a Bible verse: “And everyone that hath forsaken houses, or brethren, or sisters, or father, or mother, or wife, or children, or lands for my name’s sake, shall receive an hundredfold, and shall inherit everlasting life.” (Matthew 19:29.)

“We have to forsake all,” Eli insisted, “and God will bless us for choosing His way for our lives.”

I didn't quite know what he meant when he said “forsake all,” but I felt better.

* * *

Three weeks passed, and I was really beginning to miss Daniel. My feelings of anxiety about his absence were turning into depression. One day he called me at the Colombes mansion to inform me that he would be staying in Madrid for another month. He explained to me that he had been assigned to the Madrid colony to support them during a financial crisis.

At night, I prayed and asked the Lord to bring Daniel back to Paris so that we could talk. I didn't realize how much I cared for him. I often thought about going back to Madrid to see Daniel without permission, but Eli told me that this was forbidden. He explained that I had to stay in Paris until my indoctrination was over.

Every time I mentioned Daniel's name, Eli frowned. I knew he cared about me, since he had already asked me out for a date. He also had asked me to be his girlfriend. Though I was fond of Eli, I still had not forgotten about Daniel. I planned to see him again once I was released to go back to Madrid. I asked Eli if Daniel was really going to return to Paris.

Also, I informed Eli that it didn't seem fair that he “dumped” me as soon as I joined the COG.

"Forget about Daniel," Eli told me. "He'll be back to Paris in God's time."

It was easier said than done. I had grown to really care about Daniel and was expecting him to help me become adapted to the COG. How could he leave so suddenly and not call me more regularly? I thought. It all seemed so strange. Then it dawned on me that this was all a "set-up." It appeared that the leaders had purposely asked Eli to move into the home to train me to help me forget about Daniel.

When I approached Eli about this, he told me that my suppositions were nonsense. He promised me that the COG was doing everything in my best interest. Furthermore, he encouraged me to relax and keep my mind focused on my discipleship training. Taking Eli's advice, I tried to remove any negative thoughts from my mind about the COG.

Also, the COG leaders, Joe and Marie, assured me that they had asked Eli to move into the Colombes home to help me become acclimated to the COG rules and regulations. He was assigned to be my immediate shepherd. They confirmed Eli's emphasis on my daily reading of the Mo Letters. Most convincing was their determination that Moses David was our end-time prophet for the last days. As Eli had taught me, he was our King, and we were the end-time missionaries, called by God, for the commission of bringing lost souls into the kingdom. Indeed, they confirmed that we were a new nation. They agreed with Eli that the people in the world were systemites, who did not understand our doctrine, or our purpose.

* * *

Dinner time at the Colombes home was fun. We'd sit around the huge dining room table, which overlooked the garden, and eat French style steak and pommes frites. One night at dinner, Eli said, "Faye, you ought to change your name. You've been with us for about six weeks now." Everyone at the table nodded in agreement.

"What shall I call myself?" I asked.

Victory, a child-care worker, said, "We'll call you Destiny."

"No," I said. I informed Victory that I was not comfortable with that name.

"I've got it," Victory shouted. "We'll call you Joy."

"Yes," everyone at the dinner table shouted.

One of the leaders said, "Sure - she's always happy. We'll call her Joy."

Eli explained that everyone was required to change his or her name after they became a member.

"I like the name Joy," I said.

Everyone at the table exploded with laughter.

* * *

After dinner, Josiah, one of Les enfants de Dieu group musicians, sang a song from their album called "Perfect Man". Then, Judy sang a beautiful song called, "Peace in the Midst of a Storm." The music was uplifting, and I marveled at the clear sound of their voices. I was so impressed with "Les enfants de Dieu" that I asked Richard if he would spend some time teaching me to play the guitar.

He asked me if I had any experience. I said, "Yes," since I had fiddled with the guitar in college in the U.S. I promised Richard that with his help and with my diligent practice, I would learn quickly. He agreed to teach me a few songs over the next two months.

There were twelve adults and four children at the Colombes colony. Just about everyone, except the children, sang or played an instrument. Therefore, they heartily encouraged me to learn how to play the guitar. Most of all, I enjoyed when the children sang around the dinner table. The house was always full of people, and music filled our hearts. The children also had a love for music. They sang in the parks around Paris with their parents and helped to raise money for Les enfants de Dieu.

* * *

I had been in Paris for about seven weeks when Joseph, another shepherd at the Colombes home surprisingly told me that Daniel was coming back to Paris. Excitedly, I waited for his return. I explained to Joseph that I had left some of my clothes in Madrid at Señor and Señora Martinez's apartment. Therefore, I needed to return to Madrid to retrieve them. I also needed to withdraw officially from Schiller College.

Joseph informed me that I could leave soon. Eli had reported to him that I was doing quite well with my indoctrination into the COG lifestyle. Then, I asked Joseph if I could go back to Madrid with Daniel. He did not provide me with a concrete answer.

* * *

When Daniel arrived, I was so happy to see him. Yet, it appeared that he wasn't eager to reunite with me. His posture was aloof and his manner was so frigid. Shocked at his behavior, I didn't know why he was acting so strange, so I hugged and kissed him on the left cheek. Ignoring his reticent attitude, I showed Daniel a poem that I had written:

I'm Free

Not long ago my heart was lonely looking for something to uphold me.

I met a man who filled that gap, whom God used as my trap.

His spirit of Love, Peace, and Joy are what my soul was searching for.

He said he lived by faith—Forsook all to follow God,

a way at first I thought was impossible to trod.

But when I accepted God's Spirit of Love,

my soul felt clean, as if washed by the rain above.

The new me evolved, as the spirit of God made me whole

I was free, yes free from society's bondage and control

Ahead of me lies a life full of goals—the primary one being to win many souls.

Thank you, Lord, Hallelujah, I'm Free to do your Will as you direct me.

Daniel grabbled the poem, thanked me, and said that it was beautiful. Then, he asked me if I was progressing with my indoctrination. I told him that I was just about finished with my missionary training. Most importantly, I informed him that I had received permission from my Shepherd Joseph to return to Madrid.

"Can we go return to Madrid together?" I asked.

"Ah, I don't know," Daniel said evasively. Then, he galloped up the long flight of steps like a race horse charging toward the finished line. When he reached the top of the stairs, he was cool as a cucumber. Then, he whispered,

"We'll talk about it later."

Disheartened, I pondered the strange look Daniel had on his face. Was he trying to hide something? I wondered. Most disturbing was that it appeared the romance that had developed between us was a farce. I was shocked that Daniel was so standoffish. Why wasn't he enthusiastic about seeing me? I thought. I had not seen Daniel for several weeks. I was hurt that he didn't seem interested in spending any time with me.

* * *

Later that evening, I went up to my room to go to bed. As I walked up the steps, one of the bedroom doors was ajar. Curiously, I peeked in the door and was surprised to see that Daniel was in the room hugging a girl. I opened the door and Daniel looked like a little child who had been caught stealing a cookie from the cookie jar.

"This is Angelina," he said nervously.

"She's from Madrid. I believe Angelina will become a COG disciple. We came to Paris together to visit with Les enfants de Dieu."

"Como estas?" she asked.

"Muy bien," I answered. I looked angrily at Daniel and left the room, slamming the door.

How dare he, I thought, as I walked up the next flight of stairs to my room. It appeared that Daniel had already found another friend in just two months. I was irate with him. I thought we had a special relationship and that he deeply cared for me. *Was it all a game he was playing?* I asked myself. Furthermore, *how could he find another girl so fast?* I wondered.

I had been certain that if I joined the COG that Daniel would be happy about my decision and would make a commitment to me. Now, my mind was flooded with doubts and discouragement. Maybe I had made a mistake about joining the COG, I thought. In any case, I was sure it was time for me to leave the Colombes colony and return to Madrid. I felt assured that a change of environment would assist me to come to grips with my new life as a COG disciple.

That night, I cried myself to sleep thinking about Daniel.

* * *

When I awoke the next morning, Daniel had already left for Madrid with Angelina. He never explained to me why he was visiting the Colombes home. Also, Daniel did not tell me that he was leaving so soon. How rude of him, I thought.

At breakfast, I questioned Eli about Daniel's behavior. "Who is Angelina?" I asked.

"Oh, she's a potential recruit," Eli answered. "Daniel brought her to Colombes so that she could meet Les enfants de Dieu. But they had to leave because of a performance the COG music group has in Madrid this weekend," Eli explained.

"So soon?" I asked. "He could have stayed a day or two so that we could talk."

"Aren't you planning to go to Madrid?" Eli asked.

"Yes, in a few days," I answered.

"You can call Daniel when you get back to Madrid," Eli assured me.

"Yes, maybe he'll have more time to talk," I replied.

I told Eli that I was going to my room to start packing for my trip. I walked up the stairs still enraged about the way Daniel had treated me. When I approached the medium-sized room, I pulled out my suitcase and started packing. Just as I was pulling out my clothes from the drawer, Eli popped his head through the door.

"Joy, I love you," he said. "Will you marry me?" he asked, pushing his way through the door. Then, he fell to his knees.

"You've got to be kidding," I said.

"Get up - are you crazy?"

"No, I really care for you," he continued. "The first time we met at the Christmas party God showed me that you were my wife."

"Sure," I replied sarcastically.

Eli told me that he was serious and that he really loved me.

"I'll think about it," I said. I was not sure if he really meant what he said or if he was trying to dissuade my anger against Daniel.

"When you return from Madrid, can we go steady?" he continued. "If you are not ready to get married, can I at least be your boyfriend?" he asked.

"Yes," I said without thinking, partially because I was angry with Daniel.

"Now, let me pack so that I can get ready to go to Madrid," I said.

"Good," Eli whispered softly and kissed me on the right cheek.

* * *

The next day I solemnly left the Colombes mansion alone for the first time in several weeks. I took a yellow taxicab to the train station. Eli wanted to escort me, but I refused. I needed time to think about my new found commitment as a COG missionary. I was now free to decide to continue my pledge to be a faithful COG member or to return to student life at Schiller College.

* * *

When I arrived in Madrid, it was mid-February, 1978. I had decided that I would spend time at one of the hotels near Schiller College. The time alone would give me a chance to think about the decision I had made and what it had cost me. I knew my folks in the U.S. were very upset, so I decided not to give them a call. I did not want to visit with the counselor, Mr. Jenkins, at Schiller College. Also, I knew it was imperative that I speak with Señor and Señora Martinez. I needed to thank them personally for extending the opportunity for me to live with a Spanish family.

As I gathered my thoughts at the hotel room, I was confident that I wanted to give my life to serving God one hundred percent as a COG missionary. It was this certainty that helped me to grapple with my feelings of confusion about how to pull away from the life that I knew as a student in Madrid. Yet, I was overwhelmed with doubts about how to totally readjust to life as a COG missionary.

* * *

The first thing I wanted to take care of was a visit to the COG colony to speak with Daniel. I decided to call the home, which was near the University of Madrid. It was only a few short blocks from the student café where I had first met Daniel.

When I phoned, I said to the person who answered, "This is Joy, I am a new COG disciple."

"Hi, this is Estella," a quiet, sweet voice responded.

"Yo quiero hablar con Daniel. El esta?" I continued.

"Si, espera un momentito."

After waiting nervously for Daniel to come to the phone, I heard his voice on the other end of the line. "Hi, this is Daniel, may I help you?" he asked.

"Hi, this is Joy. Remember, you and I need to talk about my new life as a COG missionary."

"Oh, yes," he stated. "I was looking forward to your call. When can you come to the colony so that we can talk?" he asked.

"How about tomorrow at two o'clock?" I answered.

"Bueno, hasta manana."

"Esta bien," I said and hung up the phone.

Finally, Daniel had agreed to speak with me. During my indoctrination, the COG leaders in Paris forbade me to call him in Madrid. Even when Daniel arrived in Paris to introduce Angelina to the group, I was forbidden to have any detailed discussions with him.

* * *

The next day, Daniel and I met at a café near the University of Madrid. I was amazed at how he had changed. He was not the romantic, charming fellow who had introduced me to the COG about eight weeks ago. Daniel's appearance was stoic, and he seemed weary.

Perhaps he was tired from the constant singing at the student cafés over the Christmas and New Year holiday season, I thought.

"Hola, Daniel," I said, to begin the conversation with him.

"Hola, Joy. Coma estas?" he asked.

I solemnly asked Daniel about his strange behavior. Most importantly, I wanted to know who Angelina was. Daniel abruptly interrupted me and explained that Angelina was a new prospective COG member. He had invited her to Paris for the same reason he had invited me to come. He earnestly wanted to introduce Angelina to the leaders of the COG.

Finally, Daniel confessed that his job was to recruit new COG members. He apologized for the time he spent away from me. Yet, he cautioned that it was COG policy to allow new recruits to complete their indoctrination period. After about four to six weeks, he was allowed to make direct contact with a new COG disciple.

Although I was angry with Daniel, I allowed him to speak. Then, I explained to him that I was happy that I had given my life to what I thought was a good cause. I was certain that meeting the COG was a valid religious experience for me. Also, I was determined to forsake all and give my life one hundred per cent to being a COG missionary.

Chapter 6 Rambuteau

After settling my school affairs in Madrid with my guidance counselor, Mr. Jenkins, at Schiller College, I visited with the Martinez family. It was important that I visit with them to explain my call to be a COG missionary.

As Eli had warned me, they were not in agreement with my decision. During our one-hour conversation, Señor and Señora Martinez made every effort to dissuade me from returning to Paris as a COG missionary. I listened politely to their criticisms, but I had already been indoctrinated into the COG life-style. Therefore, I had decided to serve at least two years with the group. This would provide enough time for me to be on "the mission field," trusting God for my sustenance.

* * *

After packing my belonging at the Martinez's large apartment, I boarded the train and returned to Paris. I took an evening train so that I could sleep overnight. I was convinced that the twelve hour train ride would be a time of reflection about my first assignment as a new COG missionary. Also, I was apprehensive about the challenges that I might face as a new COG disciple.

* * *

To my chagrin, when I arrived at the Colombes colony, Les enfants de Dieu had decided to move to Cannes, France. I was informed that they were experiencing intense persecution from the Paris law enforcement about their "New Revolution."

The "New Revolution" changed the whole direction of living in the COG colonies.

Members were strongly encouraged to participate in "sharing" (free sex among group members) and flirty fishing ("FFing"). This practice included going to nightclubs to seek men who were willing to support our work. The COG changed its name to the "Family of Love."

The leaders at the Colombes colony did not invite me to join them in Cannes. Instead, they felt I was ready to pioneer a new COG colony with Stanley, a new COG shepherd.

* * *

It was early March, 1978, and Stanley ordered Richard, Lois, and me to move into an apartment near the Rambuteau Metro stop in Paris. Meanwhile, Stanley; his wife Briana; and their three children moved into the La Salle studio apartment. It was a thirty-minute train ride by Metro from the Rambuteau apartment. Jordan, a new COG disciple, also moved into the La Salle studio apartment.

Blair, Stanley's oldest daughter, who was six-years old, had a small frame. Tommy, his son, was four years old and was tall for his age. Lee was a very quiet two-year old. Stanley quipped that Lee's daily activities included getting into everything around the apartment.

* * *

When I accepted Stanley as my new shepherd, he told me that I should be willing to surrender to his leadership. Also, he informed us that we were to endure hardship as submissive soldiers in the Lord's army. Stanley made it clear that our job at Rambuteau was to "litness" and sing on the Metro in order to raise enough money to rent a house for the whole team.

* * *

Rambuteau was a rugged neighborhood, which seemed to be struggling to become a cleaner, safer place to live. Nearby, was the popular Pompidou Center. Various art shows, seminars, and musical events attracted throngs of tourists. Also, the nightclubs, bars, and restaurants were heavily populated every night. Therefore, I felt safer that the police station was on the corner near our apartment building.

Stanley led us through the tall, wooden doors and up a shabby stairwell to our Rambuteau apartment. The stairs were so rickety they threatened to give way under my feet. When I opened the door to the apartment, the knob almost fell off in my hand. Well, there's no need to lock the door. Anyone wanting to come in only had to give it a good push, I thought.

In the corner stood a grimy, old stove, obviously unfit for cooking. The only pieces of furniture were a wobbly chair, two moldy beds, and a small, dilapidated dresser. I walked into the run-down bathroom to check if the shower was working. To my dismay, when I turned on the faucet in the bathroom sink, only a tiny trickle of water came out.

Shocked and confused by the apartment that Stanley demanded that we occupy, I sat down in the old chair by the window. The apartment's decor reminded me of my dark spiritual state and my troubled relationship with God, and I was alarmed. I thought I had found the truth, but now I felt a deep sense of apprehension.

* * *

I was only pretending to be happy singing and "litnessing" on the Metros with Richard and Lois. Stanley's reminders about enduring hardship as soldiers in the COG weighed heavily on my spirit. Why was I staying? I asked myself. I reasoned that becoming a COG missionary was God's will for my life, but my spirit cried out.

It baffled me that although there was so much buzz-talk among the COG members, no one seemed to realize that there was a disciple who was crying out for help. Seeing this lack of concern for my emotional well-being amplified my fear.

* * *

During our two-month stay at the Rambuteau apartment, Stanley met with us frequently to check on our progress toward raising the money necessary to rent a house. We were on duty every day for twelve hours. We faithfully left the Rambuteau apartment at six a.m. Our schedule consisted of "litnessing" during the morning hours. In the afternoon, we worked on recruiting new COG members. Richard was an excellent singer and guitarist and the French people loved his music.

Most of the time I was fatigued and emotionally distraught. These feelings of anxiety made me feel like a child who had been abused by her parents. In addition, I was perplexed by the overwhelming sense of bewilderment that I felt. My condition worsened until I was unable to clearly think about my spiritual state.

One day Richard, Lois, and I met Eli while singing on the Metro. Eli was living at the Bastille colony at the Gare du Nord Metro station.

"Bonjour. How are you all doing?" he asked.

"I'm fine," I said sluggishly.

"Nous etions bien," Richard and Lois said in unison.

"You look tired, Joy," Eli said, reaching for my hand.

"I'm really drained. We have an early morning schedule to sing on the Metro," I stated. I then informed Eli that Stanley was my new shepherd.

"Why do you feel so exhausted?" Eli asked.

"Well, we're trying to raise money to rent a house," I answered.

"Stanley's expectations of your team must be very strenuous," Eli said seriously. "You look awful."

This was the first time I had seen Eli since I was assigned to be on Stanley's team. He was still very handsome, tall, and slender. He galloped down the stairs with his rugged black boots. As he approached the vending machines, Eli pulled out his money to buy his train pass.

I ran down the stairs and grabbed him around his neck. "Why don't you join our team so that you can help us get our house?" I asked him.

"Maybe," he said hesitantly. "I would like to speak to Stanley about it. But for now, I like the Bastille colony," he replied.

Eli pulled me closer to him and kissed me on the lips. Quickly, I asked Eli for his direct phone number at the Bastille colony. Then, he waved good-bye and dashed onto the train.

* * *

That evening I called Eli. I was really glad to talk to him again. During our conversation, Eli told me that he had just returned from Cambridge, Maryland, to see his immediate family and relatives. He explained that his mother and father tried to persuade him to leave the COG, but he was sure that he wanted to return to Paris.

Eli revealed to me how shocked he had been at the severe harassment that the singing group Les enfants de Dieu had suffered in Paris. He believed that the persecution stemmed from the "New Revolution."

He confirmed the information that the Paris Show Group had moved to Cannes, France, to flee from the interrogations that they had received from the police department in Paris. Eli explained that when he had visited the COG Colombes home, the leaders told him that he could either go to Cannes, France with them or find a new colony. Then he called the Bastille colony where his friends, Elaine and Larry, were shepherds. They accepted him right away.

"So you decided to stay in the COG and follow the "New Revolution" and haven't backslidden?" I asked.

"I love the Bastille colony," he said cheerfully. "Yes, I had problems with the "New Revolution" at first, but I still want to be a soldier in the army of the COG," Eli exclaimed.

Encouraged by his enthusiasm, I invited Eli to come for a visit with us at the La Salle studio apartment. "I would love for you to join our team," I said.

Eli informed me that he'd think about making a change. Also, he stated that he would let me know his decision within the next two weeks.

I hung up the phone, feeling irritated that I did not tell Eli how disturbed I was about the "New Revolution" ideas of "sharing" and "FFing." Also, I wanted Eli to know I was unhappy as a disciple on Stanley's team; but Eli had seemed in a hurry to get off the phone. I decided to call him again another day and try to meet him for lunch.

* * *

That evening Stanley came over to the Rambuteau apartment with his wife and three children. They played while Stanley informed us that we would start "FFing" at one of the clubs near the Champs Élysée called Coeur Samba. He insisted that this was a great place to meet potential supporters for our missionary work. Besides, he felt that since there were lots of tourists at Coeur Samba, we would have a great chance for meeting potential COG recruits.

I wasn't too anxious to "FF," but everyone else seemed excited. Stanley explained that Briana, Lois, and I would be the bait (the girls who went "FFing," and Stanley would be the chaperone). Though the men usually stayed home with the children while the women went "FFing," they were encouraged to routinely "FF" on their own.

As Stanley talked, I focused my attention on his wife, Briana. A young American girl in her twenties, she was medium height and very pretty. However, she always seemed somewhat withdrawn and in a daze. She never asked questions about anything Stanley said. She simply shook her head and nodded in agreement anytime he asked her to do something.

It was as if Stanley wound her up like a robot in the morning, so that she obeyed everything he said. Stanley rarely asked her opinion on anything. I was puzzled by this behavior since Stanley and Briana were both responsible for making the rules for the home.

Lois, who lived with Richard and me, was only twenty years old and very shy. Her ivory colored face was accented by a wide, tight-lipped smile. Tall and slim, she was very troubled. I often felt that it was some incident in her childhood that was responsible for her mental state. Yet, she was determined to support Stanley in his endeavor to establish a new COG colony.

Richard loved rules and regulations and avidly obeyed every Mo Letter. If "Dad" (Moses David) said "sharing" and "FFing" were okay, then he was in complete agreement with the practice. He confirmed that Dad was our prophet and the captain of our army and that he, Richard, was proud to be a soldier in the COG. Richard was very active always on the go. Because of his aggressiveness, we nicknamed him Richard Go-Slow to remind him to slow down.

As we discussed "FFing," I had all the questions, "What do I wear? What do I say to the men at the club? What kind of follow-up would be necessary?"

Stanley answered these questions very briefly.

"Joy," he said. "Wear your best red dress. Only say or do what is necessary in order to convince the men to receive Christ. As far as your other questions, let's see what happens when we get to the club."

After our initial meeting about our new method of witnessing, I thought about "FFing" daily. It just didn't seem right to me, but I went along because I was pressured by Stanley to comply with the rules and regulations of the "New Revolution." The team's rejection of my outspokenness about "FFing" was evident. However, I did not care about their rebuff. I was more concerned about my ability to get back in right relationship with God.

* * *

A few days later, I called Eli again. I wanted to know his true feelings about "FFing."

"Eli, what do you think about "sharing" and "FFing"?" I asked.

"Why, the Mo Letters say we have to do it; otherwise, we can get ex-communicated from the COG. So, we have no choice."

"Eli, we are going out on Friday night and I'm petrified," I said. I asked Eli to meet with me for lunch the following day and he agreed.

* * *

After speaking with Eli, I decided to talk with Stanley about my apprehension about sharing and "FFing." I had also decided to speak with him about his insistence that I be his childcare worker for his three children. I took the thirty-minute Metro ride and then walked four blocks to the LaSalle apartment building.

The COG team member's studio apartment was on the fifth floor. At the Rambuteau apartment, Lois, Richard, and I were able to use the bathroom inside the apartment. However, at the La Salle apartment, the COG team members had to share the bathroom in the hallway with the other tenants on the floor.

When I arrived at the apartment, Stanley opened the door. I could smell the aroma of pommes frites and bifteck, my favorite Parisian dishes. Stanley beckoned me join them, but I was too upset to eat. I had lost my appetite since I was so stressed about my role as a member of Stanley's team.

Stanley must have noticed how disheartened I felt. Staring at me, he asked, "Joy, what's troubling you?"

"Stanley, I'm uncomfortable about 'sharing.' Is this practice biblical?"

"Joy, to the pure all things are pure; all things are lawful as long as we do them with love," he said. "You see, we are a new nation, called by God to save this untoward and wicked generation. We are the chosen few . . ."

I interrupted him, "What about "FFing"?" I asked.

"Joy, these men, the 'fish' (men who we met while "FFing"), are lost," he explained. "They don't have Jesus. If you girls have to go to bed with them so that they can get saved, then it's not against God's law of love. You have to lay down your life that they may live."

Before I had a chance to answer, Stanley shoved a Mo Letter, "Die Daily," in my hand. Then, he stated that we were now called the Family and should begin to consider more thoughtfully why the Lord had called us into this new nation. "In order to understand 'sharing' and "FFing" and the whole concept of the 'New Revolution,' you have to die daily to your own selfish desires in order to save the 'fish'," Stanley continued.

"The most uncomfortable place for a Christian is a comfortable place. One of the great dangers you have right now is the feeling you've really accomplished something, so much so, that you no longer have that driving motivation, which makes you feel like you cannot stop, that you've got to keep going even if it kills you. How like death moving is. It's the ending of one life and the beginning of another. Moving is hard to do. I'm even having a real battle moving on to the next place. If I have to keep moving, I have to keep dying. You can understand why Paul said, 'I die daily'."1

"Joy, you have to share with your other brothers," Stanley continued passionately. "If they have a need, you must be willing to meet that need."

Then, Stanley continued, "since Dad has now changed our name to the "Family of Love", he felt that we should refer to our team members as such." Stanley believed that being considered as the Family would be preferable over being called the Children of God.

To change the subject, I brought up the idea of being Stanley's childcare worker. Tommy, Blair, and Lee were adorable children. However, I told Stanley that I was not sure if I wanted to be their childcare worker. Stanley contended that God had spoken to him and told him that I was the perfect person for the job.

"Stanley, you can't force me to do something that I'm not comfortable doing. I love the children, but God has not spoken to my heart that I should be their childcare worker," I said sternly.

"Joy, you are rebellious and disobedient to leadership," he interrupted. "I'm the shepherd, and I say that you will make an excellent childcare worker."

I was furious. How could he demand that of me, I thought. There was no use talking to him any longer. I got up to leave. "Stanley, I really have to go now," I said. "Au revoir."

I rushed to the door and ran down the stairs to the ground floor. I dashed toward the Metro, my mind frantically speeding like race cars dashing toward the finish line. I was angry with Stanley. His dictatorial manner was very disturbing to me. Yet, I had nowhere else to go. He was my shepherd, and the Mo Letters stated that we had to be obedient to our leadership.

* * *

When I arrived back at the Rambuteau apartment, Lois and Richard had gone out "litnessing." I was glad to be alone so I could think.

What am I doing here? I asked myself. I was a college dropout and in a foreign country, where most of the natives spoke only French and Spanish. I had learned enough French to go to the store and buy food and get to the Metro, but I was far from being fluent. Then, I thought about Stanley and how tyrannical he was. I wondered if we would ever get along.

As these thoughts ran through my head, I looked down at the "Die Daily" Mo Letter and began reading it. The letter clearly stated that the rugged COG soldier should simply follow the commands of the colony shepherds. Moses David explained this concept as dying daily for "the cause."

As I continued reading the Mo Letter, I became so immersed in the die daily doctrine that I forgot about my argument with Stanley and my doubts about the "Family."

Surely, God had called me. He would not have allowed me to drop out of college and live in self-denial as a missionary if it wasn't His will for my life, I thought. I simply needed to die daily to my will. The Mo Letter had answered my questions and gave me hope in fulfilling what I thought was my call to the COG. I decided to keep marching on. I wanted to be a soldier in this God-chosen army, even if it killed me.

* * *

The next day I met with Eli at a café near the COG Trocadero home. Eli told me that Daniel was visiting with the leaders at the colony. They were having financial problems and Daniel had returned to Paris to assist the colony with singing on the Metros to raise money.

Eli made it clear that most of the homes in Paris were experiencing financial difficulty because of the heavy persecution since the "New Revolution."

"Would you like to go and see Daniel?" Eli asked.

"No, I really don't want to see him," I answered. After all, I thought, I was becoming very fond of Eli.

"Why does Stanley insist that I be his childcare worker?" I asked Eli, changing the subject.

"Joy, as a soldier in the COG, we have to be obedient to our leaders," he answered. "Stanley is your shepherd, and you have to do what he tells you to do," Eli said as he glared sternly at me.

"But what if I don't like babysitting children all the time?"

"Well, you have to die daily to your feelings and think about the children," he answered. "Have you read that letter?" Eli asked.

"Yes, I guess you're right. I need to learn to die daily," I confessed.

Saying good-bye, Eli kissed me on the cheek and promised to ask Stanley about his joining our team. Then, Eli asked me a question that surprised me. "Joy, would you be my steady girl? Better yet, why don't we just get married?" Eli blurted out.

I didn't think he was serious. "I'm quite fond of you and would like to be your girlfriend, but I'm not ready for marriage," I answered.

This was the second time that Eli had asked me to marry him. I was unsure what his intentions were, especially since in the COG we were forbidden to marry. We could only live together as a couple.

Frightened to even consider his proposal of marriage, I said goodbye to Eli, and promised to see him again soon.

* * *

When I returned to the Rambuteau apartment, Stanley was there and happily announced that we had almost enough money to rent a home. He said he had found a little house in the Gonesse suburbs.

We walked as a team to the Metro and caught a train, praising and thanking God for the house that the Lord had for us.

The train ride was about forty minutes. The suburbs of Paris were astounding! Our team members were quiet as we anticipated the joy we would all experience once we were able to occupy the new colony.

* * *

When we arrived in Gonesse, we walked about four blocks to the house. It was a single family home, with beige shutters and a lime green door. As we approached the entrance of the house, I noticed the steps were freshly painted.

Although it was a small house, it had three bedrooms on the main floor, a bathroom, a large living room, and a dining room. As we walked down the hall, I noticed a powder room on the right. A small stairwell led to the basement, which had been made into a large bedroom. Also, I noticed a large backyard, which seemed like a great place for the children to play. We agreed that although the house was rather small, it would be sufficient and quite affordable. Stanley was ecstatic, and we shared his delight. This was a major victory for us. Our early morning singing on the Metros to raise the money to obtain the house had finally paid off.

* * *

As we headed toward the Metro to go back to Paris, Stanley explained that the house would not be available for another month. Therefore, we would have to stay at the Rambuteau and La Salle apartments until that time. "Besides, we need more time to finish raising the money we need for the rent and to purchase furniture," Stanley assured us. All of us looked at Stanley in dismay.

"Cheer up. We need to start thinking about Friday night. We're going "FFing!" he exclaimed.

My heart sank, but before I had a chance to express my annoyance about this decision, Stanley said, "We need to plan the bait."

* * *

Friday night came and with it my heightened reservations about "FFing." My curiosity peaked as I pondered what I would be confronted with at the club. I tried to be mentally prepared to move to another spiritual level. Most challenging was the fact that this would be our female team members' first adventure at "FFing."

I slowly slipped my favorite red dress over my shoulders. I put on my long silver and black earrings and slipped my matching chain around my neck. I gazed in the mirror. I was amazed at how I had coordinated my colors. Nervously, I slipped my shiny, black pumps onto my small feet.

Lois wore a beautiful pink, satin dress with sequins. Just as I was helping her choose a pair of shoes, Stanley marched in with Briana. My, did she look beautiful, I thought. Briana had on a sleek silk black dress.

Stanley looked handsome, too, in his blue and white pinstriped suit. The smell of Pierre Cardin cologne, Stanley's favorite, filled the room.

"You girls look gorgeous," Stanley said. "Are you ready to catch some 'fish'?"

"Yes, we're ready," we said in unison.

* * *

When we arrived at Coeur Samba, I was very edgy. It appeared that Lois and Briana were nervous too.

"Relax, and I will tell you girls who to dance with," Stanley said, as we walked through the majestic doors of the nightclub. It was so dark inside that it took my eyes awhile to adjust. The music assaulted my ears with its relentless pounding. The hostess seated us at a table near the dance floor. We ordered vin blanc. Then, Stanley began to brief us on what to say.

"Always tell the 'fish' that you are missionaries. Remember to invite them to receive Christ," he cautioned.

"If it is necessary, do we have to go to bed with them?" I asked.

"Only go to bed with the 'fish' if it is necessary to get them to receive Christ into their hearts," he answered.

I swallowed hard. I could feel my heart pounding relentlessly. Then, a tall, handsome, dark-skinned guy came over and asked me to dance. Stanley beckoned to me that it was okay. The gentleman pulled me to the dance floor. My, he's cute, I thought. I assumed he was from Africa since most blacks in Paris were.

"Are you from Africa?" I asked.

"Yes," he replied.

"What part?" I continued.

"Ghana. And you?" he asked.

"I'm from the United States, but I'm living here in Paris with a group of missionaries," I answered. We pranced gracefully around the dance floor.

"Missionaries? What is the name of your group?" he asked me.

"Les Enfants de Dieu."

"Oh, I never heard of them," he said. "But tell me about your group."

I told him about our cause and about our basic beliefs as missionaries. He was curious and said he wanted to know more.

"Your name?" I asked.

"Oba," he answered. "And yours?"

"Joy," I replied cheerfully.

After the song was over, Oba escorted me back to our table and I sat down. I was beginning to feel a lot more comfortable, as Oba seemed like a nice guy. Stanley questioned me about Oba as soon as I pulled my chair up to the table.

"Did you tell him about our cause and our mission in Paris?" he asked.

"Yes," I said and nodded.

"Very good," Stanley congratulated me.

"Merci," I said as I sipped my vin blanc.

Briana and Lois seemed to be enjoying themselves out on the dance floor. They were both dancing with men who appeared to be French.

When they returned to the table, they happily exclaimed that they were having fun. They informed us that they had met Jean and Pierre. They confirmed that they were two Frenchmen from Paris, who seemed interested in supporting our work.

Stanley congratulated us all and said that he was quite pleased with our performance.

* * *

Oba asked me to dance again. As the soft music calmed my emotions, I had enough courage to ask Oba for his phone number. I explained to him that I would need to follow-up with a call to him since I didn't have a phone at the Rambuteau apartment.

Oba asked me more questions about Les Enfants de Dieu. I explained to him that we needed supporters to help us with our work. Also, I told him we did not have jobs. I then confessed that we raised funds by singing and passing out literature.

Oba continued to ask me questions. He responded that he was impressed with our dedication and asked me to call him so that we could talk more the next week. I felt strange telling Oba that we were missionaries while dancing in a disco. It seemed so hypocritical. Yet, I promised to call him soon. Oba said that he was really looking forward to hearing from me.

* * *

At about two o'clock, we left the club and took a taxi home. I was relieved to leave Coeur Samba. I wasn't sure I wanted to go "FFing" again. However, during our ride home, Stanley reminded us that we were going "FFing" again the following Friday night. He also explained that we should make sure we called the contacts we made at Coeur Samba the following week.

* * *

A month later, Stanley informed us that our house at Gonesse was ready. At last we would have a decent dwelling place, and we thanked God for it.

The Metro ride to Gonesse was pleasant. Stanley insisted that we read Mo Letters during the forty-minute train ride. He was particularly concerned that we understand all of the new changes that the "New Revolution" imposed on the Family.

* * *

When we arrived at the house, we had a celebration. This was a grand day for us all. Our whole team had worked double-shifts in order to raise the money to rent the house, and we were proud of our success.

Briana and Lois cooked a wonderful beef burgundy, and we had Beaujolais wine. At the dinner table, Stanley thanked God for our new home and prayed that everyone would faithfully follow the rules of the "New Revolution," especially "sharing" and "FFing."

When Stanley explained that we would keep our usual schedule of early morning singing on the Metro, our celebration turned sour. I knew everyone needed a break, but no one dared to speak up.

Finally, I blurted out, "Stanley, do you think we can have a break this week, before going back to our regular schedule?"

"No, Joy, I think you are just being lazy," he answered. No one said a word. "In this home, we are striving for excellence, and as the old saying goes, 'Early to bed, early to rise makes a man . . ."

Before he finished, I interrupted him. "You know, you never listen to our feelings on any issue. Really, I think you are too authoritarian."

Anger glinted in his eyes. "Joy, to be a part of my home, you must learn to follow the commands of the shepherd. You haven't learned yet how to be a real soldier," he said. He shoved the newest Mo Letter, "Fighters," into my right hand. "Read this," he said. "I'm sure you'll learn that in this army we don't have time for lazy soldiers who don't know how to fight," Stanley said sternly.

I took the letter and excused myself from the table.

"Aren't you going to finish dinner?" he asked.

"No, I'm not hungry anymore," I answered. I went into the bedroom and wept bitterly. Stanley was very stubborn and had no compassion for us. Nor did he make an effort to work with us as a team. I was angry about his insensitivity to our feelings and his inability to communicate with the team appropriately.

After taking some time to pray, I dried my teary eyes. Then, I began reading the Mo Letter. It talked about the complaining Dad was hearing from the disciples about some of the rules of the "New Revolution." The disciples were tiring of the constant pressure, especially the girls who were going out "FFing" nightly. Still they continued because they felt that it was their duty and calling.

Moses David wrote in the letter: "It's a battle of love! It's not easy for these girls down there every night, but they enjoy it. It's not easy to have to love these men, and dance with them, and talk to them half the night, and sleep with them the other half! But they love it, because they know their job and their duty and their calling and their vocation and their fight and their battle!"2

The letter disturbed me greatly. Was I one of the sickening and complaining soldiers that Dad so adamantly rebuked? Life as a COG member was becoming a chore, and I was losing my zeal. After reading the last paragraph, I tossed the letter down. All the talk of being a soldier who didn't complain and his insistence that we continue "FFing" was discouraging. The letter verified the complaints Stanley had against me.

I picked up the letter and read it once more. Yes, I was like the "sick complainers," whom Dad talked about in the Mo Letter, I thought. Then, I dried my eyes and decided that I was going to be a fighter. Dad insisted that nurturers who complained about how tough it was to be a COG member would eventually "dry up and die off."

I certainly didn't want to end up being like the murmurers. Dad repeated again and again in the Mo Letter that we joined the army to suffer and die to our personal desires. Self-denial and a fighter's attitude were imperative to fully enter into the spirit of the "New Revolution."

After I finished reading the Mo Letter, I was afraid to ever complain about Stanley again. He was my shepherd, and I believed that God had placed him over me to lead me. I needed to be more submissive, I thought. I was convinced that I needed a fighter's attitude more than ever.

Chapter 7
Sold Out

During the busy months that followed at the Gonesse home, I began to lose touch with my real feelings. In order to live with my shepherd Stanley, I had to "bury my will" and "die to myself." I no longer saw life through my eyes, but through Stanley's perception of my role as a COG disciple. My innermost being mourned the jubilation that I felt at the Colombes colony in Paris, when I first joined the COG.

At the Gonesse home, my sense of identity seemed to drift away like whiffs of smoke from a gray chimney. Yet, I still managed to exist as a COG disciple. There was a great struggle to come to grips with reality, but Stanley was winning the battle. He was pulling me further into his world. Furthermore, I was pressured to submit every thought and deed to him.

At times, I would tell him how distressed I was over the rigorous witnessing schedule that we had to follow and his insistence that I participate in "sharing" and "FFing." One day, in particular, I told him that I was thinking of leaving the Gonesse home. Stanley hastily informed me that he would not give me permission to leave.

"Joy, if you leave the Lord's will, which is for you to be a member of my team, then God will punish you."

"Why?" I asked.

"Because you would be leaving God's perfect will for your life," he replied. Looking at me sternly, he continued, "Your call is to be a missionary in the COG. Also, it is important that you continue as my childcare worker."

"Okay, Stanley, I'll stay," I replied sadly.

I was afraid to leave him, thinking that God might strike me dead. Stanley had such power over me that it was hard to break. I was becoming like the rest of the team who simply obeyed everything he said. We all feared God's judgment if we dared to disobey our shepherd, Stanley.

* * *

Eli called me one day and asked if he could come to visit us.

"Joy, how are you?" he asked.

"Eli, I'm not doing too well; to put it honestly, I'm miserable," I said.

"What's the matter?" he asked with concern.

It had been weeks since I'd heard from him. I asked, "Why haven't you called me?"

"We've been so busy here at the Bastille colony. I've been thinking a lot about you lately," he answered.

"Stanley has mandated that we stay on a rigid schedule. "I'm exhausted," I said.

"Would you like to come over tomorrow to visit?" I asked. "We can talk then."

"Sure, at what time?" he asked.

"At three o'clock," I answered.

* * *

When Eli arrived the next day, he was elated about our house. He was happy to see us living in a decent home. He also told me that he was fond of Gonesse. "This is a substantial change from Rambuteau," he said as he entered.

"Yes, it's quite cozy," I replied.

As he sat down in the living room, I walked into the kitchen and prepared French tea. Grabbing the honey and lemon, I carried everything on a tray and brought it into the room. I sat next to Eli and said, "I'm having a real problem living with Stanley."

"Joy, what's the matter?" he asked.

"He is so dictatorial - he won't give us any breaks. He insists that we "share" regularly and that we go "FFing" every Friday night. I can't take it anymore."

"Have you spoken to the new leaders at the Colombes home?"

"No," I answered.

Pedro and Martha are now the shepherds of the Colombes colony. There is a rumor that they are getting ready to go to Geneva, Switzerland, to start an "FFing" colony," he continued. "I will let them know about the problems you are experiencing with Stanley," Eli assured me.

Looking at me intently, Eli blurted out, "Joy, I'm leaving the COG."

"You're kidding," I said in amazement.

"No, "I'm not in agreement with all the "sharing". Girls are getting pregnant, and couples are breaking up. It can't be the will of God," he contended.

"Eli, what will you do? You know Dad says if you leave the Family then you are a backslider."

"I don't care," he answered. "Though I agreed with "sharing" and "FFing" in the beginning, I now believe that it is unscriptural. There is so much bad fruit from it," he continued. "I simply can't take anymore; I'm really unhappy. I think you ought to leave too."

"Eli, I'm shocked," I said. "I thought you wanted to join our team, you would . . ."

He interrupted me, "Joy, I want to marry you. Let's go to Cambridge, Maryland, together, get married, and forget about the COG."

"Eli, you're crazy. Stanley says God will judge you for backsliding. It's okay to change homes, but to leave the Family is leaving the will of God," I insisted.

"Joy, I used to think the same thing, but I'm convinced now that I made a mistake. Forgive me for misleading you, but I have been wrong, terribly wrong."

"Eli, Stanley is my shepherd; I have to obey him," I answered.

"I say, get out now, before you get pregnant, like some of the other unmarried girls in the Family," Eli warned me.

"Eli, I think it's time for you to go," I interrupted.

"Joy, please come with me, leave the COG, and forget it ever happened."

"No," I said sternly. "Eli, this is the place for me; this is God's will for my life," I said as I opened the door.

Eli walked out of the Gonesse home. I could tell by the look on his face that he was saddened by my refusal to leave the COG. As Eli stood on the doorstep he said, "You sure you won't change your mind?"

"Yes, I'm sure," I said as I closed the door.

As soon as Eli left, Stanley walked into the living room to find out what he had said. He thought Eli had come for a visit to discuss joining our team. "Why did he leave so soon?" he asked.

I explained to Stanley that Eli had asked me to leave the Family and marry him.

"Joy, leave Eli alone. He will make you a backslider," he stated.

"I know. I don't know what's gotten into him," I replied.

"Did you give him the letter "Fighters?" Stanley asked.

"No, I don't think he wanted it. He seemed quite certain that he wanted to leave the Family."

"Joy, remember God has called you to be a member of the COG; and don't let anyone, including Eli, pull you away from your calling," Stanley insisted.

"Okay," I said, and I went into my bedroom. I was depressed. Eli was leaving. I wondered what would become of me. I wanted to go with Eli, but I was afraid. Stanley had convinced me that if I left, God might severely chastise me and that something bad would happen to me. I actually believed that. I knew Stanley had a grip on me, but I didn't know how to break loose from his tyranny.

Stanley had used every tactic to possess me, and he had finally succeeded in totally owning me. He had not only broken my self-will by his nasty and domineering ways, but he had also succeeded in breaking up my relationship with Eli. Stanley made clear to the whole team that to live in his domain meant total submission to his rules and regulations. Feelings didn't matter anymore. Only strict compliance to the Mo Letters and total commitment to the COG were acceptable at the Gonesse home.

* * *

The next day Eli called to see if I had changed my mind about leaving with him. Stanley was standing right next to me when I picked up the phone to speak to Eli.

"What does Eli want?" Stanley asked.

I held my hand over the telephone and answered, "Eli wants to know if I have changed my mind about leaving the COG," I answered.

"Tell him no," Stanley commanded.

I yearned to say yes to Eli, but I was terrified. Although I knew God would take care of me, I was afraid for Eli. I knew that he was leaving the COG, and I did not want his shepherd at the Bastille colony to harm him in any way. Also, I did not want Stanley to confront Eli by unexpectedly visiting him at the Bastille colony. Therefore, I answered, "No, I can't go." Then, I abruptly hung up.

When the phone began to ring continuously, I was certain it was Eli calling back, yet, Stanley forbade me to answer the phone, so it continued to ring. I didn't hear from Eli after that day for about two weeks.

* * *

It was traumatic living with Stanley during this turbulent time. I thought my relationship with Stanley would change, but it became worse.

Our team members sang daily on the Metro and "litnessed," and I even had about two "fish" on the line, yet I was still very despondent. I did not want to continue as a COG disciple, but I was trapped. I was afraid to seek support for fear of retaliation.

* * *

Briana became pregnant again with her fourth child. It was dreadful thinking of being a childcare worker for four children. I had begun to enjoy working with the children; but with the addition of a new child to care for, it appeared that my role as a childcare worker would become more difficult.

I explained to Jean Paul, who was one of my "fish," that Briana was pregnant and that we needed a car to take her for regular doctor visits. Also, I made every effort to convince Jean Paul that we needed a car to get Briana to the hospital when it was time for her to deliver the baby.

Jean Paul graciously donated to us a small, lime green car, which was in good condition. This was a real blessing since Gonesse was a forty-minute driving distance from the hospital in Paris where she went for check-ups.

Jean Paul was from Ghana, but he was a native of Paris. In addition to donating the car, he was a strong financial supporter of the Gonesse home. He came over often for dinner, and we were trying to win him to the Family as a disciple.

Jean Paul was possessive of me, even though I explained to him that I had other friends. I was commanded by Stanley not to make any emotional commitments to my "fish." Stanley made it clear that we were strictly evangelizing in Gonesse. Therefore, he insisted that we refrain from making any personal commitments to the men whom we met on Fridays at the Coeur Samba nightclub.

* * *

Finally one day the phone rang. Intuitively, I knew it was Eli. I had been expecting his call. In anticipation of hearing his voice, I picked up the telephone and spoke softly. "Hi," I said.

"Hi Joy, how are you? This is Eli."

Eli explained that he wanted to check on my decision about leaving the COG with him. He planned to return to Cambridge, Maryland, to visit with his family and finish his bachelor's degree in French. He felt assured that he could complete the program requirements in French, since he had developed a fluency in the language by living in Paris.

"I will visit you today at Gonesse. I will speak with Stanley about giving you permission to leave the COG," he continued.

"Okay," I said abruptly. "I will see you soon."

After hanging up the phone, I informed Stanley that Eli was coming to Gonesse for a visit. I also informed him that Eli wanted to chat with him. However, I was careful not to tell Stanley any details about what Eli wanted to speak with him about.

* * *

Stanley and Briana and their three children used the bedrooms in the basement where they could maintain some privacy. When Eli arrived, I asked him to sit in the living room. Then, I went downstairs to the lower level of the house to tell Stanley that Eli had arrived. When Stanley finally joined us, Eli initiated the conversation.

"Stanley, Joy would like to leave the COG and return to the U.S. with me."

Anger glinted in Stanley's eyes. "Absolutely not," he said sternly.

"Joy is unhappy with the "FFing" on Friday nights. Also, she is not in agreement with the "New Revolution" concept of "sharing." She has asked me to speak with you," Eli continued.

"Have you read the Mo Letter called 'Fighters'?" Stanley asked him.

"Yes," Eli assured him, "but I am not convinced that these practices are biblical. I am not comfortable with the new direction the COG has taken. I have decided that it is not God's will for my life. I will be leaving in about two weeks to return to Maryland and finish my bachelor's degree in French."

"Joy, I'd like to hear your thoughts, Stanley said," staring angrily at me.

"I am not ready to leave the COG yet, but I do not want to participate in "sharing" or "FFing"," I said firmly.

"Okay," Stanley said, "I know you have been battling with this, and I won't require you to continue."

"I have to go, but I am demanding that Joy return to the U.S. with me. Besides, I'd like to marry her," Eli blurted out.

"No," said Stanley sternly. Then he stood up, ran over to the couch, and grabbed Eli by his collar. Eli swung his arm and hit Stanley with his fist on the right cheek. Stanley began throwing punches at Eli. Stanley and Eli were fiercely wrestling on the couch.

A fight had broken out, and I felt responsible. With fists tightened, the men began screaming at each other.

Despite my making every effort to pull the two of them apart, Stanley and Eli continued fighting. By this time, their bodies were rolling all over the small living room. As Stanley and Eli were gnashing their teeth, Richard and Jordan ran up the stairs, thrust themselves between the two fuming men, and broke up the fight.

I screamed and asked Eli to leave. I did not want him to be in trouble at the Bastille colony. I knew that he could be ex-communicated from the COG for fighting with a leader.

Eli picked up his black leather jacket. Quickly, he ran toward the front door, opened it, screamed a few choice words at Stanley, and slammed the door behind him.

After Eli's departure, I ran into my room on the main level of the house, closed the door, and cried the rest of the day.

* * *

Two months passed, and I had not heard from Eli. I assumed that he had returned to the U.S. I was saddened by his departure from the Bastille colony. I did not have anyone with whom to discuss my disagreement with Stanley's demanding rules and regulations. Then, I heard that Brandon and Pamela had returned to Paris. They were a singing team whose music had touched the hearts of many COG disciples in Europe. They had spent one year on the mission field in various countries in Africa. Their return to Paris was necessary since Brandon had been diagnosed with a mild case of malaria and needed to recuperate.

When they arrived, they needed a place to stay. Since the old leaders had left Paris for Cannes, France, the new leaders at the Colombes colony asked if Brandon and Pamela could live with us at the Gonesse home. Stanley declined since we barely had room for our team, especially since Briana was expecting a child. We also had two new disciples who had joined our team, Joshua and Claude.

Stanley had informed us that Claude was a returning backslider from South Carolina. He was a tall, sturdy, handsome fellow of about thirty. Claude had left the Family a few years ago, but he returned to missionary service in Paris. Mysteriously, he had left his wife and daughter in South Carolina to rejoin the COG. Claude said that he was willing to forsake all in order to recommit to the mission field.

Joshua was a blond, blue-eyed Parisian. Though he was quite slim, he was tall and very attractive. He was only twenty years old. His father brought him to the Gonesse home and then left abruptly. When his father left, Joshua explained to us that he had met Jordan on the Metro singing and decided then to forsake all. His father was willing to let him join if he was sure he wanted to make the commitment.

Jordan was assigned to be his "buddy" and helped him to adjust to COG living. Also, he had a one-hour COG training session with Stanley every day before they went out on the Metro singing and "litnessing." We never told new disciples about "sharing" and "FFing" until they were completely comfortable with being a member of the Family. Then, as time passed, we would break them in slowly.

* * *

One day Brandon and Pamela came for dinner. I was very fond of them. They were a wonderful couple, who sang beautifully together. Pamela truly had a beautiful soprano voice. Born in Ohio, she had been a solo artist before joining the COG. She was short and had a slim frame. She informed me that she had been a COG member for about three years. Brandon, her partner (no one married in the COG - couples simply lived together) was a real Southerner. He loved to cook and was quite a chef. He had been with the Family for about six years and was totally sold out to the COG. Pamela and Brandon had met each other in Paris, just before going to Africa and decided to live together.

We took a walk after dinner, and I told Brandon and Pamela about how miserable I was living with Stanley. They encouraged me to leave since I was so unhappy. I asked them what team they were going to join. Both Brandon and Pamela stated that they felt comfortable at the Bastille home. However, Brandon said that the shepherds there had not officially accepted them yet.

I told Brandon and Pamela that Richard "Go-Slow" was also planning to leave the Family entirely. Stanley was furious about this and called him a backslider. Richard was having problems with depression and anxiety; therefore, I explained, this was a bad time for me to leave the colony. Most perplexing was that Richard's father was a minister, and he wanted him to leave the COG. His father was very upset about the COG's participation in "sharing" and "FFing."

I informed Pamela and Brandon that Stanley was irate. He was losing his team members and insisted that if I left the Gonesse home, it would be more than he could bear. Despite Stanley's strong opposition to my leaving, Brandon and Pamela encouraged me to go to a new home where I could be happy. I explained to them that Briana, Lois, and Jordan were like robots that never questioned anything Stanley said. Also, I told them that Stanley insisted we maintain a twelve-hour day from 6:00 a.m. until 6:00 p.m. Our work included intense witnessing on the streets and "litnessing" on the Metros.

However, I confessed to Pamela and Brandon that confronting Stanley was difficult because the other disciples were afraid to challenge him. Nevertheless, I was miserable, and I felt that my head was about to crack open from all the pressure I was under. We had been on a rigid twelve-hour schedule for about six months, and I was so drained. As a result, I was beginning to suffer severe headaches. Yet, Stanley demanded that I stop complaining and "endure hardness" in the army of the COG.

Brandon and Pamela listened intently as I poured out my heart. I told them about Eli leaving the Family and how I was heartbroken about breaking up with him. I cried until it seemed I didn't have any more tears left. I told them that "sharing" and "FFing" were hard enough, but Stanley had even said that Dad didn't overtly speak out against lesbianism. Brandon and Pamela looked at each other in disbelief.

"You're kidding," Brandon said.

"No, I'm telling the truth," I continued.

Then I told Brandon about the Mo Letter that condoned lesbianism and how there were several women couples now in the Family. Moses David had even said that some men were also considering open homosexuality in the Family. Yet, Dad adamantly stated in a Mo Letter that this was totally unscriptural and forbidden.

I desperately asked Brandon and Pamela to help me talk with Stanley because I couldn't take any more of his emotional abuse. I wanted to leave his home immediately.

* * *

When Stanley returned to the house, Brandon, Pamela, and I asked him to meet with us in the living room. As we sat, I was extremely nervous. Brandon spoke first. "Stanley, Joy has decided to leave your home because she's been unhappy for several months."

"You're kidding," Stanley said angrily.

"Joy, is this true?" he asked, looking at me in disbelief.

"Yes, Stanley," I said, looking at the floor.

"Why are you being so rebellious?" Stanley asked. "Joy, I have strictly forbidden you to leave my home. If you dare to disagree with me, you are leaving God's will for your life." I knew Stanley would be irate, but his demeanor was now overwhelming.

"Stanley, I have been in your home for almost a year now, and you and I have never gotten along," I said, as I hesitantly looked him in the eye.

Brandon began questioning Stanley, "Joy tells me that you encourage "sharing" in your home and that you do not condemn women who decide to become lesbians. Is this true?" Brandon asked.

"Yes, according to the Mo Letters, we have complete sexual freedom in the Family. All things are lawful to us. Haven't you read the Mo Letters since the New Revolution?" Stanley asked.

"Yes, I have," Pamela replied, "but you shouldn't force Joy to do something that is against her will."

"Joy simply isn't spiritual enough to understand our sexual freedom as COG members," Stanley interrupted.

Silence.

"Stanley can I make a call?" I asked to break the stillness. "I want to call Pedro and Martha at Colombes to see if they can find me another colony," I continued. As I walked toward the phone, Stanley frantically jumped up and yanked the cord out of the socket.

"If you want to leave, then leave now. Pack all of your bags and go, but I don't want you using my phone," he shouted angrily.

I left the room hurriedly, crying hysterically. I left Brandon and Pamela in the room with Stanley. Since I had already packed a few of my belongings, it did not take long for me to gather two suitcases.

Then Brandon appeared at the door of my room. "I'll help you get your suitcases into the car," he said with a sweet smile on his face.

"Okay," I said.

When I finished packing, Brandon helped me put my luggage into the green car that my "fish" Jean Paul had given me. I looked into the living room as I went out the door, and Pamela was trying to console Stanley. Stanley had his face buried in his lap. I was so relieved to be finally leaving Stanley's home. Brandon asked if I wanted him to help me make a call to the Colombes colony, and I informed him that I appreciated his support.

We briskly left the Gonesse home and walked two blocks to where there was a public phone. Brandon placed the phone call, and Pedro answered. As Brandon spoke with Pedro, he informed him that I was leaving the Gonesse home and wanted to move into a new colony. I beckoned to Brandon that I wanted to speak with Martha.

When I heard her voice on the phone, I burst into tears. I briefly informed her of the disruption at the Gonesse home with Stanley. I begged her to let me stay at the Colombes home for one to two weeks until I could connect with other prospective COG colonies. In a calm voice, Martha assured me that everything would be fine. She asked to speak to Brandon. In obedience, I gave the phone to him.

Brandon and Martha spoke for about three minutes. From the smile on his face, I imagined Martha had asked him to bring me to the Colombes home. After he hung up, Brandon and I walked back to the Gonesse home where the green car was parked. He sat in the driver's seat and informed me that Martha had asked him to bring me to the Colombes home right away.

Brandon insisted that he drive. Although I argued that I could make the trip alone, Brandon was adamant that Martha's advice should be followed. He did not recommend that I drive the forty minutes to the Colombes home alone. He reiterated that I was too upset to be alone after the way Stanley had balked about my determination to leave his colony.

Miraculously, I felt as if one hundred pounds of weight had been lifted off of me. Living with Stanley had been a nightmare, and I was glad it was over. Yet, deep inside, I was appreciative that he had turned me into a "sold-out" COG disciple. I felt ready and able to continue my journey as a COG missionary.

Chapter 8
The Struggle Within

According to Christian theology, there are only two laws that are at work in the world today: the law of sin and death and the law of life in Christ Jesus. Christians live by either one of these laws.

The law of sin and death was predominant in my life while I was a member of the COG. This is a life that is controlled by the powers of Satan and his kingdom. We cannot hear the voice of God because we are consumed by the lust of the flesh. It was the mission of the COG shepherds to completely kill the self-will of its members. This would assure that the commands of our prophet, Moses David, would be realized.

* * *

At the Rambuteau apartment in Paris, I had great moments of introspection. My innermost being was struggling with the battle between my flesh and my spirit.

At the Gonesse home on the outskirts of Paris, great changes took place in me, which required me to re-align my thinking. I had ample time to consider the road that I had traveled as a COG missionary. As the days passed, I realized that I was in spiritual trouble. As a member of Stanley's COG team, his oppressive leadership style was overwhelming to me. Therefore, I suffered from severe anxiety. Even so, I had chosen to delve deeper into the cultic doctrine. It was evident that I began to lose the Word of God, which already had planted in my heart. I was heavily pressured by Stanley to receive and obey COG doctrine, which in many instances was contrary to the Word of God.

Unfortunately, I was losing the Word, because I was not feeding myself with biblical principles. According to Buddy Harrison, in his book *Hear, See, Do*, "if we place little value upon God's Word, then we will get little or nothing out of it. In fact, we will begin to lose even the revelation we have already received. For whosoever hath, to him shall be given but whosoever hath not, from him shall be taken away even that he hath." (Matt. 13:12).1

Throughout the experience, the Lord was giving me an "inward witness" because of the spiritual irritation that I felt. What I heard and what I saw are what I did. The COG team members under Stanley's leadership were told that the Mo Letters took precedence over the Bible. Unfortunately, we accepted this delusion. Most disturbing was the fact that the COG mandated that the Mo Letters were the accepted truth for us and the Bible was just a supplement to them.

I was terribly frustrated and despondent. Most catastrophic was my struggle to obey whatever Stanley told me to do. I was commanded to live my daily life based on the concepts found in the Mo Letters, even though deep inside I was miserable. Yet, every time I expressed these feelings to Stanley, he would give me the Mo Letter "Die Daily." He said I had to "die daily" to my feelings of inner conflict and "bear my cross." This was the foundation for my COG indoctrination. I had to "die daily" to myself in order to do what supposedly was God's will for my life.

When I became frustrated, Stanley commanded that I ignore the warning signals of the Holy Spirit and to obey the Mo Letters unreservedly. In actuality, I was "dying daily" to the voice of the Holy Spirit that was warning me to repent. Yet, I pushed this warning signal away and obeyed the "Die Daily" Mo Letter instead.

The Law of Sin and Death

Kenneth Hagin says in his book, *How You Can Be Led by the Spirit of God* that "The number one way, the primary way, that I lead all of my children is by the inward witness."2

As a COG disciple, the inward witness was dying within me, and this is the primary way Jesus speaks to us. It was disturbing that I didn't even know it. I was running the risk of a seared conscience (a conscience that no longer hears the warning signals of God reminding us of our sin). My spirit was in shock because of what I had become. As a result, my actions as a COG disciple were causing me to be overwhelmed with grief and sorrow.

By "litnessing," singing on the Metros to earn money and "FFing" at the nightclubs on Friday nights, I was violating God's laws of purity and holiness and passing out Mo Letters, which were often contradictory to the Word of God.

Something inside of me (the inward witness) was telling me to go home, leave the COG, and admit that I was wrong, but pride kept me from obeying. Even Eli, whom I first met at the Colombes colony in France, warned me to get out of the COG; but I didn't listen.

Regretfully, I was afraid to leave the COG because Stanley told me that God would punish me for leaving His perfect will for my life. By contrast, if I had obeyed the inward witness (which was signaling me that something was amiss), I would have been able to disconnect myself from Stanley. Furthermore, I would have ignored the actions of other COG disciples and the Mo Letters.

In late 1977, when I first joined the COG, it was a valid religious experience, since I learned a lot about being on the mission field trusting God for my sustenance. However, by mid-1978, when the Mo Letters were widely distributed introducing the "New Revolution," which emphasized "sharing" and "FFing," I should have left the COG. It was evident that the Mo Letters were in violation of the Word of God.

In retrospect, I believe that I wanted to follow the COG because I refused to admit that I was wrong. It was easier to live the lie, to pretend that everything was okay, to feign that I was giving my best service to God. During the two years as a COG member, I felt wholeheartedly that I was living for God. Unfortunately, even though my desire was to serve God one hundred per cent, I lived mostly for one cause - -to serve the COG.

Why did I stay? To answer this question, it is important to look at my COG shepherd, Stanley, as the prototype of most cult leaders. He was strong-minded and unwavering in his commitment to the COG. A powerful, well-built man, Stanley's commanding presence was arrogant and deceptive.

He was unswerving in his stance that our COG colony give ten percent of all the income we made through "litnessing," singing, or "FFing." Regular donations were sent to the COG headquarters as a tithe offering. It was our duty as COG disciples to financially support Moses David—Dad, our prophet. We sent money to a man, whom most of us had never met, but in whom we had faith that he was hearing from God. We were convinced that Moses David was the end-time prophet, the man called by God. Most important, we believed that the COG disciples were the end-time disciples. We were called to clean up the world of sin before Jesus comes again.

Stanley proclaimed that time was running short and Jesus would soon return. Therefore, God had called out a "chosen few" to bring the world back to His Word. I was totally consumed with the delusion that God had called me into the COG for this special purpose of being a soldier in the COG army. Yes, I had found God's perfect will for my life, I thought. I felt I had reached the pinnacle of my spiritual walk with Him.

* * *

On the contrary, I had created my own world and was completely brainwashed into COG doctrine. Unfortunately, this world was dictated by the demands of the COG.

According to Buddy Harrison, "You and I have the power to create our own world by the mental image we create when we speak forth with our mouths. When we speak something out, it runs right back around into our own ears and enters our minds and hearts to produce a picture. And that picture, held firmly enough and long enough, will eventually reproduce itself in the physical realm: What you see (in your mind) is what you get (in your world)."3

In addition, The "Die Daily" Mo Letter had created an image in my mind of a rugged, unthinking soldier, who simply obeys the commands he or she receives. This image became my reality. I had to pretend that I was dying daily to my true feelings of misery in order to stand the pain that my sin had brought upon me.

It was at the Rambuteau apartment in France that my deep struggle with Stanley began. He was very oppressive and insisted that I serve as his childcare worker for his three children. Stanley reiterated that a soldier never questions. One simply carries out COG orders. Happiness was not the issue; rather strict adherence to the Mo Letters was the sign of true loyalty to the COG.

Stanley attempted to comfort me by saying that when I matured in the Lord and had greater understanding of the Mo Letters, the "joy of the Lord" would surely overtake me. Because I was rebellious to his authority, he said, my stubbornness was causing me to be melancholy.

To live with Stanley meant that I had to die to my self-will. Without a doubt, he truly carried the spirit of the cults, which seek to destroy the individual by killing the self-will of their followers. By doing this, they bring a person into complete submission to the cult. Within time, Stanley had accomplished that purpose. Every disciple at the Gonesse home obeyed his tyrannical leadership.

Therefore, when I finally had the courage to leave the Gonesse home, I was completely sold-out to the COG, and my will was buried in the commands of the cult. I had left Stanley's home, but the spirit of the cult was still with me. Most perplexing was the fact that my spiritual walk with God had greatly deteriorated.

As Deborah Davis says in her book *The Children of God, the Inside Story*, "There is a definable path to reprobation. Individuals and societies alike follow this route. It begins with natural curiosity, the temptations common to all people: the lust of the eyes, the lust of the flesh, and the pride of life. Drawn by lust, we fall into sin. Once drawn into evil, our conscience - the awakening of guilt and the law of God within us - sounds an alarm. As the conscience amplifies the guilt, we feel frustration, spiritual irritation, and a sense of alienation. These are God's warning signs, His method of drawing us to Him. The pain of guilt can be relieved only by the remission of sin. But rather than turning to God, confronting our sin, and confessing it, our tendency is to deny its reality and our accountability to God."4

I had been drawn into the COG by my curiosity and had been tempted with the pleasure of what seemed to be easy living. When there was an alarm sounding in my spirit, I was terribly frustrated and discontented. Why didn't I repent, leave the COG, and admit that I had been wrong?

Often, these thoughts crossed my mind. Yet, I denied the reality of my dark spiritual state and immersed myself deeper in the "Die Daily" and "Fighters" Mo Letters. These letters became my Bible. Every time God's warning signal alarmed my spirit, I rejected the inward witness and continued to let the law of sin and death rule in my life. When you live a life that is dominated by the law of sin and death, the result is total alienation from God and finally reprobation. Ultimately, individuals will be given over to their sin.

Davis says: "Reprobation is seen in its final, completed stage when a person begins to argue and teach others his redefined morality. A reprobate will attempt to bring others into his perversion because sin loves company."5

My lifestyle in the COG had become spiritually dangerous. I was reading and obeying Mo Letters that redefined the Word of God. The "Die Daily" letter taught us to die to the voice of the Holy Spirit signaling us by the inward witness.

The "All Things Are Lawful" letter taught us that whatever we did in love, it was not against God's law of love. Sexual immorality ("sharing" and "FFing") was encouraged in this letter, and I was forced to accept it as truth. Whenever I openly expressed my disapproval of the practice, at the Gonesse home, Stanley rebuked me publicly. He ridiculed me in front of the other members of the colony and publicly deemed me unspiritual. The "Fighters" Mo Letter admonished us to continue in the COG army even if we were miserable. Hard work and suffering were expected of any missionary in the field.

I had forsaken my former reality and teaching to accept the COG doctrine, which violated the Word of God. Truly, I was on the path to reprobation.

In her enlightening book *The Snare of the Fowler*, Frankie Fonde Brogan candidly reveals her feelings when her son, Bob, joined the COG in 1971. She writes: "They all swept through the house, emptying it swiftly of any reminder of my son: his clothes, books, bike, tape recorder, and musical equipment, including a guitar, sax, and banjo. And I didn't lift a finger, just stood there smiling and trying to act natural, keeping a tight rein on my emotions. I did tell them politely that the bedroom furniture in his room was ours, not Bob's; then I felt unaccountably ashamed when they nodded agreeably and left it sitting there.

"I learned that they were all to 'forsake' worldly possessions. Another thing each forsook was his name. Each "Child of God" took on a biblical name and went solely by that name from then on. Bob's name had not yet been selected, but the thought of this abandonment of identity shook me more than seeing all of my son's material things vanishing into the van."6

Like Brogan's son, Bob, I too had changed my name - to Joy. By doing so, I willingly changed my identity. By the time I was a loyal COG member of the Gonesse colony in France, there was no meaning in my life; and as a result, I was emotionally perturbed. In essence, my life was dominated by sin and I was not listening to the voice of the Holy Spirit.

As written in *Galatians 5:17* (Amplified Bible): "For the desires of the flesh are opposed to the Holy Spirit, and the [desires of the] Spirit are opposed to the flesh (godless human nature); for these are antagonistic to each other (continually withstanding and in conflict with each other) so that you are not free but are prevented from doing what you desire to do."

The Rambuteau apartment in France was the place where the struggle, conflict, and change in me began. By the time I left the Gonesse house in France, the law of sin and death had completely taken over my spiritual life. My flesh was violating the natural laws of God, and I was truly oblivious to my condition. The alarm was going off in my conscience. Unfortunately, I rejected this warning instead of repenting and asking God for forgiveness.

* * *

It appears that every cult member will come to a breaking point where the battle between flesh and spirit will confront them; and one will need to make a decision as to the direction one should take.

When young people join cults, often they feel that they have found God's perfect will for their lives. Therefore, they are ready to accept the half-truths of the cult. Their hearts may be sincere, but they can still be taking a wrong direction in their spiritual lives.

Many cult members make the same error that I made. They accept half-truths of the cultic doctrine, but happiness remains only a transient emotion. They can't reconcile their fleshly state with the Word of God, and so there is great conflict and frustration. They live as a cult member in conflict with the Christian principles they have been taught all of their lives. Since the flesh is always at enmity with God, the cult is a door to release sin and the lust of the flesh. God's Word states in *Romans 8:7*: "the carnal mind is enmity against God: for it is not subject to the law of God, rather indeed can be."

The Law of Life in Christ Jesus

The law of life in Christ Jesus is a life that is governed and controlled by the Holy Spirit. In *Galatians 5: 22-25* of the Amplified Bible it says: "But the fruit of the (Holy) Spirit, [the work which His presence within accomplishes] is love, joy (gladness), peace, patience (an even temper, forbearance), kindness, goodness (benevolence), faithfulness, Gentleness (meekness, humility), self-control (self-restraint, continence). Against such things there is no law [that can bring a charge].

"And those who belong to Christ Jesus (the Messiah) have crucified the flesh (the godless human nature) with its passions and appetites and desires.

"If we live by the [Holy] Spirit, let us also walk by the Spirit. [If by the Holy Spirit we have our life in God, let us go forward walking in line, our conduct controlled by the Spirit.]"

Truly, God's will for everyone is that we make him Lord in every area of our lives: spiritual, emotional, and financial. The life that is dominated by the law of life in Christ Jesus is one that immediately obeys the voice of the Holy Spirit (the inward witness) and does God's will instead of our own will. If you live your life according to this law, then it will lead and guide you to truth and joy unspeakable. It will bring you the spiritual riches of the kingdom.

Kenneth Hagin writes: "If you will learn to follow that inward witness, I [the Lord] will make you rich. I will guide you in all the affairs of life, financial as well as spiritual. (Some think He's only interested in their spiritual atmosphere, and nothing else. But He's interested in everything we are interested in). I am not opposed to my children being rich. I am opposed to their being covetous."7

We have to understand that we are spiritual beings. We have a soul, mind, thoughts, and emotions; and we live inside of a body, but the real you is your spirit. God is a Spirit (*John 4:24*), and He can communicate to only that which He is. He wants us to learn to walk by His spirit and the inward witness because this is His primary way of communicating to us - through our spirit. We cannot communicate with God through our body; we must learn to train our spirits so that we can communicate more effectively with God.

As Hagin says: "The Lord enlightens us and guides us through our spirits. If that be the case - and it is - then we need to become more spirit-conscious. We need to become more conscious of the fact that we are spirit beings, not just mental or physical beings. We need to train our spirits where they will become safer and safer guides."8

Training the human spirit is a lifelong task. Since the carnal mind is at enmity with God, we are in a constant struggle to do His will and not our own. Hagin states: "Your spirit can be educated just as your mind can be educated. Your spirit can be built up in strength and trained just as your body can be built and trained. Here are four rules by which you can train and develop your own human spirit:

1. By meditation in the Word.
2. By practicing the Word.
3. By giving the Word first place.
4. By instantly obeying the voice of your spirit."9

Training the spirit is the first step toward living the life that is dominated by the law of life in Christ Jesus. In training the spirit, we can then bring the flesh under control to the voice of the Holy Spirit and under submission to the Word and will of God.

* * *

My prayer for the cult member (or ex-cult member) who has experienced what I went through (at the Rambuteau and Gonesse COG colonies in France) is that you make the right choice and repent of your sin. God will cleanse your troubled life.

I was blind and foolish. I pray that you don't make the same mistake that I made (because I refused to admit my sin). There was still too much pride in me since I did not want to admit that I was wrong. In actuality, I was completely bewildered by the COG doctrines and totally lost, but it was easier to pretend that I was fulfilled as a cult member by feigning happiness. Therefore, I walked deeper into the sin which blinded me and dominated my life for two years.

I thought I was on the right track to spiritual growth, but I was dying spiritually day by day. God's Word says: "There is a way which seemeth right unto a man, but the end there of are the ways of death." (*Proverbs 14:12*).

God is merciful; for He forgave me, even though I resisted his warning signals for two years as a COG disciple. The day that I cried out to God, He opened my eyes so that I could clearly see the sin in my life.

After repenting, I made the decision to leave the COG. It is important to note that God's enlightenment came only after I repented and admitted that I was wrong. It was God's mighty power that delivered me from the claws of Satan and the bondage of cultist living. Matthew 7:14-15 says: "Because strait is the gate, and narrow is the way, which leadeth unto life, and few there be that find it."

* * *

Therefore, when he called me to be a minister of the Gospel, I quickly heeded His command.

No matter what path you may find yourself on, God can intervene in your life at any time and set you free.

Therefore, may God keep your path enlightened, so that every day you might seek His will for your life. I pray that you will stay close to the Word of God, always giving it first place in your life.

Beware of false prophets, who come to you in sheep's clothing; but inwardly they are ravenous wolves. Most of all, make Christ the Lord of your life, and train your spirit to immediately obey the inward witness. This is God's primary way of speaking to His children.

Chapter 9
The Tender Years

I was born in Macon, Georgia, on September 21, 1957. Macon is about an hour and one-half driving distance from the Atlanta metropolitan area. I was the fifth of six children born to my mother, Carrie Johnson. My biological father, Franklin Johnson, died when I was about three years old.

Since my father died when I was such a young age, I don't remember much about him. At the forefront of my mind were the times he regularly took me to church on Sunday mornings.

My mother was nicknamed "My Dear." She was short with a plump frame. In her mid-thirties, her dark brown hair was shoulder length and beginning to gray at the temples. She had a jovial, carefree personality; and we loved her. "My Dear" was a kind, outgoing woman. Her skin was chocolate brown, and her dimpled cheeks enhanced her wide-mouthed smile. Casual in her discipline, she had a laid-back attitude about life.

* * *

Around 1962, my mother separated from my step-father, Douglas Barnes. There was a domestic brawl that caused her to leave him. She had been injured and told not to return to the apartment that they rented in a poor section of Macon, Georgia.

Thereafter, my mother suddenly made the decision to move to Brooklyn, New York. I was around five years old. My sister Eva was just two years old. My sister Jessica was eleven years old. My brother Sean was ten years old.

Bundled in our overcoats, our happy family boarded a Greyhound bus in Macon, Georgia. The bus ride to New York City was about ten long hours. With four children to handle during the journey, my mother was determined to go forward with her life. I believe the domestic violence situation in the apartment that she rented with my step-father reminded her not to look back.

* * *

We arrived one bright winter morning at the apartment building in the East New York section of Brooklyn. A tall, light-skinned stern-faced woman was waiting downstairs for us in the lobby. My mother introduced her as Aunt Silvia. She was broad shouldered, dressed in casual wear and wore a navy blue overcoat. She stared at my mother with her dark brown eyes. Then, she burst into tears, affectionately hugged my mother and welcomed us to New York.

Josephine cuddled my sister Eva and me in her arms. Then, my brother Edwin kissed us on our cold, frostbitten cheeks. Aunt Silvia agreed to open the doors of her apartment to us. Since my sister Jessica and brother Sean were older, they were more aware of the transition we were making. My sister Eva and I were too young to comprehend the significance of a major move to the North.

Josephine, my eldest sister, was about seventeen years old. My eldest brother, Edwin, was about fourteen years old. They had already been living with Aunt Silvia. Apparently, my mother had sent them to the North years before our arrival. It appeared that she wanted them to take advantage of the educational opportunities. Also, I believe my mother was appreciative of my Aunt Silvia's support, which was vital as she struggled to raise her children.

Josephine was medium height and slim. Her long, jet-black hair always lay softly on her sleek shoulders. She had a wide-mouthed smile that glowed. Her personality was warm and friendly.

Josephine had a two-year-old daughter, Cathy, who also lived in the apartment. Though the apartment was already crowded, my mother's sister, Silvia, opened its door to us.

* * *

Unfortunately, I would often hear my mother and Aunt Silvia arguing. Although I was only five years old, I was aware that something was wrong. Josephine later explained to us that Aunt Silvia was not aware that my mother was going to stay permanently with her in Brooklyn. It appeared that she was under the impression that we were only coming to Brooklyn for a short visit. Perhaps her hidden anger about my mother's unexpected arrival in Brooklyn, explained why Aunt Silvia often stayed away from the apartment overnight. It appeared that she wanted to avoid arguing with her.

In addition, I was told later that some contention between Aunt Silvia and my mother also stemmed from my sister Josephine's two-year old daughter, Cathy. My mother was not alerted when Josephine became pregnant. Also, she was not told if Josephine was planning to marry Cathy's father, Joe. She was informed only after our arrival in New York City that Aunt Silvia had adopted Cathy. This was an effort to assist Josephine with the burden of being a teen-age mother.

* * *

Since my mother was a seamstress, she eventually found employment in a factory in the evening. She was a hard worker and did what she could to provide for us. Josephine often read bed-time stories to Eva and me. She was happy to be united with us. She explained to us that "My Dear" moved to the North to overcome her economic difficulties. Josphine told us that she was assured that coming to the North would help "My Dear" to overcome many obstacles as a poor, black single woman.

* * *

After staying with Aunt Silvia for about six months, my mother moved out of her apartment, along with four of her children. Edwin and Josephine continued to reside with my Aunt Silvia. Brave and determined, my mother found a shabby, old apartment in the Brownsville section of Brooklyn, on Pitkin Avenue in New York. The drug abuse, violence, and street gangs were commonplace in the tough neighborhood. It was God's divine protection that kept us and my mother safe.

I attended a neighborhood elementary school and did well as a student. The school was near Lavonia and Junior Street close to the "L" train.

My brother Sean was a rebellious teenager. I remember that my mother had a difficult time keeping him under control. My mother was adamant that Sean stay off illegal drugs.

Sean earned extra money as a construction worker. He was elated about the job, but had an accident. One day plaster fell into his right eye while he was working. Subsequently, he developed an infection in his eye and had to wear a patch for a few weeks until it healed.

It was during the time that Sean was recuperating from his eye injury that my mother decided to send him to Macon, Georgia, to visit with my Uncle Sam and Aunt Alice. My mother felt that Uncle Sam would positively influence Sean to go to school and remain drug-free.

* * *

Jessica made a concerted effort to assist my sister Eva and me with our homework. The burden that she took upon herself was courageous for a girl of about eleven years old, as she grew into her teenage years. She took care of the house and cooked dinner while my mother worked. Since my mother worked overnight, Jessica made sure that Eva and I went to bed on time.

Jessica even accepted the responsibility of waking up Eva and me in the morning to prepare for school. She often cooked us a hearty breakfast of oatmeal. Then, Jessica poured us a glass of orange juice and helped Eva and me to get dressed. Jessica took the short, ten-minute walk to school with us. She was amazing and possessed many adult qualities. Our family affectionately nicknamed her "Pixie."

Jessica's hair was bushy, like most teenagers growing up in the 1960's who prided themselves in wearing "Afros." Her lips burned with the message of civil rights for all African Americans. Her demeanor was arrogant, yet she was sure of her position in life. After all, Jessica was an honor roll student and was proud that she academically surpassed her classmates.

Mother Carrie's Death

When I was thirteen years old, my mother suddenly died of colon cancer. She was only forty-six years old. Jessica was now attending Tuskegee Institute in Alabama. She was studying liberal arts at the college. However, she later informed the family that she wanted to be a teacher.

My older brother Sean was permanently living in Macon, Georgia, with Uncle Sam and Aunt Alice. My younger sister Eva and I moved in with my Aunt Silvia and Josephine.

Determined to succeed after my mother's death, Josephine felt secure as the proud owner of a new Beauty Salon near the Brooklyn Museum. When she initially opened the salon, she was about twenty-one years old, but she was still living with my Aunt Silvia.

Josephine taught me entrepreneurship at fourteen years old. I managed her beauty salon during the summer when I was on school break. I learned how to work with her employees. I also learned how to do bookkeeping for the business. Most importantly, I learned that working with people was an art and a science.

After my mother's death, my older brother Edwin was now working and had found an apartment next door to the house that my Aunt Silvia owned in East New York. The house was only about two blocks from Linden Boulevard.

The family was proud of Edwin when he finally landed an important position in the government in Albany, New York. He traveled frequently, so I did not get to see him very much. He was very proud of the beige luxury Jaguar that he had purchased.

My Aunt Silvia was very strict and had a set of rules that seemed almost impossible to keep. Shocked and still grieving my mother's death, I felt overwhelmed by my Aunt Silvia's strict demeanor.

As I grew older, I felt that Aunt Silvia's inability to have children throughout her adult life mandated that she become a real authority. She was determined to make sure that as our aunt, she would have a set of standards by which we lived. Also, she strongly encouraged us to take advantage of educational opportunities to succeed in life. Aunt Silvia once told me that she felt she was born to care for her sister's children. Therefore, she was not afraid to step in and take control of us when my mother died.

Her moral values eventually led me to seek God during my teenage years. It was during the time that my "faith was seeking understanding" that I met Santiago. He was from San Juan, Puerto Rico.

After my mother's death, Santiago witnessed to me about the love of God. Immediately after Santiago prayed with me, I gave my life to Christ. After attending the Holy Redeemer Lutheran Church with Santiago for about one month, I became a proud member. Because of my love for music, I joined the youth choir. The church is located on Linden Boulevard. in the East New York section of Brooklyn.

My tears turned into joy once I understood that despite my mother's death and resulting emotional trauma, Christ still loved me. I was excited about his sacrificial death on the cross. My conversion empowered me to understand that Christ gave his life that I might live.

It was also clear to me that I needed to progress educationally in order to secure a college education. Therefore, I was determined to excel academically in school. Of particular interest was Santiago's availability to be my Spanish tutor. Santiago and I met almost every day after school to review my Spanish homework. He also spent about one hour speaking with me in an effort to enhance my Spanish conversational skills.

Santiago was medium height with straight, black hair. Although it was not fashionable for teenage boys to wear their hair long, Santiago insisted that he wanted his hair to be cut just above his shoulders. His ivory-colored skin glowed whenever he smiled at me. With high cheekbones, his dimples were radiant. Highlighting his good looks was his strong faith in God, especially since he was a devout Lutheran.

Santiago lived with his mother, Lucy, and his father, Hugo. They lived in the housing projects near Pitkin Avenue in the East New York section of Brooklyn. His older sister, Rebecca, was very kind to me. Most rewarding was that his family's commitment to teach me conversational Spanish.

* * *

Of particular significance was my first semester as a senior at Thomas Jefferson High School, in Brooklyn. My guidance counselor, Ms. Edwards, insisted that I meet with her regularly. She explored with me all the scholarship opportunities that were available to me as a high school honor roll student. With her tenacious assistance, I was eventually awarded a scholarship to study at Fairfield University in Fairfield, Connecticut.

In my second semester as a senior in high school, Ms. Edwards nominated me to deliver the graduation speech to my class as their valedictorian. Because of her nomination, my other teachers agreed. Ironically, there was another "A" student, Darnell, whose grade point average was two points higher than mine. However, Ms. Edwards insisted that because of my character and outstanding academic success at the school, I should be recognized.

Because of her support and that of my other teachers, I felt honored to deliver the valedictory speech to my classmates. In June, 1975, my name was officially added as a member of the National Honor Society.

Teenagers and Grieving

(*My Youngest Sister, Eva*)

To our family's dismay, Eva was dismissed from an honors class during her first semester in high school. She was always at odds with my oldest sister, Josephine. Eva refused to abide by the rules and regulations that were instituted at home. Aunt Silvia was adamant that we were respectful of her home. Eva was the youngest, but it was difficult to work with her as a teenager. She was very rebellious and refused to obey her curfew. I was alarmed that she refused to listen to anyone in the family, except Edwin. She was always arguing with Aunt Silvia and Josephine. I thought that they were going to send her away to a detention center.

Eva often stated that she was a free spirit and that she did not feel comfortable with some of the family values. After my mother's death, she continued to be verbally abusive. I confronted her about her behavior. Yet, I had to face the reality that Eva had to find her own identity and sense of purpose in life.

She suffered a significant burn during a meeting at school. A pot of hot coffee fell on her leg. The accident caused her to miss significant time at school. Eva eventually confessed to me that she made the mistake of not studying during her recuperation time. Consequently, her lack of commitment to her school work resulted in poor grades.

When her behavior worsened, Josephine eventually was compelled to send Eva away to Chicago to live with our extended relatives. It was during this time away that Eva could reflect on how to redirect her academic life. With a major effort, I believe Eva was capable of reforming her life.

It was only a few years ago, during a conversation with Eva that she confessed to me the details of her personal life. While a teenager, her first introduction to casual drugs came from her friends who lived in the rugged East New York neighborhood.

She also informed me that the security guard, Ike, at her high school had molested her. She contended that the crime occurred at the Children's Day Care Center (where she used to play basketball) across the street from Junior High School 463, on the corner of Dumont and Logan Streets.

The emotional scars that resulted from this traumatic situation in her life alienated Eva even more from our family. Eva's internal turmoil caused by this incident propelled her into a life of mistrust of anyone who tried to befriend her.

Often this is the case when a sexual crime is committed against a woman. They feel that if they tell anyone about the evil that has been committed against them, they will be ridiculed and rejected. Unfortunately, some women develop a common type of depression called "withdrawal." This was evident because of Eva's inability to take off the mask and be open to other members of our family.

Eva concealed her true feelings and refused to let anyone in our family help her. This is the reason that there was a lot of contention and resistance to following rules. The only person in the family that seemed to be able to reach Eva was my sister Jessica. It was during her teenage years that Eva formed a good relationship with her.

* * *

Tragedy in Our Family

Unfortunately, in April 1994, the death of my sister Jessica was a big setback for my family. We received an unexpected call from Macon, Georgia, that Jessica had been shot in the head. We were baffled about the heinous crime, since we could not fathom that Jessica could have enemies. Who then could commit such an offense against her? What was their motive?

I was alarmed because Jessica was the person who could talk with Eva in an effort to keep her connected to the family.

* * *

It was a miracle that all of our family members were able to change direction and catch a flight to Macon, Georgia. At the same time, we had to prepare for her funeral. We immediately contacted Jessica's pastor, the Rev. Donald Gregory, at Baruch Baptist Church. Pastor Gregory was very comforting when he spoke to my brother Edwin over the phone. He insisted that he would visit us at the house that Jessica and her husband Donald had bought at the bargain price of about sixty-five thousand dollars around 1986.

I was scheduled to graduate from Wesley Theological Seminary in Washington, D.C., the following month. However, I was overwhelmed with grief. Due to the disturbing news of Jessica's death, I was not sure that I could complete all of the pending school work that I needed to do to graduate. Yet, when Pastor Gregory met with us, he encouraged me to take a deep breath and make a concerted effort to finish school.

To my surprise, my family had a unanimous vote that I preach at the funeral service. Pastor Gregory was delighted, since I would be the first woman to preach in his Baptist pulpit.

As our family prepared for the funeral, Pastor Gregory asked many questions while we worked assiduously to complete all of the arrangements. I remember his consoling words: "This kind of thing happens every day," he said; "every now and then, it hits home."

Such reassuring words from Pastor Gregory were healing to our distraught family. We endured the pain and made the decision to continue even though we would miss Jessica. Her husband, Donald, was also grieving the loss. Jessica left behind two children from her first marriage to Louis; Francisco, who was nineteen years old, and Betty who was fourteen years old.

Around 1979, Louis, Jessica's first husband, died of stomach cancer. Around 1983, Jessica married Donald. They had one daughter, Diana, who was ten years old at the time of her death.

During the funeral, I sat with the other ministers of the church. Then, I was escorted to the pulpit to deliver the message. I preached a dynamic sermon on discipleship. Later, my sister Josephine announced to me that she marveled at my composure. She stated that the message was comforting to her and that she did not see a tear in my eye. She confessed to me that it was at that point that she finally realized that I was a minister of the gospel.

* * *

After Jessica's death, we had a very difficult time finding her pertinent information, even though my brother Edwin searched throughout her home. Her will, life insurances, and other important papers were difficult to locate. He later informed me that it took him almost two months to finish all that had to be done to settle Jessica's estate.

In her will, my sister Jessica named Eva as the guardian of the children. Jessica's two daughters were young and would need follow-up professional counseling. Unfortunately, they were going to be separated because Donald decided that Diana was going to live with him.

My sister Eva was afraid to stay at Jessica's home since the murder had occurred there. She decided that she was going to sell the house and purchase another property. In the interim, Eva moved into an apartment in College Park, Georgia.

* * *

From 1994-2000, I assisted Eva with contacting a professional Christian counseling service. Immediately, she made an appointment for Diana and Betty. It was the counseling sessions that kept both girls emotionally sound during their period of grief and loss.

What would become of Francisco, my sister Jessica's son? We were concerned because he would not be under our care. He had to serve time in prison because of a crime he committed.

Because of Francisco's violent behavior, all of my other family members have refused to interact with Francisco. However, as an estranged member of our family, I have chosen to forgive him.

Therefore, to date, I remain in intercessory prayer that God's perfect will be done in his life.

* * *

Eva eventually moved to Mableton, Georgia. She purchased a small townhouse which would be suitable for her and Betty. Eva made the commitment to take care of my sister Jessica's children at great cost. She had to relocate from Brooklyn, New York.

To assist Eva with the burden of raising my sister Jessica's children, I was committed to spend considerable time in Georgia between early 1995 and 2000. Subsequently, I conducted an October 1998 National Network (NNCMW) Conference at a local hotel. I invited several members of World Changers Church, College Park, Georgia.

Eva assisted me in contacting one of the ministers of World Changers, Minister Tracy Johnson. She agreed to be the keynote speaker at our second NNCMW Conference in October 1999. It was conducted at the Ramada Inn Hotel (now the Quality Hotel & Conference Center), about one mile from the Atlanta, Georgia airport.

At the time, Eva was single. But she began to court Mike. He had a flourishing karate business. Eva first met Mike when she took her son Josh to karate lessons. After dating for several years, Mike and Eva married. Thereafter, Eva decided to join World Changers Ministries Church in College Park, Georgia. Her life was changed as she accepted salvation at the church. It was in Atlanta, through the ministry of senior pastor Dr. Creflo Dollar, that Eva's life was transformed. She began to change her worldly behavior and started attending regular Sunday services.

When the war in Iraq started, Mike spent considerable time in Iraq (from about 2004-2008). It perplexed us that he was commanded to fight the war in Iraq even though he was in the Army Reserves.

* * *

On Thanksgiving Day, November 27, 2008, I received an unexpected call from Eva. Mike had been admitted to Walter Reed Hospital in Washington, D.C. He had undergone a spinal cord operation.

"Is Mike okay?" I asked Eva.

"Yes," she replied. "He walked out of the hospital and is now back in North Carolina," she continued.

Eva shocked me when she blurted out that she had witnessed soldiers at various times who had no ears, legs, or arms. War is a tragedy.

I was happy when President Barack Obama announced that he had ended the war in Iraq. He deserves credit for fulfilling his campaign promise that American soldiers would be withdrawn from Iraq by the end of 2011.

* * *

Fortunately, this was beneficial to my family. Mike has permanently returned from the war in Iraq. He and Eva can now raise together their teenage son, Josh. They reside in Georgia.

* * *

Betty, my oldest niece, is in her early thirties. She has her Associate's degree as a laboratory technician. Her younger sister, Diana, is now in her early twenties and is working as a sales associate. Donald, who was living in Macon, Georgia, unexpectedly passed away in February 2008.

Josephine's daughter Cathy is now grown. She has an adolescent daughter, Gloria who attends a private school in Brooklyn, New York.

Edwin, my oldest brother, currently resides in upstate New York with his wife, Lorrie. They have a college age daughter, Julie.

* * *

Education and Success

My success at school was partially because my sister Jessica was adamant about assisting my younger sister, Eva, and me with our homework. She often made it clear getting "C's" at school were unacceptable in our household. She was unwavering in her stance that only "A's" or "B's" were to be the custom for our completed schoolwork.

"You should always strive for excellence," Jessica said. She convinced me, even at an early age, that performing well in school was the way for a successful future.

Most challenging were the regular fights I had with my classmates. They teased me because I was a good student and was able to maintain exceptional grades. I was also angry when they continued to call me a bookworm.

Jessica encouraged me to ignore them. She said that knowledge was the gateway to making sure that Eva and I could win scholarships to college as we grew older. Jessica's positive influence in my life regarding my education propelled me into a mindset of excellence.

* * *

Our next-door neighbor, Veronica, had two young girls. She did not feed her children, nor did she bathe them regularly. Whenever she left them with Eva and me, we combed their hair. Then, we fed the children and bathed them.

My most vivid recollection of this time was that Veronica was in love with a man who we knew was a drug addict. He spent a lot of her money and then disappeared for days at a time. Then, we found out that Veronica was pregnant again with his child. Since she was destitute and already had two children, I could not understand why she wanted more children.

We were also poor, but I remember that my mother always showed us love. My mother was also a friend to me. I guess my special closeness to her explains why her death was so painful for me.

* * *

Although I was overweight as a child, by the time I reached fourteen years old, I was physically fit. I became more social and I started participating in study groups at school. I developed long-term relationships with my classmates who were also pursuing excellence.

* * *

In August, 1975, when I arrived in Fairfield, Connecticut, I found college very challenging. Since it was a predominantly Jesuit school, we were encouraged to uphold the Christian faith. The students and faculty were mostly Caucasian. I was surprised at how few minority students were on campus. All students were expected to attend Sunday worship at local churches.

Since I had won an academic scholarship, I was required to maintain continued excellence in my work at school. Therefore, for spiritual strength, I attended prayer meetings of The Way International Fellowship group.

They were offering a six-week course on spiritual gifts. I was interested in learning more about the "baptism in the Holy Spirit." Therefore, I enrolled and began taking classes weekly.

After the sessions, we were all gathered in a small room holding hands. Someone laid hands on the student beside me, and she began speaking in Spanish. She did not understand what she was saying, but I did. Surely, she was "speaking in tongues."

The leaders laid hands on me. Then suddenly, I began to speak "in tongues." According to Gloria Copeland in her book *God's Will for You*: "You receive the Holy Spirit by faith just as you receive Jesus as Lord. (*Galatians 3:14*). Christians must be taught to believe for the indwelling of the Holy Spirit. The Master had taught the disciples in the upper room on the day of Pentecost about receiving the Holy Spirit. The entrance of God's Words gives light or understanding (*Psalm 119:130*)."1

She further states: "When you pray in tongues, you are praying in the spirit." Just as English is the voice of your mind, praying in tongues is the voice of your spirit. Therefore, after you ask, speak no more English. You cannot speak two languages at once.

I Corinthians 14:14 says, "For I pray in an unknown tongue, my spirit prayeth, but my understanding is unfruitful." The Amplified Bible says, "My spirit by the Holy Spirit within me prays."2

After I had received the baptism in the Holy Spirit, I changed. I had the power to witness and to be a bold disciple for Christ. I had a greater desire to serve Him and to come to grips with God's will for my life. As Gloria Copeland writes: "But ye shall receive power, after that the Holy Ghost is come upon you (*Acts 1:8*). Something wonderful has happened to you today. Power! Power! Power!"3

What then is the will of God? To answer this question, one should understand first why God has called us into His kingdom. Are we called in the fivefold ministries (*Ephesians 4:11)* or are we called to serve as a disciple of Jesus Christ?

According to Copeland, "His Word is supernatural and it is alive! The Holy Spirit is sent to reveal this supernatural Word to you. He makes the instructions of the Father a reality. Read the Bible with the knowledge that God had it written for your benefit - not for His. He is already quite successful!"4

Finding his Word as the resource for successful Christian living, one has a roadmap to follow. On the contrary, when there is no workable plan in place, depression and confusion permeate our minds.

* * *

This was my dilemma as I pondered the possibility of life outside of the Children of God. The Bible had been taken away from me and replaced with the Mo Letters. I was told that I must obey them even over the Bible. Moses David was our prophet for this end time, and his word to us about the direction of our lives was supposedly the Word.

This false word was tainted with echoes of sexual immorality and moral degradation. Yet, I continued to struggle to stay a faithful member of the COG. Why?

My shepherds told me that being a COG member was God's will for my life. Therefore, they informed me that I should feel privileged to be chosen as God's end-time prophetess. I was told that Moses David was our leader. They were adamant that he had been chosen by God to lead us. All we needed to do was follow!

After six months in the COG, I was completely brainwashed into believing the doctrine of the cult. Most perplexing was the fact that I still felt empty. Therefore, I continued to experience many breaking points while my life in the COG unfolded.

In retrospect, as I delve deeper into the lives of those who influenced me, God's Word becomes clearer to me. We must "commit our ways unto the Lord, and He shall direct our paths."(*Proverbs 3:6*).

From the Children of God to Capitol Hill

In June, 1991, I eventually obtained my Bachelor of Arts degree in business management, with a concentration in organizational development, from National Louis University in Mclean, Virginia. Also, in May, 1994, I obtained my Master of Divinity degree in the Urban Ministry Track from Wesley Theological Seminary, Washington, D.C.

By November 1994, I accepted the nomination to be the president of the Network of Christian Women. We began conducting business meetings on the second Tuesday of the month at the Rayburn House Office Building. Former Congressman Bill Goodling from Pennsylvania was our first Congressional sponsor.

By October 1995, after a conference at the Washington Convention Center, Washington, D.C., the name was changed to National Network of Christian Men and Women (NNCMW).

The Church on the Hill started as the Christian Fellowship outreach ministry in January 1995, on Capitol Hill. From 1994 to1998, through former Congressman Goodling's leadership, we conducted prayer meetings every third Thursday of the month for political leaders and their staff members. The congressional meeting locations included the Rayburn, Longworth, and Cannon House Office Buildings.

Around November 1996, while teaching a stress management

seminar for our National Network (NNCMW) meeting at the Rayburn HOB, I met a prominent business owner, Mr. Joe Camper from Akron, Ohio. Over the course of a year, Mr. Camper generously contributed the seed money (five thousand dollars) to support the early development of the Church on the Hill.

Mr. Camper made it clear in a letter that we should include in the mission and ministry of the church an emphasis on working with congressional/political leaders and their staff. The rationale being, when the Lord touches the hearts and minds of our secular leaders, then the nation will change.

This prayer outreach ministry expanded in 2004 to Upper Marlboro, Maryland, Prince George's County, at the office of former County Executive Jack B. Johnson. Also, we extended this prayer outreach ministry to the office of the former State's Attorney, Glenn F. Ivey.

Around 1996, Mr. Jonathan Jones was very supportive by providing substantial yearly contributions to the Church on the Hill. His donations classified him as a Platinum Sponsor (who gives gifts of one thousand dollars or more).

Mr. Jones holds a master's degree in international politics. It was through his impressive leadership skills that the Christian Fellowship became a strong prayer outreach ministry on Capitol Hill!

He informed me to utilize his contributions in order to make sure I received a part-time stipend from Church on the Hill. His contributions were very important from 1997-2004, since I spent considerable time on Capitol Hill at the Congressional buildings.

Mr. Jones also worked (1997-2004) with former Congressman Bill Goodling and me to grow our Church on the Hill-NNCMW membership on Capitol Hill. In addition, our collaborative work on Capitol Hill was very instrumental in assuring the success of our outreach ministry.

* * *

Surely, we all have experienced trying economic times since the September 11, 2001, attacks by terrorists on the World Trade Center in New York and the Pentagon in Washington, D.C. Compounding the nation's economic troubles was the downfall of Enron.

In addition, the late sniper shooter, John Muhammad, who murdered innocent people throughout the Washington, D.C. metropolitan area, shocked the nation. He left most of us wondering how this could happen in America. Most frightening was the involvement of a youth, John Malvo, his accomplice, who was also convicted of murder.

The Church on the Hill had the opportunity to minister to Muhammad's estranged wife, Stephanie. In our yearlong telephone conversations with her, Stephanie's fear was abated once John Muhammad was convicted and sentenced to death in 2006.

Sadly, one of the victims was a youth from Benjamin Tasker Middle School in Bowie, Maryland. The Washington Post, Friday, December 12, 2002, article commended former First Lady Laura Bush for her visit to him at the Children's Hospital, Washington, D.C. She was making an effort to show her support during his family's turbulent experience. Though the student recovered after a month long struggle for his life, the other senseless murders committed during John Muhammad's shooting spree were a true sign that the moral fiber of our nation was deteriorating.

All of the aforementioned events are a sign that our nation desperately needs God's intervention. Even though America is facing some of the darkest days in history as a result of the aforementioned tragedies, we can still as Christians and people of faith walk in the realm of the miraculous. We do not have to turn to destructive cults, like the COG in our time of despair.

It is evident that the basis for jurisprudence in the nation's capital is the popular opinion of the people rather than what the Word of God says about an issue. Therefore, the spiritual leaders of the nation now have a greater opportunity to share the "good news" of the gospel. When all else seems lost, we can lead the people whom God sends to us, back to His Word. Truly it is our source for daily living, edification, and healing.

* * *

By November, 1995, the Church on the Hill conducted its first worship service at St. Michael's Lutheran Church in Largo, Maryland. My trusted friend Pastor Jason Cage provided the "spiritual covering" for its first service.

When I became pastor of Church on the Hill, I resigned my position with a Methodist Church in Silver Spring, Maryland, where I was the minister of education and youth. Staff members of many congressional/political leaders attended Sunday services on the first and third Sundays of the month. We conducted worship services at the former Days Inn Hotel, Capitol Heights, Maryland.

In December 1997, we conducted our second Church on the Hill anniversary service. We rented a meeting room at the Red Roof Inn Hotel in N.E, Washington, D.C. Former Mayor Marion Barry, of Washington, D.C., was the special guest speaker.

Currently, Church on the Hill (1995-present) is based in Prince George's County, Maryland. The ministry functions as a para-church corporation. Such an organization assists the traditional church in building spiritual leaders. The church also serves National Network (NNCMW) members in the Prince Georges/Montgomery County metropolitan area.

Community outreach programs, including the "Community Transition Center" meetings are conducted in Prince Georges / Montgomery County. These meetings are conducted to assist those in transition as they grapple with unemployment, underemployment and homelessness.

When the Rev. James Love officiated at my ordination service on September 24, 2000, I accepted the responsibility of serving as the senior pastor of Church on the Hill. This public recognition of my call to ministry was also a time when I vowed to be faithful to growing the membership of Church on the Hill. Through God's grace and mercy, I now can freely teach others to submit their lives to Him.

Chapter 10 My Last Days in Europe

When I arrived at the Colombes home, I was in tears. Leaving Stanley's home was like escaping from a detention center. Pedro and Martha greeted me at the front door of the house and then invited me to sit down in the charming living room. Immediately, Pedro and Martha wanted to know why I had accepted Stanley's offer to join his team. I told them that I had thought it would be a good match.

Pedro was medium height, with dark brown hair. His sky blue eyes were accented by his ivory colored complexion. As I spoke, his mouth was twisted as he anxiously listened to me review the details of the disagreements that had occurred at the Gonesse colony. Pedro's demeanor was stiff, and his shoulders erect. His eyes widened in alarm. Furthermore, it appeared that he was in shock over my unexpected return to the Colombes home.

Martha was tall and slim. She had high cheekbones, and her reddish-brown hair lay neatly on her narrow shoulders. Her emerald green eyes highlighted her gleaming white skin. Martha appeared relaxed and ready to talk about my experience. Since her manner was serene, I felt at ease as I unraveled my horrific ordeal as a COG disciple on Stanley's team.

I informed Pedro and Martha that the old shepherds at the Colombes home, Joe and Marie, had referred me to Stanley. Also, I confessed to them that the members of Les enfant de Dieu did not want me to take the journey to Cannes. Instead, they thought that it would be best for me to join Stanley's team.

I was adamant as I informed Pedro and Martha that I sincerely wanted to support Stanley. He was sure that I would make a good childcare worker. However, Briana was expecting another baby soon. I did not feel capable of being a childcare worker for four children.

Therefore, I felt overwhelmed by Stanley's insistence that I continue working with the children. As I sobbed relentlessly, I frantically conveyed to Pedro and Martha that Stanley had refused to consider me for other work on the team. Also, it appeared that Stanley was determined to train me to be on his "FFing" team on Friday nights.

As he consoled me, I cried on Pedro's right shoulder. Martha brought tissues to me, and I wiped my face. I confessed to them that I was grief stricken about the confusion that had occurred over the last few months at Gonesse. Furthermore, I felt ashamed that my experience on Stanley's team had been disastrous. Martha smiled and compassionately held my right hand. Her kind gesture relaxed me. Then, she asked if I wanted to be considered as a member on their team.

Pedro explained that our prophet, Moses David, had commissioned them to start a new colony in Geneva, Switzerland. Pedro said that they were going to depart for Geneva in about three days. However, they insisted that I stay at the Colombes home for the next week.

I confessed that seven days would be sufficient time for me to make a decision about joining them in Geneva. Inwardly, I was relieved that I did not have to make a quick determination about the next COG colony I would join. A peaceful mood overshadowed me.

* * *

For the next week, I stayed at the Colombes home and reflected on my tumultuous experience at the Gonesse colony. Ultimately, I needed a reason to continue as a COG disciple.

I was elated when Brandon called me. His voice was relaxed and comforting. He heartily informed me that he and Pamela had decided to join the Bastille colony. I informed Brandon that I was not sure about going to Geneva, Switzerland. However, I advised him that I did feel capable of working with Pedro and Martha. Yet, I was certain that I did not want to participate in "FFing."

Brandon assured me that he felt going to Geneva would be a good choice. He thought this would be a great opportunity to have a change of scenery and give me a chance to forget about my traumatic experiences with Stanley. He also reiterated that I should convey to Pedro and Martha that I did not want to participate in "FFing."

Brandon was very convincing. He insisted that I remain a faithful COG disciple. I eventually agreed with his advice and informed him that I would leave for Geneva the next week.

* * *

When I arrived in Geneva, it was around December, 1978. Two men approached me while I descended the steps of the train. They asked me if my name was Joy. I nodded and provided them with the information they requested of me. It was a letter of transfer from Pedro and Martha. The letter assured them that I had followed proper protocol by getting a shepherd's permission to move to a new COG colony.

The two tall, brawny, good looking men introduced themselves as Theodore and Michael. They kissed me on my left cheek and grabbed my luggage. Still holding me around my slender waist, Theodore explained that they would be driving me to the Geneva colony.

Theodore had rusty brown, shoulder length hair. His square-shaped face was covered with freckles. He told me that he was originally from Barcelona, Spain. He confessed that he had met the COG in Geneva while on student break.

Michael informed me that he had only been a COG member for about four weeks. Michael was a Parisian who had left Paris to work on establishing the Geneva colony. Broad shouldered, well-built and assured, he was very excited about the "New Revolution." He confirmed his loyalty to our prophet, Moses David, and vowed to work with the COG for the next few years.

While driving back to the Geneva colony, I marveled at the lofty mountaintops surrounding the city. Geneva was one of the most astounding places that I had ever seen. I remembered that it was the place of political talks and money exchanges. The strategic location of the fancy jewelry shops on the corners was amazing. The sight of wealthy businessmen sitting in the high-class restaurants confirmed it was truly a city of opulence.

* * *

When we arrived at the Geneva colony, Pedro and Martha opened the door, clutched my hands, and welcomed me to Geneva. They heartily confessed that they were proud to be the new shepherds at the Geneva colony.

The couple revealed to me that the new assignment in Geneva entailed locating a large apartment in an effort to establish a successful "FFing" colony. They had done an excellent job, I thought. The Geneva apartment was exquisite.

They invited me to sit down in the living room of the huge apartment. They had just lit the fire. As we talked, the brown logs were burning in the fireplace. Pedro and Martha informed me that it was a four-bedroom apartment. They also told me that some of their Arab "fish" supplemented the rental payments.

An amazing couple, my new shepherds gazed at me and energetically boasted that the Geneva colony was a strong team of COG members. With their leadership, they were certain that Geneva, Switzerland, was their spiritual domain. In time, they were determined to evangelize the city and make the COG a household name.

* * *

My first week at the Geneva home was spent learning about the chores that I was assigned to do. Patricia and Edna, both natives of Paris, had been COG members for two years. Patricia had an eighteen-month old boy named Stewart.

Patricia was a gorgeous young woman in her twenties. She was medium height and had long curly black hair. She was a kind woman with a confident demeanor. She was proud of being a single mother and seemed jubilant about her journey as a COG disciple.

Edna was an older woman in her forties. She had beautiful, blonde hair and large brown eyes. She had become a COG disciple because she felt called to give her life one hundred percent to serving God. Like myself, she was on a spiritual journey; and she felt the call to be a COG disciple was a valid religious experience.

During the next two weeks at the Geneva home, I learned of the prosperous "fish" (especially Arabs) that the COG family members had in Geneva. Not only were they truly an "FFing" colony, but it was also expected that I would join their team in these efforts.

* * *

Pedro and Martha informed me one Friday morning that I would be expected to go "FFing" at a popular local nightclub later that evening. During our conversation, I informed them that I did not want to participate. However, Pedro and Martha insisted that I was a spiritual baby. Over time they assured me that I would become more understanding of the practice.

Later that evening, Larry, a tall, handsome man with dark brown hair picked me up at the Geneva home. He informed me that he had only been a COG disciple for about six months.

Larry was self-assured, with a stocky build. His wide-mouthed smile glistened as he entered the apartment. Also, I could smell his Pierre Cardin cologne as he sat down in the living room of the large, lavishly decorated apartment.

I was dressed in a flashy, blue dress, and I had on high-heeled silver pumps. Long white pearls fell neatly around my neck. I wore my favorite sky blue earrings. Larry stood behind me as he assisted me to drape my sapphire blue jacket around my narrow shoulders.

Larry and I departed to our assigned nightclub. Reluctant to participate, I once again found myself in the midst of what appeared to be a "set-up." I had made it clear to Pedro and Martha before I left France that I was not interested in "FFing." Yet, I was once again expected to participate against my will.

* * *

After my first night "FFing" at the Geneva colony, I was dismayed. How could Pedro and Martha be so deceiving, I thought. We had several conversations upon my return to the Colombes colony about my discontent with the practice of "FFing." Yet, I had only been in Geneva a couple of weeks, and they were insistent that I participate in "FFing" on Friday nights.

There were no other homes to go to in Geneva. Therefore, I made the decision to stay on Pedro and Martha's team. I needed the time for personal reflection. Besides, I was thinking that perhaps I was due for a visit with my family in the U.S.

* * *

To my surprise, after residing in Geneva for four weeks, I became really ill. I decided to go to the doctor for an exam. Martha was appointed by Pedro to accompany me to the health clinic in downtown Geneva. To my dismay, the doctor informed me that I was about two months pregnant.

I fell into a deep depression. I remembered that after Eli's departure from the COG, I had been strongly attached to a COG member, Taylor at the Gonesse colony. However, I was not sure that he was reachable, since just after the "New Revolution," he had already returned to the U.S.

Since the father of my unborn child was unreachable, my feelings of isolation increased. Not only was I having an emotionally difficult time accepting the pregnancy, but my shepherds, Pedro and Martha, were obviously disheartened. They had intended for me to participate in their "FFing" excursions at the nightclubs.

* * *

Nonetheless, Pedro and Martha were concerned about my health. They asked me to attend Christian counseling sessions. They felt confident that the sessions would assist me in dealing with my anxiety. Also, Pedro was particularly concerned that I face up to the realization that I would soon be a single mother.

During our home meetings with the other members of the Geneva colony, Pedro informed me that their original intention was for me to participate in "FFing." That was obvious to me. I was once again being forced to participate in a practice that I felt was totally unbiblical.

However, since I was pregnant, Pedro and Martha decided that they were willing to make some changes. Most perplexing was the fact that the COG was experiencing heavy persecution in Europe. As a result, Moses David began writing Mo Letters commanding the disciples to flee to South America. Since I was having a lot of morning sickness, I was uncertain about taking a flight to the U.S. Such an effort could be more than I could take emotionally. Also, the constant bouts with depression had taken their toll on me.

Inwardly, I wanted to continue as a COG member because I did not know how to make it on my own. Now that I was pregnant, my dependency on the group heightened. Compounding the emotional torment I was experiencing was the fear of facing my family in the U.S. I was embarrassed to even call home to New York to inform my family that I was soon to become a mother.

Pedro & Martha

They were the prototype of what COG shepherds were expected to portray. They insisted that we were required to have an insatiable desire to win disciples to Christ. Also, we were admonished to have a strong admiration for our prophet, Moses David. This included strict adherence to the Mo Letters.

They were not worldly people; they loved God. Yet, their inability to distinguish Godly love from loyalty to a man that had lost contact with God was beyond my comprehension. I was on the mission field because I felt called to be there. I felt it was a valid expression of my love for God and His people.

However, the COG life-style, which appeared to sway further away from biblical principles, was becoming more bizarre to me. Since I saw signs of spiritual maturity in Pedro and Martha, I patiently expressed my difficulty with COG doctrine to them. They did not rebuke me. After all, Martha was one of the European media spokespersons for the COG.

Therefore, Pedro, and Martha listened kindly and understood my position. They encouraged me to continue my spiritual journey. Though they did not wholeheartedly agree, they felt it was acceptable for me to return to the U.S. They thought that a visit with my relatives and friends in the U.S. would soothe my feelings of disparity.

* * *

Pedro and Martha understood my plight. Therefore, I did not have to participate in "FFing" at the nightclubs, especially since they felt my pregnancy might alarm potential "fish," "I was relieved, since I was convinced that the COG practice of "FFing" was unbiblical. I was adamant that I did not want to participate.

Therefore, I was asked to take on the role of childcare worker for Patricia's son, Stewart. She was actively "litnessing" during the day at busy tourist attractions. At night, Patricia was either "FFing" at nightclubs or singing at cafés with Theodore, Michael, and Larry.

* * *

The daily routine of caring for Stewart was good for my morale. I felt that I was at least able to contribute to the Geneva colony. My time in Geneva was a period of deep introspection. I pondered about motherhood and what this change in my life would mean. If I left the COG, I would have to find a job to support my child and me.

Yet, I felt ready to re-enter the real world. Also, Pedro and Martha assured me that I was always welcome back in Geneva, should I decide to return to the COG. Obviously, I was torn about what direction to take.

Since many of the COG disciples were moving to South America, I brushed away thoughts of inadequacy to function on my own. I could either delve deeper into the COG doctrine or leave the organization and return to the U.S.

* * *

I was bewildered when Moses David began writing letters about the persecution that we were receiving in Europe. It seemed like good common sense to return to the U.S. However, I wondered if I should continue my journey to South America as a COG disciple.

The shepherds had declared that our prophet had spoken. Therefore, I had a dilemma. Whom should I obey?

* * *

After about six weeks in Geneva, I began writing letters to my family in the U.S. I explained to them that I was planning to return home to New York City. Most important, I had also been in contact by phone with Eli. He was awaiting my return and promised to help me when I arrived.

Of course, when I made the decision to return to the U.S., it was mandatory that I have an "exit interview" with Pedro and Martha. They warned me that once I returned to Brooklyn, New York, I would receive strong opposition and criticism from family members and friends. Therefore, to prepare for intense questioning about the COG, they recommended various Mo Letters that I should read.

Though I felt prepared to return to the U.S., I was not quite ready to face criticism from my family and friends. Despite conflicting emotions, I decided to board the airplane to return to the U.S.

Chapter 11 "Backslidden" in the U.S.A

I arrived in Brooklyn in early February, 1979. My Aunt Silvia and my sister Josephine greeted me at J.F. Kennedy airport. As I pulled my luggage off the conveyor belt, Josephine hugged me around my neck and kissed me on my forehead. Flustered, I held her around her slim waist and shed a few tears.

The first thing that she noticed was that I was obviously expecting a child. Josephine's eyes widened as she tried to compose herself. She immediately began to bombard me with questions about the COG.

Since it was obvious that both Aunt Silvia and Josephine were alarmed about my state, I attempted to console them. I made it clear that I was twenty-one years old. I defended my right to make my own decisions and informed them that I was capable of working to find employment to take care of myself.

* * *

The ride was exhilarating as my Aunt Silvia drove her blue sedan from the airport. During the sixty minutes that we drove toward the family house in Brooklyn, which my Aunt Silvia had purchased, my sister Josephine continually talked about my "brainwashed state of mind." She insisted that she would help me rid myself of the erroneous COG doctrine.

Though their comments were well accepted, I had not completely made up my mind that I was ready to leave the COG. However, I had missed the U.S. and I was enthusiastic about being home. It was good to see family again, and I was eager to find a job.

* * *

Though Aunt Silvia and Josephine expressed that they were

perplexed about my commitment to be a COG missionary, they lent a listening ear to my story. Yet, as I unraveled the details of what had happened to me in Europe, it appeared that Aunt Silvia and Josephine were still worried.

Aunt Silvia purposely reminded me that I was a bright, young woman with a promising future. "How could you allow this to happen?" she asked.

I repeatedly insisted that the COG was a valid religious experience and that I was capable of choosing my religious path. I told them that I had made a decision to drop out of school to pursue my religious journey, but that, in time, I would complete my undergraduate education.

I believe some of my family's anxiety stemmed from the fact that they had not seen me for about one and one-half years. Therefore, it was obvious that they did not understand the spiritual transformation that had taken place in my life. Most difficult was the staunch reality of my poverty.

Although I informed them that COG missionaries had forsaken all to follow the cause, it was not real for them. They were not judgmental about my pregnancy, but they were concerned about what plans I intended to make. Aunt Silvia, especially, reminded me that there would be new challenges since I was soon to become a mother.

However, I was assured that I was on a personal journey to find God's perfect will for my life. Therefore, I was ready to handle the plethora of questions and opinions, which I knew my family and friends would continue to have. Assuredly, my faith in God intrigued my family. They could not overlook my sincere enthusiasm for doing missionary work as a COG disciple.

It took a couple of weeks, but Aunt Silvia and Josephine eventually came to a consensus. They agreed that it was truly my decision how I wanted to live my life.

* * *

As the days passed in Brooklyn, I felt more peaceful about my pregnancy. Also, there was plenty of food to eat.

Eventually, Aunt Silvia and Josephine stated that they would be supportive of my decision about remaining in the U.S. or returning to the mission field as a COG disciple. However, Josephine tenaciously tried to convince me to return to school and finish my undergraduate education right after the birth of my child. At that time, however, I was sure that returning to school was not my first priority. On the other hand,

I was anxious to find work and earn enough money to take care of myself.

* * *

Within three weeks, I found employment as a clerk/typist with the government in Manhattan.

It was during this time that Eli began calling me at the family house. I did not give him any specific time that we could meet. However, I made an effort to inform him that I was pregnant.

* * *

As planned, I worked for two months in order to raise the fare I needed to go to South America. After waiting to get a response from a COG home in Quito, Ecuador, I finally received an affirmative letter. However, I was careful not to let my Aunt Silvia or Josephine know that I was considering a trip to South America. Any letters that came for me were kept safely in the bottom of my dresser drawer in the room that I occupied.

* * *

Sometimes, Josephine drove me to the subway station in the morning. Or, I would walk one block to catch the bus on Dumont Ave. At the subway, I could board the "A" train to downtown Manhattan where I worked. I am not sure what happened, but one morning while boarding the train, I had a touch of morning sickness. I had a bottle of water with me and sipped it as the train rushed through the tunnel. I felt dizzy and almost fainted.

Then, as the train approached the Jay Street stop, I collapsed into the nearest seat. I sat for a few minutes to gather my strength. An African American woman - Jill asked me if I needed assistance. She sat next to me on the train for about fifteen minutes to make sure that I was okay.

By the time my train arrived at 34th Street in Manhattan, I had gathered enough strength to walk. Jill continued her journey on the train. Waving good-bye, she gave me her phone number. She informed me that I should call her later in the day if I needed help to get back home to Brooklyn.

Pushing myself to mount the stairs to get to the turnstile of the train, I eventually pressed my way through the crowd. Reaching the top of the stairs, I was overjoyed to get a breath of fresh air. It was about 9:00 a.m. and I was due at work. Yet, it was apparent that I was going to be tardy.

* * *

Though I had encountered some early morning sickness, I felt better once I arrived at the office and was able to sit down at my desk. As usual, the phone at my desk was ringing, and I had to take a message for my supervisor, Ms. Banning.

The rest of the day was low key since my daily work activities were minimal. I was responsible for answering the phone, delivering messages, and typing minor correspondence. There were about thirty other employees in the small office. The department was responsible for assisting individuals who had questions about government policies.

* * *

I received a call one day at work from Eli. He invited me to lunch. He stated that he wanted to help me readjust to real life. He also insisted that he wanted to provide me with the phone number of a great health clinic, which would assist me to get support as I prepared for the birth of my baby.

When we had lunch at the Boston Gate Restaurant, I revealed to Eli the details of my struggle. I confessed to Eli that I was not ready to stay in the U.S. or return to school. I explained to him that my family was bombarding me with too many questions, and that I felt pressured by them.

Eli assured me that I was displaying signs of anxiety. He confirmed that my feelings of stress were part of the de-programming process. He confessed that he had similar feelings when he initially returned to the U.S. Eli's words were comforting. He even offered to go to professional Christian counseling with me. I was in tears as we talked. Yet, I was still not ready to face reality. I was also struggling with how to make the necessary changes in my life as a single mother.

Though Eli was very persuasive, I informed him that I had decided to take an offer to join a COG colony in Quito, Ecuador. Eli informed me that should I change my mind and stay in the U.S., he promised me that he would be available to talk with me. Then, he prayed with me and assured me that he would be supportive of whatever decision I made.

* * *

Three days before leaving for Quito, Ecuador, I met with Eli. He again proposed marriage and encouraged me to leave the COG. Furthermore, he was adamant that I should not go to South America.

Unfortunately, I was experiencing mixed feelings about my ability to remain in Brooklyn. My family and friends were very critical of my involvement with the COG. Their constant barrage frightened me.

Moses David had commanded a number of COG disciples to flee to South America. Therefore, I was torn between obeying the "voice of our prophet" by fleeing to South America or heeding the advice of Aunt Silvia and my sister to stay home in the U.S.

I was reluctant to provide Aunt Silvia, Josephine, and Eli with too much information. Secretly, I was making plans to go to South America should my stay in the U.S. prove to be too traumatic. Unfortunately, the pressure that was placed on me propelled me into a state of fear that my family would physically coerce me into staying in the U.S.

Also, Eli was very unwavering in his stance that he was totally against COG doctrine. He admonished me to seek the support my family was offering me and remain in the U.S.

* * *

Despite Eli's warnings and the generous provision my family had made available to me so that I could re-enter society, I was still not sure that I wanted to leave the COG. I was still perplexed. The support that Eli and my family were optimistically presenting to me appeared viable; however, I still felt that I needed the extra support systems that I thought the COG could offer me as a single mother.

For example, the COG home in Quito, Ecuador, had promised to offer me housing, financial assistance, and childcare services upon my arrival. They had also promised to find a good doctor for me and provide baby clothes and supplies when I delivered the baby.

* * *

Because of my intentions of going to South America, I resigned my position on the job as a clerk/typist for the government. About one week later, I secretly called a taxi one night and ordered the taxi driver to take me to the airport. I had made reservations for a flight from LaGuardia Airport to Quito, Ecuador. I did not alert my family or Eli about my departure to South America. I was six months pregnant.

Part Two: South America

Chapter 12
Ecuador

When I arrived in Quito, Ecuador, I could feel the warm summer air blowing in my face. It was exhilarating to be in South America and to be back on the mission field. The city is in the mountains, so that found it somewhat difficult to catch my breath.

Richard, an American disciple, and Rosita, a native of Quito, Ecuador, met me at the airport. They had a baby girl, Sonia, who was six months old. Hugging me, they both exclaimed that it was a pleasure to meet me. They were thankful that I was able to come and offer support.

The drive from the airport to the apartment was about forty minutes. During our ride, Richard made an effort to explain to me that the COG had undergone severe persecution in Quito. Also, he confessed that the authorities had forbidden the COG to practice "FFing."

"Bueno!" I exclaimed. I was not in the frame of mind to discuss my true feelings about the practice, especially since the Mo Letters were encouraging it.

"No creo que "FFing" es bueno para Quito," Rosita responded.

Richard did not say a word about our remarks. Instead, he carefully cautioned me that I should be very careful about mentioning the word COG in Quito. He continued to warn me that the police in Quito had interrogated hundreds of COG disciples fleeing from Europe to various South American countries.

When we arrived at their apartment, they showed me a small room where I could put my belongings. Rosita had made a scrumptious dinner for me - arroz con pollo.

* * *

Over the next few weeks, I learned a lot about Ecuador. As in most South American countries, the people were poor. Only the rich had washing machines. It was not uncommon to see women washing their families' clothing in huge wash buckets. They dried their clothes on a line right outside their homes.

I was baffled by the persecution that COG disciples were receiving in Ecuador. The reaction that the authorities in Quito had toward COG disciples made me apprehensive about staying. Stories of policemen raiding COG colonies and seizing property were frightening.

The general public did not speak about the group openly. Therefore, I wondered if it was possible to "litness" there in an effort to get the word out about the COG. The obvious disapproval of COG doctrines was evident in Quito, especially since many of the people were Catholic.

Richard and Rosita were just living together, as was the custom with most couples in the COG. There was tension between them because of the Mo Letters. Like me, Rosita was strictly against "FFing." Therefore, she refused to participate in the practice. On the contrary, Richard expected her to obey the Mo Letters, even if she was not in total agreement with them. Compounding the problems between the couple, Rosita wanted to get married. Obviously, this meant that Richard would have to leave the COG.

At the time, according to the Mo Letter "One Wife," COG disciples were not required to be joined in holy matrimony. They were instead allowed to live together as a couple and have children. The COG members were instructed to be sold-out to COG doctrines. This included being loyal to our prophet, Moses David, and his controversial Mo Letters. Since I was disheartened by the constant disagreements between the couple, it was clear to me that Quito would not be a good place to settle and prepare for having a baby.

I was perplexed that Richard and Rosita had never mentioned anything me to in their letter about such grave persecution of COG disciples. The churches in Quito were strongly sending a public message that COG doctrines were anti-scriptural. Therefore, the local church pastors were delivering a general warning to their parishioners to steer clear of the COG (and its doctrines).

Therefore, I decided to write a letter to the COG leadership in Guayaquil, Ecuador. I checked to see if they needed help there.

By May, 1979, I was seven months pregnant. By God's grace, I received a response from a team of three COG members. They invited me to join them in Guayaquil.

* * *

Arriving in Guayaquil was so refreshing. The atmosphere was less intense than in Quito. Over time, I knew that the fear that I felt in Quito about serving as a COG disciple would dissipate, but I enjoyed the people in Guayaquil since they were so casual in their demeanor and friendly toward Americans. The warm spring air made me feel as if I could fly like a bird.

José was a native of Ecuador, and Maria was an American disciple. They had been a couple for two years and had a baby boy named Raul. They had been in Guayaquil for about six months. José was very much in love with Maria. She, on the other hand, was only very fond of him. It was obvious that she did not intend to marry him. They were very excited about my joining their COG team. Also, they were hopeful that our team could bond well together and work toward getting a home for us to live in.

Juan was an American disciple who had been in an accident as a child. He fell out of a moving vehicle. Miraculously, he lived, but the injuries from the fall caused his right arm to be paralyzed.

The COG team informed me that they were renting two small rooms in a student facility in order to raise money for a home. In addition, restaurant owners and friends were supporting the COG team there. Therefore, I thought that perhaps this would be a good opportunity to get settled before I was due to have the baby. They agreed to help me, and I began the process of settling into the COG life-style.

* * *

Though I knew that I was near the end of my two-year commitment as a COG disciple, I was grateful for the opportunity to be in Guayaquil, sharing the good news of the gospel. Since the city is on the seashore, there were many opportunities to go to the beach. The temperature was so much warmer than in Quito. The COG members were very inviting. They were not much older than me.

It was much easier to witness in Guayaquil. The people were not as antagonistic against COG doctrine. Actually, members of our colony were told to use the name the Family rather than the COG. This was in compliance with the "New Revolution."

Within two weeks' time, a new COG member from another colony in Guayaquil, Sara, visited us at the student facility. She was six months pregnant. Sara had a heart of gold. She was very concerned about my getting proper medical care. Therefore, she was anxious to take me to the hospital in order to secure a doctor who could deliver the baby.

I welcomed her support since she was very fluent in Spanish and knew the city well. We took a bus to downtown Guayaquil so that she could show me where the public hospital was located. Since I was almost full-term, it was important that I make proper arrangements immediately.

* * *

Despite Sara's encouragement, after four weeks in Guayaquil, our COG team was still unable to raise enough money for a home. They were also unsuccessful in finding a decent public hospital where I would feel comfortable. I was worried about our living arrangements when I received a letter from a home in Caracas, Venezuela. Upon receiving the correspondence, I remembered that I had written the home before I left the U.S. It was truly a surprise to get an affirmative response from the colony.

* * *

I explained to the COG team in Guayaquil that I was leaving to go to Caracas. I was eight months pregnant and truly in need of proper prenatal care. Sara agreed with me that Caracas, Venezuela, would be a safer and more reliable place to have a baby. She emphasized that the medical facilities were more sanitary in Caracas than in Guayaquil.

Sara accompanied me to the airport in Guayaquil. I had been cautioned that it may be unsafe to travel. Despite the potential danger of flying in my condition, I stretched my faith and boarded the airplane. I was determined to take the flight to Caracas, Venezuela.

Chapter 13
Caracas, Venezuela

Upon arriving in Caracas, Venezuela, I was greeted by the Family. There was a team composed of two couples. John and Linda were an American couple.

Helena was a Mexican disciple. Roberto, her partner, was an American disciple. Helena and Roberto had an adorable fifteen-month-old baby, Louis.

The COG team was renting an expensive apartment in downtown Caracas, Venezuela. They had a prosperous "fish," Manuel, who was assisting them with their rent.

* * *

I was overjoyed when Helena confessed to me that she had baby clothes and accessories for me. She reminded me of the letter I wrote to them a few months ago. She mentioned that I had informed her in my letter that I was five months pregnant.

Helena informed me that once the colony had accepted me on their team, she decided to look for a clinic. During her search, she had also been successful in locating a competent physician. The doctor was Rafael Cordova. He was the founder of Rafael Cordova Clinic in downtown Caracas.

My orientation about the rules and regulations of the Caracas colony took two weeks. During that time I realized that the two couples had different perspectives on their work with the COG. John and Linda went "FFing" regularly on Friday nights. Helena refused to participate since she was very busy with raising her son, Louis. Roberto was supportive of Helena's decision not to be involved in "FFing."

* * *

Helena proudly boasted that Dr. Cordova and his clinic were well known in Caracas. She wanted me to be relaxed since she stated that I would have several appointments with him within the next three weeks.

This would allow the doctor to determine how soon I was going to have the baby.

Daily living at the Caracas apartment was peaceful. I was not pressured to participate in any form of "FFing" or "litnessing." Gratefully, I had been excused from fundraising so that I could concentrate on giving birth to my baby.

Helena went to the bookstore and bought all kinds of natural childbirth books for me to read. I was determined more than ever to take her advice and allow her to be my coach. She reminded me to relax. Helena, along with the other COG team members, was very encouraging and kind to me.

* * *

Linda was a beautiful blonde woman in her thirties. Tall and assured, she had a slender frame. Her sky blue eyes highlighted her ivory colored skin. With high cheekbones, Linda's smile illuminated the room whenever she spoke.

Helena was in her late twenties and was medium height. She had long black hair. Her eyes were brown, which highlighted her tan skin tone. She was a gorgeous woman with a magnetic personality.

I was baffled by the constant arguments between the two couples over "sharing" (exchanging sexual partners within the home). Since John was in complete agreement with the Mo Letters, especially the popular "All Things Are Lawful" letter, he often asked Helena to "share " with him. Since her companion, Roberto, objected to the practice, she refused John.

Linda volunteered to share with Roberto. This was an effort to help him to be more accepting of the practice, but it caused a furor among the couples. One night, I heard them discussing the details of the practice of "sharing" in the living room. An explosive argument broke out. Since my door was slightly ajar, I was startled by their intense bickering.

* * *

The concepts of "FFing" and "sharing" were continually being discussed throughout the COG colonies. I had decided that both practices were unscriptural. I had also determined that after the birth of my child, I was not going to participate in any kind of "FFing" or "sharing," even if it resulted in my being excommunicated from the Family. Therefore, I knew I had to leave the COG as soon as possible.

I was aware that my decision not to participate was totally against COG doctrine. Besides, Moses David had recently given a mandate that any COG disciple who refused to participate and obey the laws of the "New Revolution" would be excommunicated. However, by the time I had reached Caracas, I did not care anymore. I had made up my mind that I would once again follow the inward witness, and obey the scriptural principles of the Bible. I wanted to stay away from any practice that the Word of God did not allow.

John approached me one evening since he knew I felt uneasy about participating in "FFing." After my conversation with him, it was clear that after the baby was born, I would have to find another colony to live in. My conscience bothered me whenever I thought about participating in "FFing" and "sharing."

Yet, I was afraid to voice my convictions about my decision to adhere to the Christian principles I had learned as a teenager. I feared open rebuke by the COG team members in Caracas.

* * *

It was mid-July, 1979, and I was lying on the bed in my bedroom looking at television. I heard a "snap" like a balloon bursting. My water had broken. The whole bed was soaking wet. It dawned on me that I was ready to have my baby. It was ten o' clock in the evening. The labor pains started immediately after my water broke.

Helena popped her head into my room. She saw the water all over the bed, and then she yelled to Roberto, "Llama Dr. Cordova. The baby is coming."

Then, Helena prompted me to prepare for my clinic visit. She told me to select the clothes that I wanted for the baby to wear for the days that I would stay at the clinic. She also told me which personal items I would need. Since she had volunteered to be my coach, Helena decided that we would do the breathing exercises that we had been practicing together.

"Joy," Helena said nervously, "Do you have a name already chosen for the baby?"

"No," I replied. That was the last thing I was thinking about. The labor pains were getting closer. Also, the intensity of the pain interrupted my thoughts.

Then, a wide array of concerns jolted my mind. Would the baby have ten fingers and ten toes? Furthermore, would I be able to contact his father? I thought. His father was probably safely back in the U.S. Perhaps the Family would have a way of assisting me to locate Taylor. I felt confident that he would be delighted to know about the baby.

I was consciously timing the labor pains. I remembered distinctly Dr. Cordova's advice to keep an accurate record of the time between them. By now, the contractions were four minutes apart. I knew it was time to go to Dr. Cordova's clinic.

* * *

Once we arrived at the Rafael Cordova clinic in Caracas, I was having brisker contractions. Helena was standing beside me as the nurse pushed my wheel chair into my room. Helena assisted the nurse to help me get into the bed. The whole experience was heavenly. I felt safe as Helena clutched the Bible in her right hand. Whenever I had contractions, Helena prompted me to breathe in and out. Then, she would remind me to relax, as the pain grew more intense.

I remember her handing me calcium vitamin tablets as she prayed with me. She's great, I thought. Her calm demeanor helped me to stay in control and time my breathing. We had agreed that I would have natural childbirth. Also, in Venezuela the doctors did not believe in administering drugs for pain relief during childbirth. Therefore, Dr. Cordova was in agreement with Helena that I should continue my breathing exercises and relax between labor pains.

* * *

Suddenly, I fell asleep. Then, I had a dream. While dozing, the Lord gave me a name for the baby - Rafael. I slept for about two hours.

When I awoke, Dr. Cordova was yelling, "Get her to the delivery room!"

What was all the fuss about, I thought. Looking at the clock, I noticed it was almost 4:00 a.m. Dr. Cordova continued screaming, "It's time to push!"

I was still half asleep and did not want to wake up, but the pain assaulted me. The contractions were so strong that when the nurse vigorously rolled me into the delivery room, I screamed, "Please give me something for the pain."

Dr. Cordova exclaimed, "Why? The head is out. Push, push!"

Various voices joined in demanding that I push. By this time Helena was not at my side anymore. Dr. Cordova and nurses were attending to me. I pressed downward whenever I was told to push. Then, when the pain was excruciating, I made one final push and the baby was born.

I immediately started to chuckle since I was overtaken with joy. The next thing I felt was a needle in my arm, and I fell asleep.

* * *

When I awoke, they brought the baby to me.

"You have a brand new baby boy. What will you call him?" Dr. Cordova asked.

"Oh, how much does he weigh?" I asked.

"Six pounds," Dr. Cordova gleefully replied.

"I am going to name him after you - Rafael," I exclaimed.

Dr. Cordova was so elated. He grabbed the newborn baby in his arms. He held baby Rafael like a football player clutches the ball when determined to make a touchdown. Then, while holding the baby firmly against his chest, Dr. Cordova rushed out of the room with Rafael. I could hear his laughter all the way down the hall, as he shouted to his staff at the clinic, "The baby's name is Rafael." I could tell he was proud of the delivery and of baby Rafael.

* * *

I had mixed emotions over my recovery time. I could hardly move because of the pain and needed to request bedpans, but the staff at the clinic was enthusiastic, and the positive atmosphere was ample reason to recuperate. Therefore, after about three days at the clinic, I was ready to go home with baby Rafael.

During the weeks after Rafael's birth, there was an array of important things to take care of. I had to obtain immunizations for Rafael and obtain his birth certificate. This was very difficult since I also had to obtain a Certificate of Birth Abroad. Then, I had to obtain a passport for him. This effort included two different passports: American and Venezuelan. The Passport Office told me that Rafael could have dual citizenship until he was five years old. After that time, I would have to decide as his mother which citizenship he would permanently retain - American or Venezuelan.

The apartment building that we lived in had swings and a small playground. It was so relaxing to sit on the bench right outside the apartment building and rock baby Rafael to sleep. It took more than a month for little Rafael to sleep through the night. Since I had decided to breastfeed him, he woke up every four hours throughout the evening.

* * *

By the end of two months, I was exhausted. Lots of sleepless nights caused me to endure fatigue throughout the day. Caring for baby Rafael was a task. However, Helena did offer to assist me with feeding Rafael two nights a week.

Most unnerving were the constant approaches from John about "sharing." Then, too, the couples continued to argue about the practice. It was a nightmare. It was clear that this would not be a good place to raise little Rafael. I had decided that it was time to start writing other colonies and find another place to live.

* * *

After about five months in Caracas, I received an affirmative letter from a home in Curacao, which is a small island off the coast of Venezuela. I had written the letter to the home in Curacao when I first arrived in Caracas. After reading over the letter, I informed Helena and Roberto that I had been accepted at a colony in Curacao. Furthermore, I alerted them that I would be leaving their colony soon. They informed me that, although they were fond of me and Rafael, they agreed that it was best for me since I was unwilling to participate in "FFing" and "sharing."

I had convinced myself that I did not want to have a second child out of wedlock. Also, I had come to grips with the fact that somehow I needed to get my life back together again. I was now a single mother. I had a child to raise. By this time, it was evident to me that raising a child in the COG would be a mistake. The only light in the sea of darkness was my decision to leave the COG and re-enter society. I tried to be patient, since I knew I would have to plan my escape.

* * *

Three days before my departure, I received a call from my family in New York that my brother Sean had died. Apparently, he had complications from a fungus infection that he picked up while attending school in Arizona. My sister Josephine informed me that Sean had contracted the fungus disease while on a football scholarship at college. The doctors had recommended he visit a hospital in New York for treatment; but by the time they were able to make an accurate diagnosis, the fungus had already spread throughout his body. I was devastated by the news. Sean had eventually made great transitions in his life. He was only about twenty-five years old when he contracted the illness. How could he be dead at such a young age? I wondered.

Unbeknownst to me, my sister Josephine had been trying to reach me for about five months before Sean's death. Because she was unable to locate me, my family feared that I might have been killed in the Jonestown, Guyana, scandal. During our phone conversation, I informed Josephine that during the time of the Jonestown scandal, I was in Geneva, Switzerland. She was relieved. Then, she asked me about my baby. She wanted to know if I had given birth. I proudly informed her that baby Rafael was about five months old. She was happy to hear the good news.

Josephine reminded me that I had only written the family a brief letter giving them my address when I reached Ecuador. She had no idea that I had taken a flight to Caracas, Venezuela, when I was eight months pregnant.

Chapter 14
Curacao

My flight to Curacao in January, 1980, was delightful. Rafael was six months old and I felt capable that we were able to take the journey. The airline flight attendant was very affectionate. She was concerned about taking care of my needs since she saw that I had a baby in my arms.

* * *

Upon arriving at the airport in Curacao, I was certain that I would find fulfillment there. I was elated to be able to spend the last days of my journey as a COG missionary in such a beautiful place.

Jeremy and Susana, both American disciples, met me at the airport. They introduced me to Dominique, their five-year old son. Jeremy was Caucasian, with blonde hair. He was medium height and very handsome. The denim jeans that fit loosely on his legs accented his medium frame. He wore a firmly starched pinstriped shirt and a red cap. His sneakers were blue and white. Casual and inviting, he shook my hand and thanked me for accepting their invitation to come to Curacao!

Susanna was the daughter of an interracial couple. She was medium height and heavy set. Her dark, curly hair bounced softly on her broad shoulders. She had dark brown eyes and ivory-colored skin. She was one of the most beautiful women I had ever met in the COG. It was no wonder that Jeremy told me that he was madly in love with her.

The drive to their home was about thirty minutes. Jeremy and Susana told me that they were renting a single-family house, from a "fish."

* * *

Upon arrival at the COG colony, Susanna explained to me that she had made the decision to forsake all and become a COG disciple about two years ago. She said that a group of COG singers had been performing at an event in downtown Curacao. They handed her a few COG flyers, and she was immediately interested in joining a COG colony. She explained to me that her parents were natives of Curacao. She met Jeremy when she joined the COG. Thereafter, they decided to be partners. Within the last six months, Susanna informed me that she and Jeremy had been asked by the prophet, Moses David, to start an "FFing" home in Curacao.

The subject changed quickly to what my intentions were should I decide to remain in Curacao as a member of their team. I explained that I had been a COG disciple for about two years. I was adamant about the fact that I would probably devote a few more months' time in Curacao as a COG missionary. Thereafter, I assured them that I planned to return to the U.S.

Jeremy and Susanna stated that they were in agreement with my plans. Almost ignoring my true feelings about the practice of "FFing," Susanna explained that she would need my support with her full-time "FFing" on the island. She made it clear that she wanted me to be available on Friday nights when either she or I would accompany Jeremy to the nightclub in downtown Curacao. This would facilitate one of us staying home to take care of baby Rafael and Dominique.

* * *

Reluctantly, I did go to the nightclub twice during the time I was in Curacao with Jeremy; but I didn't meet anyone that I was interested in witnessing to. However, during a casual trip by bus into town, I met Nelson, who was a native of Curacao. He became very attached to Rafael and me. Over the next few months, our relationship grew.

I explained my feelings for Nelson to my shepherds, Jeremy and Susanna. They rejected my desire to pursue a serious relationship with him. It was clear that COG disciples should not become romantically involved with systemites because they did not understand our mission.

Despite their rebuke, Nelson and I eventually became seriously involved. We had decided on a yearlong engagement, after which we would get married on the island of Curacao. We secretly met at various downtown restaurants in Curacao for dinner. I was forbidden to bring Nelson to the COG colony. Besides, he did not want his friends to know that we were developing a serious relationship. Also, I did not want Jeremy and Susanna to know that I had asked Jeremy to assist me in leaving the COG.

In preparation for escaping from the COG, I asked Nelson to open a post office box in downtown Curacao so that I could receive mail from my family. Any mail that would come to the colony would be opened by my shepherds before being distributed to me. Therefore, having mail sent to a post office box would assure that Jeremy and Susana did not retrieve and open my personal mail.

* * *

Over the next two months, Nelson and I decided to tell Jeremy and Susanna about our wedding plans. When we met with them, they were not supportive of our decision. Furthermore, they made it clear to me that to marry outside of the COG was forbidden.

After about 3 months of opening the post office box, Nelson handed me a letter from my sister Jessica. Usually only the shepherds of a colony are allowed to distribute personal mail. As I read the letter, I was shocked that Jessica's husband, Louis, had died of stomach cancer. She was devastated. I carefully read the letter again. It was about five pages and full of details about her loss.

Most shocking was Jessica's insistence that I move to Rolling Meadows, Illinois. She confessed that she needed emotional support. Also, she emphasized in the letter that she was desperate for help with babysitting for her two children, Betty and Francisco.

Upon responding by letter, I informed Jessica that she should take a flight to Brooklyn, New York. I agreed to meet her at the family house. Because I needed time to get acquainted with Jeremy and Susanna, I informed her that I would plan to see her in New York within about three months. I explained that I needed the time to sufficiently take care of my personal business before I left the island of Curacao. I made sure to tell Jessica in the letter that I was engaged to Nelson. I asked her to participate in the wedding. I also informed Jessica that after the wedding, Nelson may want me to live in Curacao for another year before I could permanently return to the U.S.

* * *

I enjoyed living in Curacao. Jeremy and Susanna were cordial to me. However, their loyalty to Moses David bothered me. I had been a COG disciple for two years, and I was not convinced that Moses David was an end-time prophet as they proclaimed. Supporting my suspicions, the Mo Letters were increasingly disturbing.

Therefore, I informed Jeremy and Susana that in a few months, I was going to visit my sister Jessica. I was careful not to provide them with the specific date or time of my departure. I feared their rebuke should I leave their domain without "approved leave" from my duties as a COG missionary.

One day when Susanna was not at the colony, Jeremy expressed his concern about my new friend, Nelson. He asked me what Nelson thought about my decision to go to New York. I told Jeremy that I was only going to the U.S. for a visit and that I was planning to return to Curacao. I reinforced my need to attend to two traumatic family issues: the death of my brother, Sean, and the death of Louis, my sister Jessica's husband.

* * *

During my entire time in Curacao, I noticed that there was a lot of conflict between Susana and Jeremy. She had decided that it was her "call" to become a full-time "FFer." Therefore, she would be engaged in "FFing" as a way to obtain consistent income. However, Jeremy resented her constant "FFing."

Numerous arguments broke out between the couple. Also, Jeremy openly confessed that he was unhappy with one of Susana's "fish" - Julio. Though he disliked him, Susanna argued that Julio was very supportive by paying some of the rent on the house. Therefore, since full-time secular employment was difficult to find in Curacao, Jeremy realized that he had to support Susana's desire to continue "FFing." He had to tolerate Julio until they could find other means of paying the rent on the house and supporting their small family.

* * *

To my outrage, Moses David began writing letters to the COG members about "child fondling." They arrived on a monthly basis and were considered to be our guide as COG disciples. He explained in his letters that he felt that child fondling was biblical and that children were cured of behavior problems when parents fondled them periodically.

Avid about my spiritual stance, I approached Jeremy. He also believed that "child fondling" was scripturally wrong; he called it child incest. However, Susana insisted that when Jeremy became more spiritual he'd understand.

* * *

Unable to find spiritual fulfillment and totally perplexed by the new Mo Letters on "child fondling," I wrote a letter to my sister Jessica. I explained to her that I was alarmed and that I needed professional Christian counseling. I informed Jessica that she should only use the post office box number for corresponding with me. This would assure that our plan for my escape from the COG would remain a secret. I had reached the point that I knew that divine intervention was needed to permanently leave the COG.

Not only were the Mo Letters getting more surreal, I was beginning to have sleepless nights. My conscience was troubling me, and I was fervently seeking God about redirecting my life. Indeed, I was at another breaking point.

* * *

Over the next few weeks, I began a regimen of regular intercessory prayer. I had decided that the COG had become repulsive. I had to figure out a way to get out of the group. My only dilemma was that I was engaged to Nelson. I was not sure if he would consider moving to the U.S. with me.

In numerous follow-up letters, Jessica informed me that she would assist me should I decide to leave the COG. She wrote letters to me continuously, just in case I was not receiving some of them.

* * *

When I told my shepherds that I had a set a date to visit my sister Jessica in New York, they encouraged me to also visit with my other family members.

When confronting Jeremy and Susana about my travel plans to visit my sister, they began to read various Mo Letters to me. Then, they used scripture to support their opinions about backsliders, who refused to answer their call as COG missionaries.

During the entire time that I spent in Curacao, even though Jeremy and Susana informed me that I had permission to permanently leave the COG, they did not provide me with any money. After all, I had been in the COG for at least two years. Therefore, I had fulfilled my time requirement in the organization. Most important, I had built my self-esteem and was comfortable in my role as a single mother. Therefore, I was ready to face family and friends in the U.S. I was ready to go home.

* * *

I ignored Jeremy and Susanna's warnings about being a backslider. I was convinced that I had made a terrible mistake in joining the COG. I earnestly prayed and admitted my sin to God and asked for His forgiveness. Although my stay in Curacao had been brief, I realized that it was critical that I make changes to my life for Rafael's sake. Through my desperate cries for change in my life, God opened my spiritual eyes.

It was early May, 1980, and Rafael was ten months old. I had finally come to the end of myself. Only God could redeem me and redirect my life back to the path of righteousness.

First, I placed a call to Nelson to inform him that I was breaking our engagement. Although he was confused and upset about my decision, he informed me that he understood. He encouraged me to go to the U.S. and take care of the family issues that were so distressing to me.

Then, I placed a phone call to Jessica indicating that I had changed my mind. I was not going to meet her in Brooklyn, but that I was leaving the COG permanently. Therefore, I had decided to move in with her in Rolling Meadows, Ill. Jessica heartily agreed since she was still suffering from grief because of Louis's death.

* * *

It was early in the morning (about 2:00 a.m.), when I secretly escaped from Jeremy and Susana's domain. I called a taxi that picked me up in front of the house. With baby Rafael safely in my arms, I alerted the cab driver to take me to downtown Curacao. The taxi took me to the postal store where Nelson had assisted me to open the post office box. Jessica had also agreed that this was the perfect way for us to communicate with her while I was planning my escape from the COG.

Swiftly, I picked up the airplane ticket that my sister Jessica had sent me. Then, I hurried to the convenience store and retrieved the money that Jessica had secretly wired to me. Quickly, I flagged down another blue taxi and told the driver to take me to the airport.

Fortunately, the airport was not crowded. This was probably due to the fact that it was so early in the morning. Without hesitation, I found the gate where I needed to board my flight. The destination was O'Hare Airport in Chicago. I carefully stepped into the airplane, quickly found a window seat, and plopped down. I clenched little Rafael firmly in my hands and wiped away the tears that were streaming done my face. Amazingly, I felt that a big burden had been lifted from my shoulders.

* * *

The revelation came to me that fear had driven my motives while I participated as a COG missionary. Therefore, for two tumultuous years, I had been a victim of mind control and deception. Yet, once I made the decision to permanently leave the COG, I was completely set free from the destructive web of the COG and delivered from the stain of cultist living. Miraculously, I felt completely whole again and ready to re-enter society.

Part Three:
U.S.A.

Chapter 15
The Breaking Point

After sacrificing my life by serving on the mission field for two years, I arrived in Chicago with Rafael securely in my arms. Miraculously, I was back on American soil, having narrowly escaped the bonds of the cult. It was late May, 1980, and I felt like I had just been released from prison.

My escape had been carefully planned by Jessica and Eli, who felt it was important that I leave Curacao in the early morning hours. Therefore, I had jetlag and was very tired when I arrived at O'Hare Airport.

Finally, I was re-united with my sister Jessica. She hugged me and began sobbing uncontrollably. Also, I poured out tears of joy because of my safe return to the U.S. I reclaimed my birth name - Faye.

Yet, I felt great sorrow because of Jessica's loss. She was still grieving because of her husband's lost bout with stomach cancer. I had never seen Jessica so depressed. We had long been separated by cruel fate, yet our hearts were jubilant that we were able to finally reunite. Although Jessica had no family members in Illinois, all of Louis's family members were there to support her. Yet, Jessica informed me that she still felt lonely.

Upon his death, Louis left behind Betty and Francisco. I reminded Jessica that she had to remain emotionally strong to support her two children. Betty was almost nine months old. Francisco was about three years old. He had always been a quiet child. Although he seemed distraught about his father's death, I don't believe it was real for him yet.

I was almost twenty-three years old, and I still had a lot of energy and vigor. One thing I had developed during my two-year stint as a COG missionary was endurance and determination. I was convinced that my spiritual setback would not completely destroy my personal relationship with God.

Most difficult was to admit that I had been wrong, terribly wrong.

The reality of my plight hit me like a victim whose bank has just been robbed by brazen perpetrators. I had no money and I was a college drop-out. However, for the first time in twenty-four months, I was ready and willing to listen to my family members. Also, I was prepared to receive the Bible again as the infallible Word of God.

* * *

Jessica continued to inquire if I had had any contact with Jim Jones and the Jonestown, Guyana, suicides. She informed me that this catastrophe had been published in the newspaper. However, I reiterated to Jessica that during the time of the Jonestown suicides, I was in Switzerland. The Children of God were just beginning to make plans for spreading their doctrine in South America.

* * *

Now that I was back on American soil, I had a new set of problems to face. I had no job skills, except that I was fluent in Spanish. Thankfully, knowing the Spanish language qualified me to interview for a job at a nearby hotel as a night manager. The only problem with the job was the fact that I had to leave Rafael at home with Jessica.

Betty cried a lot at night. Jessica informed me that Rafael also woke up often at night because of Betty's continuous sobbing. Jessica found it increasingly difficult to manage two babies throughout the night. I decided to quit the night manager job at the hotel and to take a full-time job at a McDonald's Restaurant.

The most painful reality was my daily struggle with depression and guilt. I felt confused and often overwhelmed by motherhood. I also found it difficult learning to make a budget and to be financially responsible. While a COG disciple, our shepherds confiscated all of our money at the end of the day. We were only given a small allowance for daily sustenance. Now, however, I would be responsible for learning to stay on a budget. Fortunately, Jessica made it clear that she would help me.

* * *

What bothered me most were my daily battles with hopelessness; I knew that I had to keep close to God in order to fight. Also, I was constantly having feelings of remorse for losing my scholarship as a Study Abroad student. Too often, I felt bewildered and often inundated by the reality of my life in Rolling Meadows, Illinois. Also, I was not making enough money at McDonald's Restaurant to take care of all of my financial responsibilities. Jessica did not charge me for rent or utilities. However, she made it clear that I would be responsible for purchasing food and clothes for Rafael and myself.

Because of my poverty, it was necessary to find a thrift store so that I could purchase discount clothes for Rafael and me. I was a size eight, so it was easy to find suitable clothing at the thrift store. Additionally, I also went shopping at discount marts where I found personal care items, diapers, and other necessities at greatly reduced prices.

I was also discouraged by the fact that I did not have a bachelor's degree as I had anticipated receiving after my junior year abroad in Spain. This was a painful reality that haunted me daily.

* * *

After one year, I met Crystal, a former member of the COG in Palatine, Illinois. Crystal had a three-bedroom apartment. She asked me to move in with her. She was also a single mother of three young children. I did not discuss my decision to accept Crystal's offer with Jessica. Since she had informed me that she was returning to Brooklyn, Jessica insisted that I leave Illinois with her. But, I had made the decision that I was not yet ready to face my family members in New York.

When I informed Jessica of my decision, she promised me that she would assist me if I would reconsider. She also assured me that she would help me by babysitting Rafael whenever I needed her support. However, I tried to make it clear to Jessica that I would need God to intervene in my life.

* * *

When Jessica began packing for her return to Brooklyn, I informed her that I had found a friend, Crystal, who was also a single mother. I told her that I had made the decision to move in with her. By that time I had been working for McDonalds for over a year. I had received a couple of raises and I was making enough money to pay rent. Also, Crystal was my age and we had a lot in common.

* * *

After Jessica decided to return to the family house in Brooklyn, I sometimes felt discouraged about my daily battle as a single mother. Yet, I was unwavering in my decision to succeed in life and had daily prayer and Bible readings. I was determined that I was not going to rejoin the COG.

The book of John was particularly enlightening to me. I found the scripture to be full of promises that I wanted to instill in my life. I was convinced that I could heal my personal relationship with God.

Most important, I had forgiven myself. Also, I promised God that I would dedicate my life to Him. I also wanted to find a church home so that Rafael and I could obtain spiritual training. I had also forgiven the COG members, whom I had met at the Colombes colony in France for their deception.

Of significant importance was my ability to be a good roommate for Crystal. She was such an encouragement to me. Crystal had also been disenchanted with the COG doctrine of "sharing" and "FFing." We supported one another in our quest to be totally cult-free and were determined to raise our children, even as single parents. Nonetheless, I was at another breaking point.

Chapter 16
"Not My Kid"

According to Deborah Berg, in her book, *The Children of God: The Inside Story*: "Coming out of a cult is more difficult by far than being in. While in, it is a simple matter of keeping one's head in the sand and staying blind to reality. But in emerging from a life of falsehood and sin, it becomes a painfully excruciating experience to face life as it truly is, accepting that you have been wrong, terribly wrong."[1]

Unfortunately, the deception of religious cults is increasing in our society and has become a major problem. Many who join spend months, even years, in a euphoric state. Then, they suddenly decide that they must escape the bonds of the cult, which has held them in bondage.

How does one lose his or her identity in the bond of a destructive cult? More importantly, how can parents who have fervently believed, "Not My Kid," cope with the reality that indeed their son or daughter has been influenced, even brainwashed, by a destructive cult?

In writing this book, I delved more deeply into the circumstances that led me to join the COG. I engaged in profound introspection; even more importantly, I examined the motives of those who provoked me to join the COG.

After about two years of being brainwashed into believing the doctrines of the COG, I escaped with no intention ever to return again. In addition, after being cult free, I confessed that I would never find myself in the bonds of another cult that would take away my freedom to be in service to the Lord.

I often went over the series of events that changed the course of my young life as a student in a foreign country. I had won a scholarship to study Spanish as a Junior Year Abroad student. I had become a Christian at about fourteen years old. How then, could I have been so deceived?

To answer this question, Deborah Davis writes: "Ironically, NBC had just shown the highly praised' First Tuesday' documentary to the

American public. This portrayed the COG to be a very puritanical, Christian organization - which, at the time of the filming, was basically true. When producer Bob Rogers and the NBC crews were filming at TSC, we lived morally chaste lives. But by the time of its release, Mo had returned from Israel and things had changed irrevocably."[2]

It was late 1977, in Madrid, Spain, when I first met the COG. Daniel, a member of the Paris Show Group, was singing with other COG members at a student café. He had an offering receptacle that they passed around to take a collection after they sang. Then, he approached me and asked for my phone number.

Why not? I asked myself. He is so cute, I thought. Little did I know that meeting the COG at that scenic student café would dramatically change my life for the next two years.

* * *

I accepted Daniel's invitation to go to Paris, to the Colombes home for the Christmas holiday. I told the COG members that I was not sure that I wanted to join the COG. Also, I informed the COG shepherds that I needed more time so that I could discuss my decision with my guidance counselor at Schiller College in Madrid.

Despite my reservations about the COG, I was pressured to join the group. The COG members surrounded me at the large dining room table and quoted from scripture.

Because I felt coerced by the COG at the Colombes home, I conceded to the demands that I join. "Why should you wait? "they exclaimed. The Paris Show Group members insisted that the time for me to join the COG was December 1977. Besides, they insisted, God had opened up the door for me to be a part of their group. They boasted that they were "celebrities" and their music had made them famous in Paris. Therefore, they informed me that it would be a privilege for me to join the COG at the Colombes colony.

* * *

After I joined, around March of 1978, the organizational structure of the COG began to change drastically: Mo Letters were written about "flirty fishing" ("FFing"). "Sharing" (sexual freedom among group members) was permissible. COG shepherds were expected to lead and be examples for the disciples of the "New Revolution." Supposedly their acceptance of the "New Revolution" deemed them as spiritually mature. We were now one body and all things were lawful.

When the "New Revolution" emerged as the new direction for the

COG, I was a brand new COG disciple. I was in shock at first over the myriad of Mo Letters about the organization's new path to follow, but to leave suddenly would mean that I was admitting that I had made a mistake. At the time, I wasn't ready to confess that I had been led astray.

In addition, the COG shepherds at the Colombes home told me that I could not leave until my "indoctrination" was complete. This included daily reading of the Mo Letters with Eli. He eventually moved into the Colombes colony to assure my indoctrination process was successful.

However, I was expecting Daniel to deepen our relationship once I had finally joined the COG, so his sudden distance from me was confusing. He returned to Madrid soon after he knew that I was safely in the hands of the COG leadership in Paris. Also, Daniel was careful not to tell me that he was a COG recruiter. Daniel was very convincing. Therefore, I thought the Lord was leading me. According to Kenneth Hagin in *How Can You be Led by the Spirit of God*, "The Lord enlightens us and guides us through our spirits. If that be the case - and it is - then we need to become more spirit-conscious. We need to become more conscious of the fact, that we are spirit beings, and not just mentors or physical beings. We need to train our spirits so they will become safer and safer guides." [3]

Circumstances confirmed that my heart had been broken. I was falling in love with Daniel, yet I was deeply saddened when one day at the Colombes home I saw him with Angelina, whom he had apparently invited to visit the colony. They seemed close and I was wondering why he hadn't approached me, asked to take me out for the evening, or embraced me since I had finally accepted his invitation to join the COG.

Then, it dawned on me that this young lady was another one of Daniel's recruits. He had probably met her at a student café in Madrid, Spain. It appeared to me that she would also be convinced to join the group and expected to submit herself to their wayward lifestyle.

* * *

Though the behavior I saw in the cult was bizarre, young adults who join religious sects need time to understand the consequences of their behavior. For example, women involved in some destructive cults are expected to bear children out of wedlock. This could be detrimental since dependence on the cult is increased.

According to Deborah Davis, "My first breaking point occurred at Vienna when my dad introduced the 'Old Church, New Church' prophecies. As I review my ten years in the Children of God, I can see that I have experienced about eight breaking points. These are the times when circumstances and events cause a person to question why he is doing what he is doing, why he is in the COG, why he is following Moses David. I believe that during these breaking points, God - through the influence of the Holy Spirit on my conscience - was trying to help me to see the truth. Being a fiercely proud person, I was not yet in a position to face the truth about my father and what we are doing for the Lord." [4]

* * *

Davis's experience as the daughter of Moses David, and mine, were so similar in nature. While I pondered why the cult was so attractive to me, I was faced with the reality that other people's children would also find the COG a supposedly easier way of living. In the COG, you did not have to make decisions about the day-to-day activities, since most colonies had a shepherd who supervised us corporately. Also, a "buddy," who watched our every move, was assigned to each disciple.

COG members followed a rigid schedule. Therefore, there was not much time for a lot of thinking about your spiritual state. Unfortunately, you simply followed and obeyed the rules (as outlined by the Mo Letters). Moses David was our prophet, and he communicated to us through these letters. The shepherds rebuked COG disciples who refused to obey COG rules and regulations. Ultimately, other COG members labeled you as "unspiritual."

Still, when my name was changed to Joy, I was expected to be happy when a lot of my personal freedoms were being taken away. For example, when I tried to leave the COG in Curacao, I was given permission to return to the U.S. Yet, my shepherds did not provide me with any financial support.

* * *

Therefore, I suggest to parents who have children who are involved in destructive cults to have patience and remain in intercessory prayer for them.

I spoke to my sister Josephine about her feelings while I was a disciple in the COG. She told me that she felt that I had forsaken our family and that the letters she received from me were disturbing. However, she felt sure that I would come to my senses and find a way to come to grips with reality and return home to the U.S.

I believe that it was her fervent prayers for my deliverance and those of my friends that loosened the bonds of cultic influence on my life. Also, Eli interceded on my behalf. His support in assisting me to be deprogrammed from the cultic mentality became strong in the years following my escape from the COG colony in Curacao.

* * *

It will take about one and one-half to two years for a young adult to be completely deprogrammed from the bonds of a cult. This was the case with me. Also, young adults who leave destructive cults must be exposed to the delivering power of the Holy Spirit. Being associated with a local church, finding other believers to fellowship with, are essential for Christian maturity.

Consistent Bible study with a book like the like *The Purpose Driven Life*, by Rev. Rick Warren, will make the difference in helping young people to rid themselves of the bonds of a destructive cult.

In Linda Davis's case, she and her husband, Bill, were delivered from the bonds of the cult through a seminar entitled "The Institute in Basic Youth Conflicts." It was a six-day seminar in which they gained a complete and lasting deliverance from the effects of the cult and the bondage of sin. According to Davis, "The Bible was given back to us as the inspired Word of God - something we could trust in, the Light of Truth by which to guide our lives once again."[5]

Chapter 17
The Cult Influence

"Yet I returned knowingly to all this," Deborah Davis writes. "The circumstances had not changed. There was a method in all of my father's madness - this I now painfully knew to be true. But where can I go? I rationalized. I had conquered the battle over physical suicide alone in the hotel room. But in going back I had lost an even greater battle: I was committing spiritual suicide."1

I had been influenced by the same destructive cult - the COG. When I refused to participate in certain unscriptural practices, I was rebuked, deemed "unspiritual" by the shepherds, and sometimes openly chastised for my rebellion.

It was about four months after I joined the COG that I realized that I had made a terrible mistake. Yet, by the time I realized that I had made a wrong turn in my spiritual journey, I was already at the stage where constant brainwashing techniques into accepting the cultic life-style are used.

Why are these techniques effective? How do they keep a young person under control? More importantly, how was I, a bright, young African American exchange student with a promising future, become so deluded in my spiritual walk with God?

To answer these questions, let's examine the supposed attributes of communal living that make the lure of the cults very attractive to young people:

1. Shared financial responsibility
2. Greater self-awareness
3. Dropping out of society
4. Freedom to express oneself sexually

Shared Financial Responsibility

One of the aspects that lure young adults to the COG is the idea of shared financial responsibility. Often those who are approached by cult disciples are between the ages of seventeen and twenty-five. They are usually students who need financial support to continue their education. Therefore, the concept of shared financial responsibility is very attractive.

The tragedy with the COG is that, although they tell disciples that finances are shared among members, they also intercept money coming in for a disciple and distribute it evenly among its own members. Why should they take money sent by the family members of disciples and use it for the work of the cult? This is of particular significance since the Christian community teaches that money should be used for the purpose for which it is designated.

The COG disciples obtained funds from daily singing on the metros. In Madrid, their singing in the student cafés and nightclubs was also a very popular way to raise funds for the cult. Some received compensation for being childcare workers. Also, there were many supporters of the COG who contributed monthly to the organization.

All these methods were effective ways of bringing funds into the colony. Therefore, each disciple was responsible for participating in one of them to support COG colonies. Yet, these COG practices were not always completely effective in bringing in the funds necessary to maintain a COG colony.

Consequently, women were expected to go flirty-fishing ("FFing"). This involved a group of girls going with a male chaperone to nightclubs, where they would dance with men, use every effort to witness to them, and ultimately bring them to Christ. Once the men were convinced to support the work of the COG, they were renamed "fish."

The problem with this method is that "FFing" sometimes resulted in immoral conduct. Young girls were often pressured, and in some colonies forced into this practice against their will (as in my case). They were told if they were selected as an "FFer," then it was their duty to be a fighter and obey the command of our prophet, Moses David.

David taught the disciples (through the Mo Letters) that as COG members, they were expected to obey him. Therefore, as COG disciples, we were only able to receive divine revelations from God through Moses David. Disciples were deemed unspiritual and rebellious if they denied his role as the prophet who pointed the direction.

Despite my strong opposition to the practice, my shepherd at the Rambuteau apartment, Stanley, insisted that I participate in "FFing." He was in total agreement with our prophet Moses David. Despite opposition from the religious community, the practice of "FFing" flourished throughout Europe. By the 1980's, the COG was named the "sex cult of the eighties."

Deborah Davis writes, "Flirty Fishing prospered elsewhere. Moses David's annual statistical newsletter for 1979 reported the growth of his new 'ministry':' Our dear "FF'ers" are still going strong, God bless'm, having now witnessed to over a quarter-of-a-million souls, loved over 25,000, of them and won nearly 19,000 to the Lord, along with about 35,000 new friends."

"The organization of David Berg had run an amazing gauntlet since the days of Huntington Beach - from witnessing to "litnessing" to Flirty Fishing. The evil that was imbedded in my father's heart in 1968 and earlier was now being planted in the hearts of hundreds of thousands of people throughout the world."2

Many young people who have entangled themselves in destructive cults like the COG because of the illusion of shared financial responsibility must reconsider their decision. If the cost they must pay is too great, then why take the risk of being sexually exploited by a cult leader, who really has his own personal interest in mind?

The answer is found in understanding God's perfect will for your life and then making a decision to stand firm in the place that He has called you. If you do this, God remains true to His Word, "But my God shall supply all your need according to His riches in glory by Christ Jesus," (*Phil. 4:19.*)

Greater Self-Awareness

Once I left the COG, I wrestled with the spiritual state that I found myself in. I was a young African American woman, who now had a son, Rafael, whom I was responsible for raising. This was the reality that I was faced with on a daily basis. How could I build my own self-awareness and move toward the divine destiny that the Lord had in store for me?

In his book, *The Gathering Place,* Dr. James Love addresses the question as follows: "Therefore, from a psychological perspective, one principle of empowerment is the development of a positive self-image.

Empowerment must emphasize the biblical principles that humankind is created in the image of God (*Genesis1:27*). As a creation of God, each person has a unique gift and calling that God knows. The real challenge in life, therefore, is to discover the reason why we were created and then fulfill that purpose."3

In COG doctrine, self-awareness was supposedly found in the confines of a "family unit," a colony. Your whole life was dominated by the demands of communal living, sharing all things in common, as was done by the early disciples.

Therefore, it was difficult to come to grips with one's self. The shepherds of the home strategically arranged your life. We had to follow a rigorous daily schedule. As COG disciples, it was impossible to find self-awareness. If you were tired and asked for the day off, you were labeled by the cult as a weak soldier and immediately handed Mo Letters, which encouraged you to continue on as a strong force in the Lord's army. Therefore, even though the cult taught the disciples that one could find greater self-awareness by entering into the glorious world of communal living, it was a lie. This lie dominated my life for two years preventing me from fulfilling God's perfect will.

According to Deborah Davis, "Cults seek to destroy the individual, as we have already seen. Moses David has used a two-pronged approach to accomplish this goal within the Children of God. The first means he has used is the Mo Letters. By declaring these the Word of God, he has stifled the creative mental powers of his followers. They no longer have to think for themselves, read the Bible and apply it dynamically to their personal lives, or do any form of corrective prayer. Their only function is to read the Mo Letters, let Mo do all of the communicating with God, and follow what Mo writes. It is simply a question of obedience."4

Dropping Out of Society

In their book *Why Cults Succeed While the Church Fails*, Enroth and Melton state: "I feel that there is something of an authority vacuum in our society, and I think it in part relates to our family structure as well as to the church. There are lots of people out there looking for this sense of authority. Some of the young adults who get involved in these groups relate to cult leaders, especially masculine cult leaders, as parent figures. The cult becomes a surrogate family for them."5

In my case, the authority figure who influenced me most while I was in the COG was Stanley, my shepherd at the Rambuteau apartment in Paris. My father had died when I was about three years old. Therefore, I was seeking a male authority figure in my life.

I believe this was the reason that I allowed Stanley to intimidate me and force me into a life of "FFing," even when subconsciously, I knew it was wrong. In addition to feeling trapped, I also felt that I had no choice but to comply with the rules and regulations of the group. During my indoctrination at the Colombes home in France, I had subconsciously pledged to support the missionary effort of the COG.

Does God lead us into sin, so that good could be done? The answer to this question is "No." God does not take away our right to choose evil over good. Yet, even when we choose to sin, it is His goodness that leads us to repent and continue to again accept the Word of God in our lives as His will.

According to research done by Enroth and Melton, "Among the people who join cults, nine out of ten will leave the group within two years."6 To validate this point, I was a COG member for about two years. This was enough time for me to have a burning desire to be set free from cultist living.

After the "New Revolution," I was perplexed at the way that the "royal family" was feuding over the relationship of Deborah Davis, Moses David's daughter, and her partner, Bill Davis. The Mo Letter "Alexander the Evil Magician" revealed the details of her father's discontent about her relationship with Bill. Davis points out the destructive language in this Mo Letter: "It doesn't matter if it kills Deborah, she'd be better off [dead] . . . one way or the other, God's will be done."7

What evil could Deborah or Bill do that would make her father want her dead? It was strange to me that such private family matters were made public. It was early 1978, when the letter was written and distributed to the members of the Family. I was at the beginning of my indoctrination period; therefore, I was not given permission to tell Eli, my buddy, or the other COG leaders what I truly felt about this letter.

However, as time progressed, I continued to probe into the motives of those who were influencing me. Even though I felt the COG was somewhat of a surrogate family for me, I also knew deep within myself that I was being used for their selfish purposes.

What I really felt inside did not matter to my shepherd, Stanley. To add to my feelings of depression and anxiety, I felt trapped by Stanley's dominating demeanor. Who could disobey his orders without public rebukes? Even when I voiced my opinion about our rigorous daily schedule, I was rebuked and called a weak soldier in the COG.

Freedom to Express Oneself Sexually

According to Deborah Davis, "At about the age when youth are most likely to join a cult (seventeen to twenty-five), the sex urge is in fact at its height. The desire to create, to build, to reform, and to improve society is very strong. At the same time, most of these youths find themselves in college or the beginning stages of a career. When the sexual drive is high, what direction should it take?"8

The answer is found in scripture. God made the body to glorify Him. When Moses David (through the Mo Letters), directed the members of the COG to release their creative energies in immoral and perverted practices, he violated the Word of God. There is no validation in scripture for child incest (called "child fondling" by David), "sharing" (free sex among group members), flirty fishing (soliciting support for the group--through sex if necessary).

Does God allow us to express ourselves freely through our sexuality? Or, does He require us to channel those urges and desires in positive ways? We need to look within to find the answer.

Getting busy with the work of the Lord surely propels us to engage in the work of the kingdom rather than the works of the flesh. We are called to "go into all the world and make disciples of every nation." We are also called to change the world.

The COG gave us an opportunity to do so. These energies were channeled through the practice of "witnessing." That was the chief practice of the disciples until late 1973.Then, early in the spring of 1974, the disciples began practicing "litnessing." During this time, many disciples confessed that they never touched anyone, nor did they have the desire to do so. They were redirecting their creative energies into Bible study, witnessing, and "litnessing."

This was the case when I joined the COG; I was impressed with their dedication to saving souls. However, about three months after I became a disciple, Moses David staged his sexual revolution. Things really began to change, and I found myself in a whirlwind. I was constantly in a state of shock, and I could not fathom that I had been deceived into thinking that I had given my life for a good cause.

Rev. Rick Warren provides a sound paradigm for understanding why God does not take away our free will to choose good over evil. He states: "God is not a cruel slave driver or a bully who uses brute force to coerce us into submission. He doesn't try to break our will, but woos us to Himself so that we might offer ourselves freely to him. God is a lover and a liberator; and surrendering to Him brings freedom, not bondage. When we completely surrender ourselves to Jesus, we discover that he is not a tyrant, but a savior, not a boss, but a brother, not a dictator, but a friend."9

It was late 1979 when I finally understood that I needed to find a constructive way to release myself from the bonds of the cult. Moreover, my sister Jessica had been in contact with me. She explained to me in no uncertain terms that I had to leave the island of Curacao and join her in Rolling Meadows, IL. Her husband had died of stomach cancer, and she needed my emotional support.

It was her influence that led me to seek a way of getting out of the COG. Therefore, when I was sure I was ready to leave the cult, to re-enter society and once again take the Bible as the authority of God, it was just a matter of finding an opportunity to escape.

So one morning at 2:00 a.m., in Curacao, I packed my bags, without my shepherd's knowledge, and called a taxi. When the taxicab arrived, I beckoned the driver to take me to downtown Curacao where I retrieved the airline ticket that my sister Jessica had sent to my post office box. Then, the cab driver cruised down to the convenience store, where I obtained the money my sister Jessica had wired me. Then, I ordered the taxicab driver to take me directly to the airport. I was now ready to catch a flight back home to the U.S.A.

I was sure the Lord was leading me out of the COG. Most important, I was ready to leave. Truly, it was my time to regain my identity, express myself fully by once again turning my thoughts, my will, and my sexuality over to God. My life was again in His hands, and I promised the Lord that if He would deliver me from the bonds of the COG that I would give my life fully to serving Him.

According to Rev. Rick Warren, "On the path to spiritual maturity, even temptation becomes a stepping-stone rather than a stumbling block when you realize that it is just as much an occasion to do the right thing as it is to do the wrong thing. Temptation simply provides the choice. While temptation is Satan's primary weapon to destroy you, God wants to use it to develop you. Every time you choose to do good instead of sin, you are growing in the character of Christ."10

Chapter 18 Readjusting to Real Life

Crystal and I had been roommates in Palatine, for a year. Unexpectedly, I received a call from my sister Josephine that my Aunt Silvia had died of pancreatic cancer. I did not have the money to attend her funeral so I offered my condolences. However, with courage and serenity, I was making plans to return to New York in the next few months so that I could begin the process of readjusting to real life.

No doubt my experiences with the COG had been traumatic. I knew that being bombarded with questions from family members would be my biggest challenge. Yet, it was time to face all of my family members in New York, confess my sin, and continue on my journey.

* * *

When Eli mysteriously called me one day in Palatine, I asked him who gave him my phone number. He didn't answer, but I assumed my sister Jessica provided it to him. She had been in Brooklyn for about a year. She was also anxious for me to return to Brooklyn, resume my former identity, and completely disconnect myself from the COG.

During our conversation, Eli informed me that he had now reclaimed his real name - Andy. He asked about Rafael. "How is your son?" he probed.

"Fine," I answered.

Then, he asked me if I would consider returning to New York City. Surprisingly, he asked me again if I would marry him. The selling point was that Andy had been cult-free for two years. For this reason I knew he was capable of assisting me to rejoin society. I had an insatiable desire to be completely deprogrammed from the stench of cultic brainwashing.

Still, with fear in making such a transition, I took a deep breath. I thought about his invitation and felt assured that I was making a good decision; I informed Andy that I had decided to return to Brooklyn. Also, I accepted Andy's proposal of marriage.

* * *

Andy met me at La Guardia Airport in New York. When little Rafael saw Andy, he swiftly ran to him. Andy swooped him up into his arms and kissed him on the right cheek. Rafael laid his head on Andy's shoulder. They immediately connected with one another. Although extenuating circumstances at the Gonesse colony in France had separated Andy and me, I was thankful for this miraculous reunion!

Most challenging was the reality that I would have to spend the next few years readapting to real life. I knew that this modification in my life-style would be gruesome. Yet, for the first time in two years, God enlightened me that I could be cult-free. With God's grace and mercy, I could successfully readapt to society. My primary focus was to keep a steady job and be a productive member of society. Most important, was my determination to be a faithful wife to Andy and a good mother to little Rafael.

* * *

In the COG, Andy and I had not been permitted to marry since couples just lived together. They bore children, yet never exchanged marriage vows.

It was mid-1981, when Andy and I decided not to have a traditional wedding. The Justice of the Peace married us in the courthouse in downtown Manhattan during our lunch hour.

Still skeptical of becoming involved with institutional religion, I began watching a TV program called "Ever Increasing Faith," based in Los Angeles, California. Dr. Frederick K. Price was the preacher. This program helped me to have faith to begin a new life that was guided by the Holy Spirit.

Living in New York was a difficult adjustment. Andy had already been living in a rented apartment near the "A" train in Brooklyn. The only problem was that we did not have any furniture, or enough money to survive in New York. Moreover, I had to find a babysitter for Rafael. This was a significant change. In the COG, there was always a designated person within the colony to help with childcare.

Now that I was adapting to real life, I understood that finding proper care for our son was our responsibility. Through perseverance and a few references to support my efforts, I was able to find a competent babysitter for Rafael in Brooklyn.

To our advantage, Andy's parents, Raymond and Gene Allison, offered to support us financially as we made the transition to becoming cult-free. Therefore, Andy and I were able to get settled into our apartment as newlyweds. They also assisted us with our rent. They even provided us with the funds necessary to purchase furniture and appliances.

* * *

Andy took a six-month course in word processing on the Wang computer in midtown Manhattan near West 42nd Street. Most firms, companies, and organizations were beginning to offer courses to the public. This was an effort to supply the demand of the public to learn word processing.

Before 1982, in the offices in New York, we had always used typewriters. It was remarkably evident that this antiquated method of using the typewriter for typing office correspondence was being phased out. Word processing machines could now do the work by automating office correspondence. Thus, the word processing boom began to permeate the professional offices in New York City and subsequently around the country.

* * *

Eventually, Andy found a job as a word processor with American Express Company. What a breakthrough for him. Also, I found a job as a temporary word processing secretary, which allowed me to build my typing skills.

Call to Entrepreneurship

Andy had been working with American Express Company for about one and one-half years. He repeatedly spoke of starting his own business. At first, the idea seemed foreign, especially since he was earning a good salary. I also was working steadily, and we were able to pay our bills and live comfortably. Initially, I was not interested in starting a business.

Despite my apprehension, Andy began talking with some friends at work about the new word processing explosion. He informed me that he and his friends were certain that the market for word processing in San Juan, Puerto Rico, was lucrative! IBM had developed a new word processing system (Display-writer). Andy was sure we could provide computer consulting and training services there.

Because I needed advice, I called Andy's parents in Cambridge, Maryland, on the eastern shore. I explained to them that Andy and I were experiencing a breaking point in our marriage. Andy spoke with his parents separately; and then, I asked for the telephone and attempted to explain this decision to his parents. They listened attentively, but did not immediately offer any advice.

After hanging up the phone, Andy tried to erase any doubts I was having about his new business adventure. He informed me that Wayne Johnson, who was an IT specialist, had made a profitable business contact for him in San Juan. A computer company was offering him a job.

Despite my fears, I had confidence in Andy. Not only could he type about 90-100 w.p.m., he was also a computer genius. So, I reasoned if the job offer fell through, I knew Andy was competent enough to start his own computer training enterprise!

* * *

I eventually agreed to move to Puerto Rico in support of Andy because I was committed to the marriage. This decision was also an effort to encourage Andy to accept the job offer and to support our new business endeavor. It was early 1982, and Andy was anxious to tap into the word processing market in Puerto Rico.

Still, I had a lot of questions about the move. Provoked by the need to take parental responsibility, I tried to explain to Andy that I wanted to settle down and raise little Rafael. He was three years old, and I wanted to make sure he had good day-care services. It was evident that Andy and I would be diligently working during the day.

In preparation, Andy was determined to help me to develop the mindset for entrepreneurship. He told me there would be ample time for us to work together with the goal of eventually building a successful enterprise. He instilled a few business-building tips into my mind. Andy's tenacity allowed me to open up my mind to this "new call." I decided to proceed on faith and move in an entirely different direction.

We spent the next six months preparing for our trip to Puerto Rico. We had to decide on the type of living arrangements we would have. Also, we had to confirm where to find an affordable apartment to rent in Puerto Rico.

* * *

After we packed personal belongings, we gave the few furniture items that we had to friends. We made sure our personal paperwork was taken care of. Also, we made sure to update all of little Rafael's immunizations.

Before we left for Puerto Rico, we visited Andy's parents in Maryland. He wanted to explain our decision to take on this new business venture. He felt confident of our success in Puerto Rico; besides, he had a viable job offer. He was excited about our prospects. Andy was very convincing.

Though his parents were happy for us, they were not sure why we could not settle down in New York and raise Rafael. Nonetheless, they maintained their composure as parents. I knew they were nervous about our decision to move to Puerto Rico. Yet, they accepted our decision. His parents smiled at us and told Andy that it was our personal choice. They also stated that they would pray for us during our time of transition.

Chapter 19
There is Life after the Cult

Upon arriving in Puerto Rico, we were astonished that the small information technology company suddenly withdrew the word processing job offer. We immediately contacted Wayne Johnson in New York for an explanation. He provided us with details. The company that had originally asked us to relocate to San Juan, had experienced unexpected financial problems. Therefore, they had to cancel Andy's job offer. Wayne apologized for our inconvenience, but he wished us much success in Puerto Rico.

Wayne did provide some solace and peace to us. We had done all the right things for a successful move. Therefore, we were sure God had a purpose in our moving to Puerto Rico. Andy and I were faced with the dilemma of buying a plane ticket back to New York or of using our limited funds to remain in San Juan.

* * *

After prayer, Andy and I made an unwavering decision to use our faith, stay in Puerto Rico, and look for an apartment. We asked God for a miracle as we took a stalwart stance against our circumstances.

Since we only had enough money to buy food and live in a hotel for one month, we needed to move fast! Therefore, we decided to browse through the student district of San Juan. We were sure that the apartments would be cheaper. After walking for about one mile, I needed to find a restroom.

We entered a grocery store and asked if they had a bathroom. A young woman with sandy brown hair approached us. She introduced herself as Señorita Priscilla Gomez. She pointed toward a white door.

* * *

After I used the restroom, Señorita Gomez asked us if we were there to look at the one-bedroom apartment that was available.

"Where?" we asked.

"Upstairs," she said kindly. Then, she collected a bunch of keys from the counter. Señorita Gomez escorted Andy and me and little Rafael up two flights of stairs to the second floor. She opened the door of the apartment, briskly walked into the living room, and asked us if we liked it.

Andy liked the apartment, but I was not too fond of it. I asked Priscilla who the landlord was. She shoved a piece of paper in my hands with the name Angel Vasquez written on it. The paper had two phone numbers. Andy informed Priscilla that we would call Señor Vasquez later that day.

Determined to press on, Andy and I walked out of the grocery store and continued looking for an apartment. After walking another mile, we were exhausted. Also, Rafael was getting tired. Andy picked him up and laid him on his shoulder, where he fell asleep.

We decided to call Señor Vasquez. We stopped at a pay phone on the corner and Andy dialed the number. When someone picked up the phone, Andy said: "Hola, soy Andy. Puedo hablar con Señor Vasquez?"

"Si," the person on the other end responded, "Yo soy Señor Vasquez."

Andy asked him if he had another apartment for rent. They talked for another five minutes before Andy hung up the phone.

Andy informed me that Señor Vasquez was going to meet with us in about an hour. He had a one-bedroom apartment in the student district of San Juan, which he wanted to show us.

* * *

The bus ride was about fifteen minutes. After descending from the bus, we walked about four blocks to the address that Señor Vasquez gave us. It was located on a noisy main street where there was a lot of traffic. We noticed, however, that the building was very clean. Although the neighborhood was busy, we needed an apartment right away.

* * *

When Señor Vasquez arrived, he shook our hands and escorted us up the steps of the apartment building. He opened the door and invited us to come in. "Do you have any references?" he asked.

"Si," we responded. Andy handed him the name and phone

number of Elena Maldenez. Wayne had given us her name and address before we left New York.

Señor Vasquez handed us the keys to the apartment. He told us that he had never rented an apartment to anyone without first checking their references or verifying their employment.

However, he told us that he was a Christian, that he trusted us, and that he believed we would make good tenants. He said he would give us a month-to-month lease.

Thankful for the apartment, Andy handed him one month's rent. Señor Vasquez said that he did not need a deposit. We signed the lease. Then, we walked briskly out of the apartment, ran down the stairs, and left the building.

* * *

After he departed, we went back to our hotel. Andy and I went into a time of intercessory prayer. We were thrilled that the Lord had provided the apartment for us. It was a wonder that we could find an apartment in one day. Yet, we knew God was able to able to supply all of our needs, according to His riches in glory. (*Phil. 4:19.*)

The day had been exhausting. Therefore, that evening, we tucked in little Rafael and then, we decided to get dressed for bed, and drifted to sleep.

* * *

The next morning we pondered upon the reality that we did not have any furniture to move into the apartment. We were totally unprepared for living in San Juan without any form of permanent employment. Therefore, we decided to visit a local church to ask for help. We found Fe Es La Victoria in the downtown San Juan yellow pages phone book. With tenacity, Andy and I, with little Rafael, boarded the bus to take the thirty-minute ride to the church. Girded with prayer, we asked God to increase our faith. The bus ride was very scenic. We passed by some of the tourist attractions. We took a deep breath and decided to make San Juan, Puerto Rico, our home.

When we arrived at the church, a young man, who appeared to be in his thirties greeted us at the door. He introduced himself as Pastor Juan Rodriquez. He graciously invited us into his office. We met with Pastor Rodriquez for about an hour. I cried most of the time as we disclosed our disappointment about the failed job offer. Still, we informed him, we were interested in starting a word processing enterprise.

Pastor Rodriquez was very compassionate toward Andy and me. He agreed with us that we should remain in Puerto Rico. He promised that he would intercede for us and assist us to make contacts in San Juan. He persuaded us that in time, God would reveal His perfect will to us. He assured us that the members of the church would assist us to obtain furniture for our apartment.

Another man, perhaps in his early forties, joined us in Pastor Juan's office. Pastor Rodriquez introduced him as Marco Manchez, an architect. Then, Pastor Rodriquez told Marco that we wanted to start a word processing business. Marco informed us that he was a businessman and that he had an office on the Condado, a popular tourist area in San Juan. He said he would consider letting us share the office space to start our enterprise. What a miracle!

Thereafter, Rev. Juan gave us his testimony of how he had become a pastor. He had been a college dropout when someone witnessed to him about the grace of God. He started to attend regular church services and then received a "call" from God to the ministry. He informed us that he had been the senior pastor at Fe Es La Victoria for only two years.

Pastor Rodriquez prayed earnestly for us. He invited us back to church the following Sunday. To our surprise, as we left the church, Pastor Rodriquez provided a one hundred dollar contribution to assist us. Amazingly, it was enough money for us to buy groceries and take care of our living expenses for the next month.

Andy, little Rafael, and I returned to our new apartment in the student district of San Juan.

* * *

Meeting with Pastor Rodriquez convinced Andy and me that the Word of God was being taught at Fe Es La Victoria. We were sure we would be strengthened spiritually if we made the commitment to attend regular worship services. Through faith in God, we asked Him for the vigor necessary to overcome the challenges of living with limited financial resources in Puerto Rico.

* * *

Andy, Rafael and I returned to the Fe Es La Victoria Church the following Sunday. By faith, we took our bold stance as soldiers in the Lord's army. We felt within our hearts that the God of heaven would take care of us, even in San Juan, Puerto Rico.

Although we were far away from Brooklyn, New York, Fe Es La Victoria was a buttress to our spiritual program. Over the next few weeks, we regularly attended Sunday worship at the church. Even though the worship services were conducted in Spanish, I understood the messages. Andy was fluent in French, but he could comprehend some Spanish.

Also, we participated in their weekly Bible study. Most important, through the dynamic Word of God that Pastor Rodriquez taught, we were confident that God was omnipresent.

* * *

We did not see an immediate change in our circumstances. Andy could not find any employment in San Juan. Also, I looked for work with no success. To our surprise the unemployment rate there was very high at that time (about twenty-five percent).

In addition to regular Sunday worship attendance and Wednesday Bible study, Andy and I began a spiritual program of fasting and praying two days during the week. We also had regular visits at our apartment from the members at Fe Es La Victoria, who encouraged us to stay faithful in the Master's service!

* * *

After about two months in San Juan, we still had not found permanent work. We were frustrated as we came to grips with the fact that maybe we had made a mistake. Since we had a son who we knew needed our support, Andy called his parents and asked if they could send money to help us. With compassion they responded by sending us the rent money via Western Union. We were relieved that we could pay the rent and had a roof over our heads.

We struggled with buying groceries. We approached a few merchants at the Farmer's Market, which was a short walk from the student district. When we explained our situation, they graciously provided food to us. What a miracle-working God! Even in Puerto Rico, God was strengthening our faith!

* * *

Encouraged by the mercy of God, Andy and I started working on a business plan for the word processing computer training center. We decided to call it Office Automation Service Center. Since Marco Manchez was impressed by our persistence, he was determined to allow us to share office space with him.

Marco bragged about his new architectural firm on the Condado. He informed us that his office was on the ground floor of a condominium complex. Marco informed us that he could use the extra money for business expenses. Therefore, he encouraged us to move into the office as soon as possible.

Marco's mother, Maria Manchez, owned six condos in the same building where his office was located. Señora Manchez invited Andy and me to rent one of the condos on the sixth floor of the complex. Señora Manchez offered it to us at a discount.

* * *

Finally, we had a breakthrough; and our time of fasting and prayer had been beneficial. Since we were determined to succeed in Puerto Rico, we also worked on finding potential clients for our Office Automation Service Center!

With permission from Pastor Juan, we passed out fliers at Fe Es La Victoria. Subsequently, many of the members of the church signed up for computer training classes at the center. As we persevered to win the battle, we continued to work on a setting up a successful enterprise by developing our business and marketing plan.

* * *

Within thirty days, our business plan was complete. We accepted Marco's offer to move to the condo. Packing up our personal belongings at the apartment that we were renting took about seven days. We had to get permission from Señor Angel Vasquez to end our month-to-month lease. Thankfully, he agreed that he would support our new business venture by releasing us from our lease.

Amiably, Señora Manchez had furnished the condo at the complex. Therefore, it was not necessary to purchase anything except appliances. By faith, we moved into the two-bedroom apartment on the sixth floor.

* * *

It was ironic that Marco's cousin, Roberto Sanchez, worked for the San Juan division of IBM. They were in need of computer training professionals to expand the training services for their new word processing computer (Display-writer). Roberto, at Marco's recommendation, suggested our company to his supervisor at IBM. Andy and I were assured that since we were faithful in writing our business plan, we had won the bid for the contract!

It was obvious that things were finally beginning to work out in our favor. Our patience and perseverance had paid off. Andy and I had decided to plunge forward in obedience to our call to entrepreneurship.

The IBM contract led Andy and me to expand our enterprise on the Condado! Moreover, we had enough money to take care of our monthly expenses, as well as being blessed to afford a regular maid to assist me with housekeeping. After about four months in Puerto Rico, we were financially secure.

After we moved into the condo, we were able to get our work at Office Automation Service Center done more efficiently, since the office was just downstairs on the main level. Most exciting, when we woke up in the morning, Andy and I had a fantastic view of the ocean just across the street!

* * *

During our one year stay in Puerto Rico, Andy and I also met a few ex-COG members who had been members of Les Enfants de Dieu in Paris. They had left the COG while in Europe after the "New Revolution" and had returned to the U.S. to visit their families. Strangely, they had decided to rejoin the COG.

Why had they made this decision? To answer this question, one should look at the power that the cult mentally has on an individual. In killing the self-will of a person, cults have the ability to transform people into unthinking robots.

While in Puerto Rico, Andy and I were surprised to see the internal struggle that ex-cult members suffer. By that time, it appeared that the COG was receiving worldwide persecution, for instance, on sexual freedom. It was very disturbing that ex-COG members in Puerto Rico continued to belong to an organization that promoted sexual immorality.

Lessons Learned in the Call to Entrepreneurship

Andy and I had made the decision to defy the economic challenges in Puerto Rico by answering the call to entrepreneurship! In addition, we had time to do research on why people join cults. This became increasingly important to us as we struggled to be cult-free even in the midst of our new challenges.

Therefore, we had time to ponder the following:

1. Why do people join cults?
2. Why do they leave after about two years?
3. Why do Christians rejoin destructive cults?

Why do People Join Cults?

According to Enroth in his book *Why Cults Succeed While the Church Fails*: "The reasons that people are attracted to cults are social in nature. People join cultic groups because they meet very real human needs."1

I joined the Children of God because it provided for me a sense of a normal family life that I did not have while I was growing up. With the early deaths of my father and my mother, I was an orphan by the age of thirteen. My sense of anxiety within my family structure was intensified when my mother died. I was so young, and I was overwhelmed with grief. My mother and I had become friends, and her death perplexed me. I often wondered why was this happening to me.

Then, my sister Eva and I moved in with my Aunt Silvia and my older sister Josephine. Aunt Silvia's strict rules only intensified my feelings of displacement. I loved my Aunt Silvia, but we did have a hard time getting along. By age eighteen, after graduating from high school, I was determined to leave home and go to college at Fairfield University, in Fairfield, Connecticut.

My decision was based on the fact that I wanted to get away from what I then thought was a strict authority figure, who dominated my life in a negative way. Though my Aunt Silvia meant well, at the time I thought some of her disciplinary tactics were harsh.

Enroth further states: "Potential converts –whether to new religious movements (like the Unification Church) or to older, more established cults (like the Mormons)--are attracted to what they perceive to be nice, friendly people who seem to care for them and affirm them as worthwhile individuals. They are attracted to the sense of family, the sense of community, the sense of purpose that these groups capitalize on."2

Often the mistake that cult members make is that they join a group before they research the mechanics of how they function. Enroth writes: "The average converts don't join the Latter-day Saints, for example, because they discovered an exciting book called the Book of Mormon. Likewise, the young people who join the Moonies rarely do so because he or she was introduced to a book entitled "Divine Principle." People are attracted because of that group's image of wholesomeness, clean-cut Americanism, and concern for family values. Young adults are drawn to the Moonies because the recruiters they meet seem to be sincere, committed, and excited about their group. Doctrinal considerations are overshadowed by personal considerations. Indoctrination into the teachings of the group comes later."3

It was for personal considerations that I continued my journey as a COG member for about two years. According to Enroth: "Among the people who join cults, nine out of ten will leave the group within two years. That's the turnover rate at present. We have counted some thirty to thirty-five thousand people who have become members of the Unification Church, but there are only five thousand of them around today. Approximately thirty thousand came and went pretty quickly."4

Why do People Leave Cults after Two Years?

As I continued to explore the motives of the people in the COG, it was clear that Stanley's behavior was influenced by the Mo Letters. My encounter with him was perplexing, especially since I was assigned to work with him by the leaders of the Colombes colony. Often during our "family meetings" at the Gonesse home in the suburbs of Paris, Stanley rebuked me. He contended that I was disobedient to authority and had not reached spiritual maturity. Therefore, I could not understand the Mo Letters, which began revealing the blatant details about our sexual freedom - hailed as an attribute of the "New Revolution." Stanley's domineering presence was intimidating, I was commanded to accept the COG rules and regulations, which contradicted the biblical principles I learned at church as a teenager. Yet, we affectionately called him "Dad."

We were told that Moses David was our prophet. Therefore, he supposedly spent his time hearing from God about the direction of the COG. What was perplexing to me during my time with the group in Europe and South America was the fact that this so-called "man of God" was tearing families apart. For example, the letter he wrote to his daughter, Deborah Berg, entitled "If the Truth Kills, Let it Kill," in early February of 1978, was devastating to me.

Therefore, to witness such blatant disputes among the "royal family" members was bewildering to me. They were deemed to be a model to the rest of the COG of what family life was really all about. Furthermore, my mind could not fathom how a man who should love his daughter would want her dead. In her book *The Children of God: The Inside Story*, Deborah Davis states: "Rachel is the executioner and I sent her to be the hatchet man, and she's either got to save them or kill them, one or the other! I know this business. . . you run the risk of killing the victim.

You tell her to get busy and kill them! Kill them! The quicker the better! I mean if they can't stand the truth they ought to die and be dead! Let's hope maybe they'll go to Heaven and not to Hell!"5

Wanting to stay faithful to the prophet, her partner, Bill, was banished by Moses David to Martinique, a small French island in the Caribbean not far from Venezuela. "The trip to the airport was the longest ride of my life," Deborah writes. "I felt as if I were accompanying Bill to his execution. When he was finally put on the plane, my world caved in. I wept until the tears could no longer flow, slipping ever deeper into mental shock; I was dangerously close to catatonia."

"For four months I lived in a lost, isolated world. The daily activity of caring for the children was the one thing that kept me in touch with reality. Sometimes I would wake up and wonder if I were truly alive, if this was all a dream. I simply lived to get the next letter from Bill. Each one brought me back to a state of half-life. But in spite of it all, I couldn't bring myself to believe the growing perception that we were going to leave Dad and the movement. How could we possibly do that?"6

* * *

It was such heart wrenching disharmony within the Family that led me to rethink my decision to be affiliated with the group. Not only was the royal family not working harmoniously together, the Mo Letters were getting progressively more bizarre. They were filled with sexual connotations, perversion, and hints of child incest. Surely, after I read some of these Mo Letters, I was faced with a dilemma. I would need to either leave the COG or immerse myself deeper into a life of sin and confusion.

* * *

My decision to leave came after my stint in Curacao. I was once again confronted by my shepherds, Jeremy and Susanna, about Flirty Fishing ("FFing"). I had decided not to continue the practice. Therefore, our arguments centered on my decision. Of course, this was now a common COG practice throughout Europe and South America. Why such practices were allowed in the COG was baffling to me.

Yet, it was all part of the "New Revolution." One of the reasons the practice of "FFing" spread so quickly was that women in the COG were often coerced to participate in the practice.

* * *

After I fought to protect my sexuality, I was tired of defending my personal decision not to involve myself in "FFing." Whenever I had meetings with Jeremy and Susanna in Curacao about not participating in "FFing" and leaving the COG, a Mo Letter was thrust into my hands.

After two years as a COG missionary, Curacao would be the place of repentance. Unable to come to grips with my life as a COG missionary, I knew I had to leave the organization. My sister Jessica financially supported me. Also, it was her decision to be patient as she worked with Eli, Nelson and I that made my escape successful.

Why do Christians Rejoin Destructive Cults?

Coming out of a destructive cult is extremely difficult. If an ex-cult member does not have the family support needed for successful deprogramming, it is very likely that they will return to cultist living. Also, a young adult who usually has dropped out of college to join a destructive cult is now faced with the following realities: How do they re-adapt to society? How do they cope with depression? How do they find gainful employment (since many do not have job skills)?

The answer to these questions can be found in scripture. *Ephesians 6:10-12* states: "Finally, be strong in the Lord and in the strength of his power. Put on the whole armor of God, so that you may be able to stand against the wiles of the devil. For our struggle is not against enemies of blood and flesh, but against the rulers, against the authorities, against the cosmic powers of this present darkness, against the spiritual forces of evil in the heavenly places."

The Christian who loves God and wants to follow His ways will win. A primary factor in my deliverance from cultic brainwashing is that I eventually came to grips with the reality that Jesus is Lord.

The pressure to rejoin the cult is heightened when family members bombard you with questions like, "Why did you do this to the family?" An ex-cult member wants to provide an answer, yet one is difficult to find. The reasons that young people may join a cult include a myriad of circumstances in their lives.

In addition, the society that we must re-enter does not always provide resources for a person who has been taught to condemn the church system. In addition, they have been told to beware of people outside the cult (they were called systemites).

Who then can one turn to for solace? Truly, it was the unadulterated Word of God and the strong support of family and friends that compelled me to re-adjust to the real world and become a productive member of society. Ultimately, God delivered me from the COG. Therefore, I am compelled to tell others about His goodness and His willingness to set them free.

Chapter 20 Politics and the Church

Before leaving Puerto Rico in early 1984, at the recommendation of Wayne Johnson, we transferred ownership of the Office Automation Service Center to Elena Maldenez. She was a friend of Mr. Johnson. We wanted to reward her for being resourceful and providing a reference for us. Her support allowed us to rent our first apartment in the student area of San Juan, Puerto Rico.

We visited with her regularly in San Juan during our time there and she became a good friend. During our year-long stay in Puerto, Rico, we encouraged Elena to take control at our Office Automation Service Center, learn the administrative aspects of running the business and work towards growing it.

In addition, Elena had been an inspiration to us while Andy and I struggled to come to grips with our stay in San Juan. Our one-year stint there was truly an answer to a call to entrepreneurship.

* * *

Andy and I eventually returned to New York. His parents were ecstatic and encouraged us to stay in Brooklyn. They emphasized the necessity to obtain an apartment and settle down, especially since we were responsible for raising little Rafael.

It was late 1984, and I was anxious to get settled. However, for Andy, it was more difficult. He was a constant traveler. Therefore, I knew within approximately one to two years' time, he would approach me about moving to another location.

* * *

It did not surprise me, then, that Andy eventually decided to move to the Washington, D.C. metropolitan area in late 1984. He said that he wanted to be closer to his aging parents in case of any health issues that might occur.

We contacted Andy's sister, Betsy, and her husband, Rev. Keith Layman. They had two young boys. Robert, who was about five years old and Warren, who was three years old. They lived in the southeastern section of Washington. We considered living close to them because we felt that Rafael would have playmates. Also, we felt that Betsy would be able to assist us as we transitioned into living in Washington. Therefore, we found an apartment near Minnesota Ave., about three blocks from Betsy and her husband.

We joined Evangel Temple (now Evangel Cathedral, Upper Marlboro, Maryland) in the northeast section of Washington, on Rhode Island Avenue. The late Bishop John L. Meares was the senior pastor.

I had completed a two-month teacher training program at Brooklyn Tabernacle in Brooklyn. The Rev. Pete Storms was the senior pastor. The two-month teacher training program culminated with an awards assembly. I was proud to receive my teaching certificate from the church! His guidance and profound wisdom during that time was an encouragement to me. Since receiving the certificate from Brooklyn Tabernacle, this was my grand opportunity to convey the Word of God to children. I felt equipped to begin teaching children's Sunday school. There were many challenges, yet I felt compelled to use my ministry gift of teaching to provide instruction and guidance to young children.

My support at Evangel Temple (now Evangel Cathedral) as a Sunday school teacher spanned from 1984 to 1987. During that time, Rev. James Love was the superintendent of the education department.

* * *

Although Andy and I lived in Washington, he continued traveling to New York City. He had a computer contract there with a medium-sized law firm. He had to travel to New York every week and sometimes only came home on the week-ends. I continued to teach regular Sunday school at Evangel Temple. I also participated in other church activities. The Bible study was a tremendous support system for me. Finally, I had found a church home after being cult-free for two years.

* * *

Andy was not progressing spiritually. Therefore, around 1985, we began having marital problems. Many difficult issues surfaced, which caused me to question his ability to continue living a Christian life-style. Most disturbing was his insistence that he continue his computer contract work in New York. I urged him to look for a contract in the

Washington metropolitan area. However, he refused and insisted that weekly travel to New York was more lucrative.

I asked Andy to attend counseling sessions at Evangel Temple. I thought we could solve our marital issues if we could have formal counseling with a ministerial staff person. However, Andy again refused. He contended that we could solve our own marital issues without the church intervening.

Since we had marital problems our issues were overwhelming to me. I started Christian counseling sessions with one of the ruling elders at Evangel, Dr. Lawrence Rawlings. He was patient and listened to me as I explained the marital issues that confronted us. Since Andy traveled to New York frequently, we did not have the prayer time that we needed to strengthen our marriage. Although we attended worship services together on Sunday, Andy did not attend any Bible study courses that were offered by the church. I was satisfied with my spiritual growth and was progressing in my commitment to live a Christian life-style. However, Andy was not making the spiritual progress I had expected. He also had friends who did not go to church, thereby not encouraging him spiritually.

Unable to come to a mutual agreement about our differences, Andy and I separated around 1986. He moved out of our apartment in southeast Washington, and found his own dwelling place in New York City.

We continued to correspond by phone, but Andy still refused to attend any marital counseling sessions with me. Many of our marital challenges stemmed from Andy's lack of submission to spiritual leadership. Andy also battled with moral issues during his journey as a Christian. Had he pursued Christian counseling to address these problems, I believe our marriage would have been strengthened. Because of Andy's refusal to make changes to become a spiritually mature Christian, and our irreconcilable differences, we eventually divorced in New York in June 1989.

* * *

In late 1987, Dr. Lawrence Rawlings had given Rev. Ralph Walters, who had been on the ministerial staff of the church for a number of years, permission to leave Evangel Temple. Rev. Walters was only in his late twenties, but he felt called to start a new church; and he sought the blessing of Evangel Temple as he embarked on his new endeavor.

Rev. Walters and his wife, Kim, wanted to start this dynamic new work, which would focus on building spirituality. In addition, the new church would concentrate on developing a strong youth and children's ministry. Therefore, the ministerial staff of Evangel Temple approved twelve church members to leave Evangel Temple and work with the couple to support the new work. The new church was eventually named Emmanuel Covenant (now Crossover Church, Hyattsville, Maryland).

In early 1988, I had another formal meeting with Dr. Rawlings. I wanted to discuss the feasibility of leaving Evangel Temple to support Emmanuel Covenant Church. Dr. Rawlings did not advise me to leave Evangel. On the other hand, he informed me that should I decide to depart to work with Rev. Walters, he would pray for me and wish me much success. He also firmly stated that should I decide to return to Evangel, the church would graciously receive me back as a member.

After prayer and seeking God about the direction I should take, I made the decision to leave Evangel in early 1988 to support Emmanuel Covenant Church.

* * *

I worked with Pastor Walters for about three years and developed a strong Sunday school program for children. I also worked with the church to establish a viable evangelistic outreach ministry. Emmanuel Covenant initially had worship services in an elementary school in Silver Spring, MD. Thereafter, they moved and began conducting worship services at a new elementary school in Prince George's County, Maryland.

During the three-year period that I was a member of Emmanuel Covenant Church, the Lord taught me the secret of obedience. Although I did not always agree with Pastor Walters, I submitted to his spiritual leadership. My tenure there focused on my desire to strengthen my spiritual walk with God.

* * *

In September 1990, I decided to finish my undergraduate degree. I enrolled in an accelerated bachelor's degree program at National Louis University, McLean, VA. I went to school two nights a week for two hours. Each class was intensive. The curriculum included college level courses: business management, statistics, economics, and marketing.

Part of the core curriculum required that I submit written essays on my life experiences, which would count toward course credits. Through this aggressive program, which gave me extensive writing preparation for graduate work; I earned my bachelor of arts in business management in June, 1991.

* * *

In November 1987, I met Mr. Leroy Ramara on a city bus in Washington. We became friends; and after about one year, we began seriously dating. He was a member of the Mt. Vernon Methodist Church Place UMC in Washington.

Leroy was from Sierra Leone, Africa, and was very attentive to me during this time. After dating for about one and one-half years, Leroy proposed to me. He requested that I ask Pastor Walters about conducting premarital counseling sessions with us.

I informed Pastor Walters that Leroy had asked me to marry him. Thereafter, we began a three-month, premarital counseling program with him. Part of this program involved intensive counseling sessions centered on the issues that married people face in the first few years: money management, communication, intimacy, and scheduling.

Throughout these sessions, I made it very clear to Leroy that I had a very demanding schedule and that I was concerned we might have difficulty in our marriage. This was partially because he also had a very challenging work schedule. Leroy was a carpenter and worked long, difficult hours. His work schedule required him to wake up very early in the morning, at about four o'clock a.m. He had to be at work by six o'clock a.m.

I was also anxious about our ability to reconcile that he was a staunch Methodist. I was born Baptist, but I had spent many years in the Pentecostal church. Leroy, however, assured me that he would leave his church and join Emmanuel Covenant Church.

* * *

After our marriage on November 4, 1989, at Evangel Temple, we bought a townhouse in the Lake Arbor community, Mitchellville, Maryland. We only had one car, so it was important that we coordinate our schedules to accommodate my decision to attend Wesley Theological Seminary. I was excited about the possibility of completing a master of divinity degree.

Because of issues surrounding my decision to attend Wesley, Leroy changed his mind and decided to return to Mt. Vernon Place UMC. He had already been a member of the church for about nine years. Although he wanted to return to his church, Leroy said that he would still be supportive of my starting my theological education at Wesley Seminary. After marital counseling, I decided that it was best to alleviate marital discord by also leaving Emmanuel Covenant Church. In January 1991, I joined Mt. Vernon Place UMC.

* * *

I officially enrolled at Wesley Theological Seminary in September 1991. Mt. Vernon Place UMC provided me with a two-year Urban Ministry scholarship. The late Dr. Margaret Pittman, a longtime member of Mt. Vernon Place UMC, had donated substantial funds to the school to set up the program. I was encouraged by Dr. Pittman to enroll in the three-year urban ministry track at Wesley! I was required to attend school full-time.

The former pastor of Mt. Vernon Place UMC, Dr. Roger Lanes, also recommended me as a ministerial candidate. With Dr. Pittman's financial contribution to Wesley Seminary and Rev. Lanes's spiritual support, I embarked on my journey as a first year theology student at Wesley Seminary, Washington, D.C.

As I began on my pursuit of ministerial training, I initially enrolled in four courses. As a full-time student, I was required to take five; but I subsequently took a course in summer school in order to obtain the necessary credit hours.

As time progressed, I began to feel more capable of handling the challenging graduate level work. By my second year of seminary, I increased my course level to five courses per semester. This was the requirement in order to graduate in three years.

I had begun working with a study group of other urban ministry track students. We were determined to finish our coursework in the three-year time period. We had all vowed to work as a team and obtain our master of divinity degrees.

The Church's Ministry of Healing

The first prominent person who greatly inspired me to answer this call to a ministry of healing was the Rev. James Love. Surprisingly, one day we met at the Wesley Seminary bookstore. He was well known at Evangel Temple because of his tenure as the Dean of the Bible School.

Since many of the students knew that Rev. Love and I had obtained extensive training at the church in charismatic theology, many of the Methodist students stopped us on our way to various classes. They asked us to lead them to receive the "baptism with the Holy Spirit," with the evidence of "speaking in tongues." (*1Corinthians 12.*)

Rev. Love did not know that I had enrolled at Wesley just one year after he had decided to matriculate. Yet God miraculously designed our paths. Wesley Theological Seminary would be the place where God would shape both of us as pastors (and ultimately as leaders of His people).

After a one hour discussion, Dean Kilmore suggested that the program would include elective courses on spiritual gifts. During the meeting, I delivered a signed student petition to Dean Kilmore. This indicated that there were a number of students at Wesley Seminary who were adamant that they wanted the spiritual gifts courses implemented into the curriculum.

It was late 1992, when the Rev. James Love and I approached Dr. Henry Kilmore, Academic Dean at Wesley Seminary. When meeting in his office, we asked Dr. Kilmore about the feasibility of implementing a "spiritual gifts" series at Wesley. To our surprise, Dean Kilmore was ecstatic about leading the seminary in the direction of teaching seminarians about the Gifts of the Holy Spirit. He asked us, "How can I help you?"

Therefore, Rev. James Love and I eventually worked to implement the following courses:

- Holiness and Pentecostal Movements (history and theology)
- Spiritual Gifts for Congregational Ministry
- The Healing Ministry of the Church

During my second year at Wesley Theological Seminary, a United Methodist Church agency awarded me with the Crusade Scholarship. Also, Mt. Vernon Place United Methodist Church provided a theology student scholarship to me. These awards made it possible for me to continue my seminary education.

We explained to Dr. Kilmore that the students were asking us more extensive questions regarding the gift of prophecy or laying hands on the sick for healing. Such in depth questions confirmed our belief that the students at Wesley were hungry for a greater knowledge of spiritual gifts.

Dean Kilmore later suggested that he work with Rev. Love and me to select the teachers for the courses. We unanimously agreed on the staff members to be involved. Dr. Darrell Lombard would teach the holiness and Pentecostal movements' course. He was the church history professor. Therefore, Dr. Kilmore felt that he would be an excellent resource to prepare the course syllabus. The course was taught for the first time in September, 1993.

During my third year at Wesley Seminary, I was asked by Dr. Lombard to give my testimony of receiving the baptism of the Holy Spirit. I was thrilled to offer my personal experience and knowledge of spiritual gifts to the class.

Dr. Art Thomas would be the perfect professor to teach the spiritual gifts for Congregational ministry course. He was an ordained Presbyterian minister, who had decided to transfer over to becoming a United Methodist pastor. His knowledge about accepting the baptism of the Holy Spirit was very extensive. He worked tirelessly to provide Wesley seminarians with the coursework necessary to implement a viable spiritual gifts program at their respective churches.

Dr. Theresa Holloway would continue to conduct healing services at the Wesley Seminary Chapel on Wednesday mornings during Lent (the church season before Easter).

Dr. Holloway also met with me regularly at her Wesley Seminary office once a week to teach and pray with me for the anointing in the healing ministry.

When Dr. Lombard later taught the Holiness and Pentecostal Movements' course at Catholic University, I sat in on a class session at the school. I was thrilled to meet the famed Rev. Joseph Douglas, pastor of Greater Mt. Calvary Church in N.E. Washington, D.C. He had enrolled in the course as a prerequisite for obtaining his doctor of ministry degree from Catholic University.

Dr. Lombard has since taken a job as academic dean of a prominent school in Seattle, Washington!

Dr. Theresa Holloway retired from the seminary as professor of Christian education, around May 2007. Wesley Seminary hosted a marvelous retirement reception for her at the school.

Currently, Dr. Art Thomas is a full-time United Methodist pastor of Concord St. Andrews UMC, Bethesda, MD. He continues to teach courses on spiritual gifts at Wesley Seminary every other year in the summer. The last course was taught in July 2012 at Wesley Theological Seminary.

During the summer, Dr. Thomas has also taught the spiritual gifts course at The Ecumenical Seminary, in Baltimore, Maryland.

The Rev. Dr. Kilmore has since left Wesley Seminary to answer the call to work at another prominent theological seminary.

* * *

In the book *God the Economist*, Dr. Douglas Meeks writes: "To call

God the Economist means that the God of Israel and of Jesus Christ is fundamentally identified through what God does in relation to household building and arrangement. Calling God Economist is in no way meant to denigrate God, but rather to express God's life and work with biblical concreteness."1

Because of the popularity of the courses, Wesley student enrollment increased significantly. Part of the reason for the growth of the Wesley student population was that the students were now referring some of their friends from various Pentecostal churches to matriculate at Wesley!

To date, Wesley Seminary, Catholic University, and the Ecumenical Seminary continue to offer various spiritual gifts courses to students. The courses are taught during the school year and also during the summer. These offerings are a major milestone in theological education.

The change in direction of each school was a direct result of the hard work that Pastor James Love and I accomplished (as well as noted faculty members) between September 1991 and May 1994.

As a result, over the years, Wesley Theological Seminary has increased the number of courses being offered in Charismatic Theology! Therefore, many seminarians are now graduating with the ability to incorporate the divine healing power of God into their prospective churches. Also, many United Methodist Churches conduct praise and prayer (or contemporary) worship services at either an early Sunday morning or a Sunday evening worship service.

* * *

After graduation in May, 1994, the birth of the Church on the Hill was centered on the revelation I received from God. It was clear that there should be a church that would pray and intercede on behalf of political leaders/congressional members and their staffs. Such a church would reach out to our political leaders in times of triumph and trials.

Since I became pastor of Church on the Hill in November, 1995, I have been blessed to host a number of distinguished men and women who have been called to public service. Such a call involves one's ability to be led by the spirit of God (gift of discernment), as He uses them to govern the United States of America!

As I began to walk out this great call of God on my life, the Lord began to place dynamic and anointed individuals in my path. These spiritual leaders would not only assist me to comprehend this great call, but also to answer it on a daily basis.

Spiritual Gifts and the Cult Influence

I believe that life after the cult experience requires one to readapt to a wholesome Christian lifestyle by joining a local Bible believing congregation. In addition, according to Dr. Francis MacNutt, in his book *Healing*, there are four facets to healing, which need to be incorporated into the Christian lifestyle: spiritual, inner, physical, and deliverance. MacNutt's theory is that we are whole persons, and when an individual approaches us for healing we need to ask ourselves, "1) What is the basic sickness, the basic problem? 2)What is its basic cause? 3)What kind of prayer, or what kind of natural remedy, should we use?" 2

My desire after I left the Children of God was for inner healing (often called the healing of memories). It was apparent after reading MacNutt's book that I had found a valuable resource on my journey to personal wholeness.

My curiosity continued to grow about the validity of the healing ministry when I participated in a "Healing Weekend" at Virginia Beach, Virginia, in the early 1990's. Dr. MacNutt and his wife, Judith, were guest speakers at the conference. Their message of healing and wholeness further confirmed that God had truly delivered me from the emotional bonds of cultic living.

I also became aware at the conference in Virginia Beach that God would use me in the healing ministry. This was further confirmed when Cindy Jacobs, President General of Intercession, Colorado Springs, Colorado, spoke. You can read more about her ministry in her book *Possessing the Gates of the Enemy.*

After her message on intercessory prayer at the conference, she asked those who wanted prayer to come to the altar. I stood in the prayer line, as Cindy Jacobs prayed over me. She then prophesied that I would "be an effective minister" and that God had called me to preach!

It was after this prophecy from Cindy Jacobs for my life that I felt confident that despite my adversity, God still loved me and wanted to use me to spread the good news of the gospel.

God's power for healing the whole person is extraordinary! He heals in ways that we are not always expecting Him to work. God continues to work His power in my life even now in my current ministry.

In retrospect, when I first left the Children of God, I was unable to find any churches that I trusted in the Rolling Meadows, Illinois, metropolitan area with resources to assist me. This realization aroused my sense of duty as an ex-cult member to incorporate divine healing into the mission and ministry of the church. Therefore, once I started the church, I came to grips with the call to the healing ministry. It was apparent to me why the Lord would require me as a pastor to incorporate healing as one of the primary focuses of the church. The Lord reminded me, "to whom much has been forgiven, the same loveth much!" (Luke 7:47.)

Therefore, in 2001, the Church on the Hill officially began the School of Healing (now known as Body & Mind Seminars: A Healthier You). This ministry was essential since one of the congregants, Ms. Tori Bruceton, was healed of breast cancer during one of our healing services.

As the Church on the Hill grows, our healing seminars will continue to provide basic training to our members and friends. Seminars are conducted in various locations in the Prince Georges County, Maryland.

To date, the Church on the Hill continues to answer the call of God to extend its ministry of healing to a lost generation who need to find their way back to a God. We will continue to make a concerted effort to heal, restore, and equip others for service in His kingdom!

* * *

After graduating from Wesley Theological Seminary in May, 1994, I initially accepted a full-time position as Minister of Education and Youth at a prestigious United Methodist Church in Silver Spring, Maryland. At the same time, when the adhoc committee was formed (two network members, including the late Cynthia Roy) I was asked to be the president of the Network of Christian Businesswomen. Ms. Roy had served as president of the organization for a few years after Ms. Delia Stanford moved to Atlanta, Georgia.

As a requirement for graduation from the seminary, I wrote my master's thesis on "Housing and Homelessness." Since 1995, I have been encouraged to host a variety of activities to address the conditions of the homeless (as well as those in transition) in the Washington, D.C. metropolitan area.

The Church on the Hill outreach ministry has included hosting the following events: Homeless Prayer Breakfast (1995-2000) in Washington, D.C. and Prince George's County, Maryland; Warm Nights Volunteer participation (1995-2000) in Prince George's County, Maryland; and Community Transition Center in Montgomery County, Maryland in March and September 2008.

The purpose of the Community Transition Center meetings is to encourage Prince Georges (and Montgomery County churches) to provide space at their respective congregations where multiple services to those who are homeless or in transition can be administered to. The meetings also will host seminars where dialogue among the community and clergy/spiritual leaders could take place. This would enhance our approach as a community of faith to deal with the growing problem of homelessness in the Washington metropolitan area.

Through our Community Transition Center meetings, the Church on the Hill validates that we have intrinsic value. As Dr. Douglas Meeks states in *God the Economist*: "This struggle can be seen in the great economic acts of God: the exodus, the creation, and the resurrection. Each economic act calls forth corresponding economic acts on the part of God's own economist, the human being."3

National Network of Christian Businesswomen

When the Network of Christian Businesswomen had its first meeting in the late 1980's, on the premise of economic development for all, I was appointed by Evangel Temple leadership to be the recording secretary. Ms. Delia Stanford, founder, confirmed the appointment.

I was excited about being a member of the organization since I had started a Shaklee vitamin business. I was sure that learning about entrepreneurship would benefit me as I developed the business.

The income from the business was greatly needed during my matriculation at Wesley Seminary. My theory proved to be right. I sold vitamins to many of the students at Wesley and even managed to attain the level of Assistant Supervisor. I also trained one of my Shaklee associates to assist me with my growing enterprise.

After accepting the nomination to become the president of the organization in November 1994, I was determined to change the structure to include a strong business development component. I resigned my position with the United Methodist Church in Silver Spring, Maryland. By this time, the adhoc committee had changed the name to the Network of Christian Women.

Since I was adamant about accepting men into the organization, the Network of Christian Women with the support of former Congressman Bill Goodling, officially launched the Network of Christian Men in June, 1995.

We had previously conducted our business meetings at a congressional facility near the Cannon House office building, however I decided that if we were to acclaim national status we should begin conducting our meetings in the halls of Congress. This included the Rayburn, Cannon, and Longworth House Office Buildings.

In early 1994, Mr. Edward Dawson, who initially introduced the Network of Christian Women to formal business development training, introduced me to Mr. Luke Washington. He was hosting his business meetings for the National Association of Public Accountants at the Rayburn House office building.

One day he phoned me because he had seen my brief TV interview on the Channel 7 evening news about my stress management seminars. I had been conducting the seminars for a few years at the Washington Convention Center and Library of Congress; Washington, D.C. Former news reporter Jim Clark aired the story.

Luke provided me with the address and phone number of Congressman Bill Goodling. He suggested that I write a letter to Congressman Goodling, asking if we could use the Rayburn House congressional building for our network business meetings.

To my surprise Congressman Goodling answered affirmatively. In November, 1994, the National Network began conducting business meetings on the second Tuesday of the month at the Rayburn House. By January 1995, Congressman Goodling suggested that we host the Christian Fellowship evening prayer meetings for congressional members and their staffs on the third Thursday of the month. Also, we eventually extended this ministry to include noon day prayer for congressional/political members and their staffs.

The Christian Fellowship meetings paved the way for the Church on the Hill, Inc., a non-denominational growing church. By November 1995, the Church on the Hill conducted its first service at St. Michael's Lutheran Church in Largo, Maryland. The Rev. Jason Cage, who has since accepted a call to another pastorate in Ohio, provided the spiritual covering for the service.

* * *

By November 1995, the Network of Christian Women hosted our first National Network Convention at the Washington Convention Center in Washington. The Rev. Dr. Corinthia Boone (whom I had first met around 1984 while she was a staff member of Evangel Temple), was the keynote speaker. She is known for her association with the

National Day of Prayer. We hosted delegates from Texas, New York, and the Washington metropolitan area.

* * *

A particularly exciting occasion for me was the invitation in1996 by a staff member, Ms. Rosa Lawrence, to attend the birthday celebration of the Rev. Jessie Jackson. This momentous event was conducted at Bee Smith Restaurant at the Union Station metro, in northeast Washington.

I was honored to meet Rev. Jackson. Also in attendance were former Mayor Marion Barry, Washington, D.C., and former First Lady Hillary Clinton. In addition, I was pleased to meet Jessie Jackson, Jr. at the event. Eventually, he would follow in his father's footsteps. He ran for election and became a representative for the state of Illinois. In 2011, because of an illness, he resigned his position.

In December 1997, former mayor Marion Barry attended our second Church on The Hill Anniversary celebration at the Red Roof Inn Hotel in Washington. He gave his testimony of how the Lord had healed him of prostate cancer (through the ministry of Church on the Hill). Encouraged by his miraculous recovery, I offered a word of prayer at the event for his continued good health.

Most notably, former County Executive Jack Johnson (Prince George's County, MD.) presented me with a Proclamation in December 2001. We were celebrating our sixth Church on the Hill Anniversary. This Proclamation was in recognition of my community service. The event was conducted at the Ramada Inn Hotel (now the Comfort Inn), in College Park, Maryland.

By March 2008, the Office of the County Executive awarded the Church on the Hill with its first state grant. We were able to use the funds to restructure the Church on the Hill and to strengthen our business development services throughout the National Network (NNCMW). This included the setup of a viable small business mentoring program.

Many noted congressional/political leaders have benefited from our Church on the Hill outreach ministry or have attended our worship services (and other events) in Washington or at the A.D. Headen Chapel of the Refreshing Spring Church, Riverdale, Maryland. These include: former Congressman Albert R. Wynn (D-MD); former State's Attorney Glenn Ivey - Prince George's County, Maryland. (healed of a cancerous tumor on his kidney); former Deputy State's Attorney J. Patricia Wilson Smoot (office of the former State's Attorney Glenn Ivey); Ms. Jill Downing, former Chief of Staff of Attorney Ivey; former Council member Kevin Chavous, Washington, D.C.; Mr. Bill Boston (former

Community Liaison for Congressman Wynn); and Rev. Tim Warner (Office of County Executive Isaiah Leggett, Montgomery County, Maryland).

Congressional/political leaders who have visited with us and to whom we offered prayer healing at our Christian Fellowship prayer meeting at the Rayburn/Cannon House Office Buildings include: Mr. Mike Rious, former grants coordinator for former Congressman Albert R. Wynn, Congressman Louie Gohmert (Texas), former Congressman Wally Herger (California) and Congressman Phil Crane (Illinois).

* * *

On Sunday, March 11, 2007, we were blessed to host the Rev. Dr. Barry Black as our guest preacher at a prominent Seventh Day Adventist Church in Silver Spring, MD. This was a dedicatory worship service for our Church on the Hill expansion project in Silver Spring, Maryland.

Dr. Black is the sixty-second Senate Chaplain of the U.S. He is also the first African American to hold this distinguished position. Dr. Black is a devout Seventh Day Adventist. Therefore, we wanted a church of this faith expression to support us for this momentous event. His encouraging message called "Give God Your Best" enlightened all who attended the worship service.

In his book *From the Hood to the Hill*, he outlines the lessons he learned from what he calls a "stuttering start."

"**First**, I discovered that God is an equal-opportunity Giver of gifts.

Second, I learned that invested talents multiply.

Third, I learned that with the help and encouragement of others I became energized to achieve the improbable.

Fourth, I learned that work brings increase.

Fifth, I learned that humble beginnings can be surmounted when faithfulness is demonstrated."4

The American Judicial System

During November 1995, after its first worship service, the Church on the Hill was initially established as a para-church corporation. At about this time, former President Bill Clinton was accused of having an affair with a young intern, Ms. Monica Lewinsky; and the country was deeply troubled. Sometime between late November 1995 and April 1996, this young intern had several inappropriate encounters with then-

President Clinton. In February 1997, she was among the guests at an evening taping of President Clinton's radio address. By October, she had asked him for help to find a job in New York. In December, she came to the White House to say "good-bye" to everyone. However, by then she had received her subpoena in the Paula Jones case.

During this time I was working as a contract executive legal secretary at Akin, Gump, Strauss, Hauer & Feld, in Washington. The partner whom I worked with at the firm for about three to four weeks was looking for a full-time secretary.

The work at Akin Gump required me to have regular daily contact with Mr. Vernon Jordan, former President Bill Clinton's confidant, who was also then being harassed by the media. One of the major civil rights figures in American history, Mr. Jordan was "of counsel" at the firm, even though he was living in New York. The questions the media had were about his involvement in assisting Monica Lewinsky to find a job in New York, specifically whether he had obstructed justice by his actions. This was important since she had received a subpoena to testify in court against former President Clinton.

At lunch time one day, I addressed Mr. Jordan in the lobby of the office building at Akin Gump. I informed him about the Church on the Hill and my desire to be in intercessory prayer for him, for the President and his family, and for Ms. Lewinsky. I invited Mr. Jordan to our Christian Fellowship prayer meeting on Capitol Hill at the Rayburn House Office Building. He declined since he felt that the environment at the Rayburn would be hostile toward him, due to the scandal (which appeared to be tearing the nation apart).

Throughout the time Vernon Jordan was receiving intense scrutiny from the press, I was responsible for providing "prayer coverage" for him. Also, I often spoke to him during the day about strategies to use to deal with the constant bombardment from the reporters.

Unfortunately, personnel from various newspapers were encamped around almost every entrance and exit of the office building where Akin Gump rented office space (near Dupont Circle in N.W., Washington, D.C.). Yet, with the support of security (and myself), Mr. Jordan was able to use selected entrances and exits of the building. This was an effort to protect his privacy.

Overall, I believe Vernon Jordan handled this adverse situation with care. Throughout the scandal, I remained confident that the results would be positive.

* * *

I was overjoyed with the true spirit of Christianity displayed by former Congressman Bill Goodling. By November 1995, he was the first political leader to sponsor the Church on the Hill on Capitol Hill at the Rayburn House Office Building.

Because of his Christian hospitality in dealing with the Clinton scandal, as well as other urgent issues, former Congressman Goodling was very popular on Capitol Hill as a U.S. Representative. During the time of the Monica Lewinsky scandal, former Congressman Goodling provided strong spiritual leadership on Capitol Hill. This was proven when he invited Clinton to one of our Church on the Hill Christian Fellowship Thursday evening meetings (even though the former President graciously declined his invitation to participate).

Former Congressman Goodling informed us that Clinton was distraught by the constant publicity and public scorn regarding his impeachment by the House of Representatives. Because of their faith in God, members of the Church on the Hill (who at that time were predominantly staff members of the congressional/political leaders), would have graciously received him.

* * *

Former President Bill Clinton's impeachment case was officially opened by Chief Justice William Rehnquist in the Senate. The prosecutors made a three-day presentation of their case.

Then Clinton's legal team began its three days of response, led by Chuck Ruff, the White House counsel and a former U. S. Attorney. He argued for two hours that the charges against the President were untrue. He made every attempt to persuade the jury that even if the senators thought they were true, his offenses did not come close to meeting the constitutional standard for impeachment.

Most notable were the arguments of one of his appointed attorneys, Cheryl Mills, a young African American graduate of Stanford Law School. She should be noted for her brilliant handling of the obstruction of justice charges against the President.

Dale Bumpers closed the defense. He made recognition of the fact that Clinton had already been punished enough for his mistakes, and that world leaders had stood up for him. Therefore, the Senate decided not to formally impeach the forty-second President of the U.S.

Was their decision to allow Clinton to remain in office a political tactic? Or, was the grace of God extended to him in an effort to show divine omniscience? I believe we serve a God who forgives. This was shown with Clinton. He was a man who had routinely performed with excellence, especially in his stance on civil rights for the Black community and for women. Also, he had shown strong political leadership in the U.S. and abroad.

Clinton delivered the keynote at the July 2011 commencement for students at Walden University (on-line school). I have matriculated and taken graduate courses in their mental health counseling program (September 2011-2012).

There was renewed optimism for our country as we celebrated the election of President Barack Obama in November 2008. His election as our forty-fourth President was a proud day for African Americans. Most inspiring, Barack Obama was the first African American man to be elected as President of the U.S. He brought new confidence in our government as he delivered his Inaugural Address on Tuesday, January 20, 2009. His theme of "Yes We Can" has brought new expectation of equal opportunity for all. After the November '12 election, he was elected for a second term as President of the United States. His inauguration date was Monday, January 21, 2013.

* * *

Following the advice of former Congressman Goodling when he retired in early 1998, I wrote former Congressman Albert R. Wynn (D-Maryland) about becoming a sponsor of Capitol Hill. He responded affirmatively. He was our congressional sponsor from late November, 1998, through June, 2008.

Bill Boston, his former community relations coordinator, suggested that I ask for support from the business community. Since the National Network (NNCMW) would provide strong business support for area businesses, Mr. Boston suggested that I make calls and discuss our business development programs with the community. In return, it was suggested that they offer their support of the church by contributing into our general fund. My son Rafael, who was sixteen years old at the time, began making calls.

A noted Capitol Heights business owner, Mr. Jonathan Jones, responded. He eventually became a platinum sponsor (gifts of one thousand dollars or more) of the Church on the Hill. His seven years (1997-2004) of substantial financial support provided a part-time stipend for me as pastor of the church. Also, his total contributions provided the necessary financial support to accelerate the growth of the Church on the Hill in Prince Georges County, Maryland.

To our surprise, we received positive responses from about fifty business sponsors in the community. Subsequently, we have designed and distributed Church on the Hill Sponsor Directories for our business sponsors in Washington, Prince George's County (1996-present), and Montgomery County, Maryland (since 2005).

To date, the Sponsor Directory has been an excellent tool for the Church on the Hill. Contributions by our sponsors, have assisted us in sustaining our ministry by providing funding for our general operating expenses.

* * *

The successful launching of the Church on the Hill also stems from noted businessman Mr. Joe Camper, a platinum sponsor from Akron, Ohio, who gave seed money of five thousand dollars in early 1996. His generous contribution provided funds for the start-up costs of the church. In letter dated April 11, 2006, he wrote: "We know that changed hearts and the influence of an indwelling Holy Spirit are a person's only hope for a better future. The same can be said of our nation. Only changed hearts of those who are leading us will secure a future for us (and those who are to follow). Please keep Mr. Blake and myself apprised of your effort and accept the enclosed gift for your organization as recognition for those efforts. May you always be found faithful in the Master's service and in His will for your life."

With Mr. Camper's financial support, The Church on the Hill was able to obtain its 501(c) (3) status in September 1997.

* * *

From 2003-2009, Church on the Hill utilized the A. D. Headen Chapel of the Refreshing Spring Church for Sunday afternoon worship services from 3:00-5:00p.m. Some of the members of Refreshing Spring also continue to participate in our National Network (NNCMW) events.

Through our aggressive Building Fund program, we plan to purchase our own facility by 2015-2016. Currently, we have a Church on the Hill administrative office in Prince George's County, Maryland. Also, Church on the Hill Sunday worship services are conducted one Sunday a month in Prince Georges County, Maryland.

* * *

To date, the Church on the Hill continues to have a strong call to conduct the following ministries: Body and Mind Seminars: A Healthier You (conducted quarterly in PG County, Maryland). Sessions include training in stress management, reclaiming your health, and natural healing. Our other ministries include:

Intercessory Prayer: provides a platform for Christians to come to the throne of grace with boldness, believing God to pour down His spiritual blessings upon His people.

Men's Ministry: is designed to financially and spiritually empower our men and provide opportunities for Christian fellowship.

Women's Empowerment Rally (annual event): is designed to economically empower women by encouraging them to become entrepreneurs. During our October 22, 2011, rally at the Christian Life Center, Riverdale, Maryland, State's Attorney Angela Alsobrooks delivered the keynote address. The Rev. George Shaw is the senior pastor. The state's attorney discussed how her position allows her to combat domestic violence. She also vowed to aggressively prosecute criminals to control violent crimes in the community.

On Saturday, October 27, 2012, we conducted the Women's Empowerment Rally at a facility at the Vista Gardens Marketplace in Bowie, Maryland. Ms. Aida Clark-Edwards, Chief of the Domestic Violence unit at the Office of State's Attorney was the keynote speaker.

Community Transition Center: quarterly meetings to address the homeless crisis, including those in transition.

Since the inception of Church on the Hill, there have been scores of environmental and financial disasters, which have caused many to look for additional resources in order to survive in a constantly changing economic system:

September 11, 2001: In addition to the thousands of deaths, particularly of American men, the terrorist attack on the World Trade Center caused economic hardship for many Americans.

War in Iraq 2003-2011: this war caused thousands of Americans, mostly men, to lose their lives. As a result, many women and children lost crucial financial support.

Enron: The company's scandalous failure in 2005 caused many to lose their retirement savings.

Hurricane Katrina in 2005: Centered in Louisiana and neighboring states, caused many to lose their personal belongings, homes, and life savings.

Wild fires in California in 2000: Caused many to lose their homes.

Hurricane Ike in 2008: Caused flooding and loss of property along the Gulf Coast.

Lehman Brothers declared bankruptcy in 2008, followed by Washington Mutual's failure. Even more perplexing was Wachovia bank's failure. Wells Fargo took over the bank after a brawl with Citibank. These events accelerated a downward spiral in the economy.

The U.S. stock market crash in 2008, which precipitated the bailout of Merrill Lynch by the federal government, shocked the nation when the DOW Industrial Average dipped to one of its lowest levels since the Great Depression. Former President George W. Bush convinced Congress to institute a seven hundred billion dollar bailout plan in order to prevent the country from sinking deeper into recession. Unfortunately, many people lost thousands of dollars in their 401(k) retirement savings plans.

In 2008, while Barack Obama and John McCain were in an intensive battle for the U.S. presidency, they left the campaign trail for a few days. They visited with former President George Bush to discuss the bailout plan. The House of Representatives did not initially pass the bill. However, after some revisions were made, they did support former President Bush in voting for the seven hundred billion dollar bill.

Again in 2008, three major car companies sought a $17.4 billion dollar bailout by Congress. The Senate denied their request. Therefore, former President George Bush interceded, agreeing to work tenaciously with the car companies to lend them the necessary funds to avoid total collapse of the industry. If they had claimed bankruptcy, millions of jobs could have been lost.

On Thursday January 8, 2009, during a morning NBC news report, the CEO of General Motors reported that a major restructuring would take place. They had already received four billion dollars from the federal government and were due to receive another 5.5 billion dollars. Their total support from the federal government would be 13.4 billion dollars through March 31, 2009.

These financial disasters have had many worried about their 401(k) retirement savings and their financial portfolios. Most disturbing, is the overwhelming number of people who have been unemployed over the last eight years.

The aforementioned disasters have significantly increased the number of calls for professional Christian consultation that I have received in recent years. Some of the people have been referred to the Refreshing Spring Church (and other local churches) for social services, including support to prevent home foreclosures. In addition, other local churches have experienced an influx of people who need emergency health and human services, as well as financial support to survive.

Where then should the church focus its mission and ministry to address these needs? To answer this question, the Church on the Hill has addressed these issues through its aforementioned advocacy programs. In addition, through our National Network (NNCMW), we will continue to assist individuals to start, grow, and expand their enterprises.

Health Care Reform

According to a November 4, 2009, report, "The Congressional Budget Office said on Wednesday that an alternative health care bill put forward by House Republicans would have little impact in extending health benefits to the roughly 30 million uninsured Americans, but would reduce average insurance premium costs for people who have coverage.

The Republican bill, which has no chance of passage, would extend insurance coverage to about 3 million people by 2019, and would leave about 52 million people uninsured, the budget office said, meaning the proportion of non-elderly Americans with coverage would remain about the same as now, at roughly 83 percent."

The article further stated: "Across the country the American people are calling on Washington to pass responsible reform that will lower health care costs, Representative Mike Pence of Indiana, the number three House Republican, said in a statement late Wednesday. Yesterday, House Republicans answered that call by putting forward commonsense health care legislation that reduces the deficit, lowers premiums, and ensures coverage for those with pre-existing conditions." (Huntington Post, 4 November 2009).

Mission and Ministry of the Church on the Hill

The Church on the Hill focuses on the ability to transform people's lives. Therefore, we will continue our ministry of healing (physical, emotional, and spiritual) through our evangelistic outreach (through the Internet, fliers, and word of mouth). Those interested in joining our growing ministry would be those who have a call to pray for our congressional / political leaders; feel compelled to offer intercessory prayer for our nation (that God would redeem us and restore America's greatness); have a call to entrepreneurship (including a desire for economic empowerment); and have a call to mitigate the problems of the homeless and those in transition in our nation.

Full Membership Requirements:

1. Be a born again believer.
2. Accept the Bible wholly and undivided as your guide for living.
3. Commit yourself to a life of spiritual growth.
4. Commit yourself to the life of Christian service as led by the Holy Spirit.
5. Faithfully attend church services.
6. Support the church with your tithes and offerings.
7. Endorse the church Covenant.

Associate Membership Requirements:

1. Commit yourself to a life of spiritual growth.
2. Commit yourself to a life of service in the church as led by the Holy Spirit.
3. Faithfully attend regular church services.
4. Support the church with your offerings.

The Church on the Hill (through the NNCMW Public Relations Committee) will maintain its stance that in the face of turmoil (or any human misfortune) we will continue our support. This entails regular visitation with congressional/political leaders (and their staff members) on Capitol Hill and in Upper Marlboro, Maryland.

Chapter 21
When God Calls

A prominent Evangelist, Dr. Peter Leonce, writes in his book *Prayer Will Knock it Down, But Praise Will Knock It Out* that: "It is the spiritual man on the inside that causes you to have a smile on your face when everything is going wrong. So if you are going to beat discouragement and overcome it, the first thing you have to do is very simple - you have to believe the promises of God."1

It was one summer in the 1990's, when I was visiting Georgetown in northwest Washington, D.C., that I saw the acclaimed movie, The Color Purple, starring Oprah Winfrey and Whoopi Goldberg. The protagonist in the movie, Celie, had been abused as a child by her stepfather. As she grew into adolescence, she eventually bore two children by him, whom he took away from her at birth. Therefore, she was not able to raise her own children.

As a teenager, her stepfather sold her into an arranged marriage to "Mister" (Albert). Unfortunately, even though he married Celie, Albert still pursued a relationship with her teenage sister, Nettie. He accepted Nettie into his home and continued making sexual advances toward her. Nettie ignored his propositions and refused to sin against her sister by being intimate with her husband. Celie and Nettie had a very close relationship. Unfortunately, Mister's anger heightened against Nettie, and he expelled her from his home because she refused to be intimidated by him.

Mister was violent and very abusive emotionally toward Celie. She withstood his abuses until Shugg Avery, who was a singer, befriended her.

* * *

Shugg's fervent affirmations of Celie's character helped her to realize that she had intrinsic value. This sparked Celie to once again find a reason to live. For the first time in years, she had a smile on her face and realized she was a beautiful African American woman.

With Shugg's continuous emotional support, Celie began to understand that she must tenaciously learn to build her self-esteem and acquire a feeling of self-worth. Shugg reiterated to Celie that she could make it on her own. She encouraged her to leave Mister and to start a new life. She assured her that she could truly blossom as a woman. Shugg made it clear that Celie had to free herself from an abusive relationship with Mister. It was through substantiating her womanhood that she could once again find inner peace and wholeness.

* * *

The movie climaxes when Celie confronts Mister at the dinner table where family and friends are gathered. Celie openly confesses to Mister that she is leaving him. It is a miracle that Celie, who has been shy and withdrawn throughout her young adult years, is finally able to face up to Mister with the support of Shugg.

Celie verbally rebukes Mister for the years of domestic violence against her and for taking her sister, Nettie, away from her at a young age. She boldly proclaims that she is leaving him to sing with Shugg Avery. Angry and shocked at her accusations, Mister rebukes her and states, "Over my dead body!" The scene intensifies when Celie puts a knife to Mister's throat. She openly lets him know that he cannot longer intimidate her with threats of physical violence.

* * *

Mister had constantly beat Celie and ridiculed her. This dramatic scene proved that Celie finally understood that she needed to be set free from Mister's control over her life. Becoming an independent woman was essential if she wanted to be free to express who she was as a person. Therefore, she concluded that she had to leave him.

* * *

Celie's stepfather had impregnated Celie. Then, he stole her children from her immediately after their birth. Mister had forced Nettie to leave his home because she refused his sexual advances. Miraculously, a missionary couple had taken Nettie into their home. The missionary couple adopted Celie's two children and was living in Africa.

To our surprise, the movie ultimately reveals that indeed God met Celie's need. Even though she did not have the opportunity to raise her two children, she was eventually reunited with them.

When her stepfather died, Celie inherited his house. Even though she had suffered a catastrophic childhood, God blessed Celie. He took care of her children through the intervention of two faithful missionaries. Truly, the wondrous works of God were manifest in her turbulent life.

During these intense scenes of the movie, I heard a still, small voice whisper to me, "Faye, I am calling you to the ministry." It was God, and I was sure He had a plan for my life.

* * *

According to Dr. Leonce, "You can praise your enemy to death. You can praise your way out of your situation and into victory. Praise will take you to the valley of blessings.

Steps to receiving the victory through praise:

1. Begin at the point of the problem - identify it, face it squarely, and be honest about it.
2. Cease all trust in the flesh. Admit your impotence.
3. Concentrate on God.
4. Continue before God, waiting in His presence until God acts or speaks.
5. Confess the truth of God boldly.
6. Commit to obeying God.
7. Collect the riches."2

* * *

According to Napoleon Hill, in his book *Think and Grow Rich*, "one of the most common causes of failure is the habit of quitting when one is overtaken by temporary defeat. Every person is guilty of this mistake at one time or another."3

* * *

I was determined not to be defeated any more in my personal life even though I had been misled into believing the doctrines of the COG.

It was early 1980 when I experienced another breaking point. When I finally left the COG and took a flight from the island of Curacao to Chicago, my sister Jessica picked me up from the airport. During the forty minute ride to my sister Jessica's home in Rolling Meadows, IL, I was sure that God was going to work out everything according to His will.

* * *

When God calls you into full-time service for Him, He is faithful in placing outstanding people in your path to support you. One of these people is Evangelist Dorothy Goode, a dynamic woman of God. She is a board member of the Church on the Hill-National Network (NNCMW). Also, Evangelist Goode is a radio personality. She has a broadcast on Wednesday and Friday evenings on WYCB (1340 AM).

Evangelist Goode has been a member of Peace Way Ministries for about thirty-seven years. There she energetically serves as associate minister and worship leader. In addition, she serves as a board member of the foreign missions work for the Church in the Republic of Haiti. She strenuously supports her husband, Minister Darnell Goode, Jr., who serves as the assistant pastor.

From September 2003 through February 2009, Evangelist Goode assisted me at the A.D. Headen Chapel (Refreshing Spring Church) in conducting our worship services from 3:00-5:00 p.m. Her bold preaching of the gospel of Jesus Christ was well spoken of amongst our growing membership.

Evangelist Goode is the oldest of eleven children. She celebrated her forty-third wedding anniversary in 2012. She is the proud mother of three children, six grandchildren, and one great granddaughter.

She attended the Samuel Kelsey Bible Institute in Memphis, Tennessee, for two years and received her ministerial certificate. In addition, she attended ministerial classes at what is now Evangel Cathedral in Upper Marlboro, Maryland, and Jericho City of Praise in Landover, Maryland. She is also an independent beauty consultant for Mary Kay Cosmetics and Avon products.

Evangelist Goode was re-elected as a board member of the NNCMW on Thursday, June 7, 2012, in Prince George's County, Maryland. During her ten years as an NNCMW member, in addition to holding various other positions in the organization, she has shown strong support as the NNCMW aggressively expands into the Atlanta, Georgia metropolitan area.

Because of her stalwart support, in 2013, the National Network (NNCMW) will change into a Limited Liability Company (LLC).

Model Church

The Refreshing Spring C.O.G.I.C., Riverdale, MD

Rev. Dr. James E. Jordan, Jr., Senior Pastor

At the heart of our Prince George's County Business Development outreach was the September 2003-August 2009 work that the Church on the Hill and the Refreshing Spring Church performed as we wrestled with the side effects of the economic downturn. With the onset of massive unemployment, many flocked to the church in search of answers for the calamity that had plagued many households.

Congressional members found "prayer support" in the Church on the Hill as they wrestled with making aggressive political decisions during a time of war with Afghanistan and Iraq.

The community at large found their answers at the Refreshing Spring Church as Pastor Jordan encouraged the congregates to "stand firmly in the Lord." Relinquishing the life of sin, establishing a pattern of personal and corporate Bible study, and using our faith to understand the power of praise and worship, are the stepping stones and keys to spiritual growth.

Pastor Jordan has served as senior pastor of the renowned Refreshing Spring Church of God in Christ since September 1995. Pastor Jordan also serves as the chairman of the board of the S.E.E.D. Community Development Corporation and oversees the development of the Spring of Life Wellness/Family Life Center. Furthermore he is a board member of the Collective Empowerment Group of Prince George's County and the Riverdale Ministerial Alliance.

Dr. James Jordan's unwavering support of women in ministry is commendable. Since 2003, he has counseled me during some of the most tumultuous times in my service as senior pastor of Church on the Hill. His adamant, but gentle, reminders that I needed to "stand firmly in my place despite the adversity that I may experience" has become a profound reality to me.

The mission of his ministry of Refreshing Spring Church is to establish a desire in the hearts of men for the Word of God. Pastor Jordan is committed to equipping the saints for the work of the ministry focused on the whole man--spirit, soul, and body.

The vision is fulfilled through the development of the satellite ministries in the U.S. and abroad. In recent years, this large congregation serves several churches throughout the Washington, D.C. metropolitan area; Laurinburg, North Carolina, and India.

The church's local ministry includes a food bank, as well clothing, prison, and homeless ministries - all functioning to extend the kingdom of God by working to make people free from all that keeps them bound.

Pastor Jordan lives by *Proverbs 3:5-6*: "Trust in the Lord with all thine heart; and lean not into thine own understanding. In all thy ways acknowledge Him and He shall direct thy paths." Pastor Jordan continues to achieve all of his goals including satisfying the mission of his ministry to establish a desire in the hearts of men for the Word of God as a foundation for personal salvation and discipleship.

Business Development Outreach

National Network of Christian Men & Women (NNCMW)

In addition to the current community development ministries that the Church on the Hill offers, we have taken a major stance on economic development since November 1994, through the National Network - NNCMW.

When I became the national president in November 1994, I vowed to assist the NNCMW membership to develop business plans to enhance their enterprises. A roadmap for success, a business plan provides direction for a successful enterprise.

The primary purposes of the NNCMW are the following:

Education--To schedule seminars and workshops to develop a business person's professional skills and spiritual growth.

Outreach-- To provide an atmosphere where Christian professionals can share the gospel of Jesus Christ in a non-threatening environment with non-Christians and disciple them. This form of witnessing entails leading others to a personal relationship with God. Those of other faiths will also feel welcome in the NNCMW. We conduct business development training, area chapter meetings, and other monthly events.

Information Services-- Political/congressional issues and events that impact them.

Networking-- To provide a forum for Christians to share talents, skills, and resources drawing upon professional contacts. Regular networking will improve and enhance their enterprises.

Technical Assistance- To provide management and technical services to members in areas such as legal, insurance and business management.

National Network (NNCMW) Committees

There are four standing NNCMW Committees:

Public Relations— We will serve as information officer to the public; publicize upcoming events and meetings in the form of various media, such as public service announcements, fliers, and ads; and will promote the organization at conferences, conventions, and other events.

Membership—We will serve as information provider to prospective and current members. The committee will keep a current roster of members' names, addresses, and phone numbers and will provide updates to the national office on a monthly basis.

Special Events—We will provide the planning and execution of special events for the organization, such as the annual chapter Christmas celebration, special fund raising events, prayer breakfast, and national conferences. It is the job of the chairperson to make sure that special events are within the boundaries of the NNCMW Statement of Faith and the vision of the president.

Publications—We will provide fliers and other printed materials for the chapter and be responsible for submitting articles on chapter events for use in the NNCMW newsletter, as well as for publishing and distributing the NNCMW newsletter to members and friends.

National Network of Christian Men & Women (NNCMW) Membership

Corporate Member:

Is a Sponsorship membership. Corporate membership rates will vary according to the number of employees of the company / firm / organization.

***Pastoral President's Club Member*:**

Over the last four years local pastors have become members of the National Network (NNCMW). They are recognizing the need to learn more about entrepreneurship, the rationale being that they can better assist the business owners in their churches to answer "the call to entrepreneurship" by establishing local NNCMW chapters in their congregations. Pastors will receive a six chapter binder, which includes information on obtaining federal, state, and local grants.

***President's Club Member*:**

The President's Club Membership is a supporting membership. In addition to regular member benefits, members will receive a special President's Club five chapter binder with vital information to facilitate the expansion of their enterprises. They will also receive special recognition during the Annual Member Rallies. Although traditionally conducted (1995-2008) in June on Capitol Hill, Rallies have been conducted in Prince George's County, Maryland, since 2009. Also, by September 2014, an Annual NNCMW Member Rally will be conducted in Atlanta, Georgia.

Regular: Is open to Christian individuals who work in the marketplace. These persons from various levels of the business and professional sector will be voting members and eligible to hold local offices and serve as conference delegates.

Special: Is available to individuals, not yet a part of the work force, who are enrolled in college or any other institution of higher education. They will not be voting members. However, they will have the opportunity to make contact with individuals already in the business community in the areas of study they are pursuing.

Since 1994, the NNCMW has provided these aggressive business development services to members of various congregations in Washington and in Prince George's and Montgomery Counties, Maryland. The NNCMW also has membership in New York, N.Y., and Atlanta, Georgia. The Church on the Hill/NNCMW Board has agreed that expanding our NNCMW membership nationwide will greatly benefit our growing NNCMW membership. Also, in the upcoming years, the Church on the Hill-NNCMW Board intends to extend membership internationally.

Therefore, those who seek to start a successful enterprise should first have a change of heart and mind. Once the decision has been made to answer the call to entrepreneurship, the NNCMW will provide the vital business development resources for the aggressive business owner necessary to start and expand a flourishing enterprise!

Developing the Mindset for Entrepreneurship

The following attributes suggest the appropriate mindset for entrepreneurship:

- personal desire to move beyond your present job situation
- commitment to working daily toward building your business
- willingness to complete the necessary work to expand your enterprise. For example, you will need a business manager to successfully manage your growing enterprise
- a business marketing professional will be needed to assist you to develop a viable business marketing plan for your enterprise. You will need to advertise your products (or services) to obtain a viable customer base.
- a commitment to continue business development training

Also, it may be necessary for entrepreneurs to locate reliable venture capitalists for their enterprises. Or, local pastors/ministry leaders will need to find sponsors to provide financial support for their non-profit, or community outreach organization.

Adequate financial statements are necessary for obtaining a small business loan from our contacts at the SBA, Washington, D.C. and Prince Georges County, Maryland.

After one has developed the mindset for entrepreneurship, a formal business plan should be written. A suggested format for writing a business plan is as follows:

Cover Sheet

Table of Contents

Executive Summary Mission Statement

Company History

The Business (Name and Type)

Description of the Business

Industry and Market Description, including the following "five P's of Marketing":

Positioning-- Convey to your target group exactly why they should do business with you.

Packaging-- Create interest and excitement about your product or service by packaging and presenting it in a creative way.

Promotion-- Get to know as many business professionals as possible to find those who will endorse your product or service.

Persuasion-- Work on your technique to turn cold calls into sales opportunities.

Performance-- Develop loyalty with your customers to keep them coming back by providing a product or service that is high quality and service that is second to none.

Management Team

Competition and Feasibility Study

Location of Business

Personnel

Financial Data

Suggested financial statements:

1. Balance Sheet
2. Break-even Analysis
3. Projected Income Statements
4. Cash Flow Projections
5. Profit/Loss Statements
6. Business Income/Loss Tax Returns

Future Projections

Summary

* * *

Full Gospel Baptist Church Fellowship (FGBCF)

(Washington, DC, Metropolitan Area)

Pastor Dawn Burrell of New Creations Church and Ministries Lanham, Maryland, invited me to attend the FGBCF breakfast at the Marriott hotel in July 2004, in Greenbelt, Maryland. I replied affirmatively since I was confident that I would enjoy the prayer breakfast.

Pastor Burrell had informed me that Dr. William Bennett was involved with the FGBCF. Also, he was former Mayor Marion Barry's Religious Affairs Director. I remembered that Dr. Bennett had been instrumental in assisting the Church on the Hill as we prepared for a visit from former Mayor Marion Barry at our Church on the Hill second

Anniversary in 1997. This momentous event was conducted at the Red Roof Inn Hotel, Washington, DC.

* * *

Upon entering the Marriott hotel, I was greeted by Pastor Lanier Twyman of St. Stephen's Baptist Church, Temple Hills, Maryland. I was impressed with his compassion and kindness. Also, I was excited about the prospect of growing and developing the Church on the Hill.

After serving myself breakfast from the buffet, I sat down at the table. The ambiance was solemn and inviting. The demeanor of the pastors (all male) around me was kind.

Suddenly, a tall, medium weight, impressive man sat next to me and introduced himself as Bishop Michael Kelsey. His kind demeanor was inviting, especially since I was expecting to meet Dr. William Bennett. I was very nervous as Bishop Kelsey addressed the other pastors at the table. Then, he asked us individually to tell him about our churches, as well as our call to ministry. Also, he wanted to know who had informed us about the FGBCF.

Bishop Kelsey cautioned the pastors not to be nervous. That was an understatement since I was so nervous that I could not stop shaking. However, over the next thirty minutes, eating the delicious buffet style breakfast eventually calmed my tension. I was elated, yet humbled by an offer from Bishop Michael Kelsey to become the spiritual covering for Church on the Hill-NNCMW.

I felt blessed that the FGBCF would also provide an opportunity for me to join the organization. Most impressive was the fact that God had allowed an anointed bishop to step into my life. His kind demeanor and words of wisdom were a guiding light to the Church on the Hill.

His guidance was important, since we were preparing to extend our ministry to the Silver Spring metropolitan area. Since staffing would be a major concern, I would need more spiritual support as we expanded.

* * *

A few months later, in September 2004, I made the decision to become an individual member of the Full Gospel Baptist Church Fellowship (FGBCF). I resigned my associate membership with the Methodist Church. At that time, as the State Bishop of the FGBCF, the Rev. Dr. Michael Kelsey remained our "spiritual covering" until 2009.

According to Hill, in his book *Think and Grow Rich* "procrastination, the opposite of decision, is a common enemy, which practically every man must conquer. . . . Analysis of several hundred people who had accumulated fortunes well beyond the million-dollar mark disclosed the fact that every one of them had the habit of reaching decisions promptly, and of changing these decisions slowly, if, and when they were changed."4

* * *

According to Hill, "Those who have cultivated the habit of persistence seem to enjoy insurance against failure. No matter how many times they are defeated, they finally arrive up toward the top of the ladder. Sometimes it appears that there is a hidden guide whose duty is to test men through all sorts of discouraging experiences. Those who pick themselves up after defeat and keep on trying, arrive; and the world cries, 'Bravo!' I knew you could do it!"5

It is with this premise that despite my many adversities, God's protection continues to be a mighty fortress. As a staunch reminder of His grace and mercy, I daily accept the challenge of the clarion call to being senior pastor of the Church on the Hill. I will also continue to serve as National President of the National Network (NNCMW).

The church will continue to be a guiding light to those in the valley. When they triumph over their trials and tribulations and get the victory, we will encourage them to remember that God is still in control. They can stare at the beacon of light as their faith seeks understanding and remember that there is a Church on the Hill.

Chapter 22 Women and the Twenty-First Century

Between 1995 and 1997, my son Rafael and I worked tirelessly to pioneer the Church on the Hill as a nondenominational growing outreach ministry. Also, I reconstructed the National Network of Christian Men & Women (NNCMW). We placed an emphasis on business development in an effort to assist entrepreneurs in writing "winning" business plans. This was essential since many were seeking business loans to expand their enterprises. Non-profit ministries/community organizations were gathering viable advisory boards in an effort to apply for federal, state, and local grants.

* * *

Unfortunately, my husband Andy passed in November 1997, at the young age of forty-one years old. He died of complications from his bout with liver disease.

Rafael, though distraught about his surrogate father's sudden death, also confirmed my call to pastor the Church on the Hill. He was enrolled at the University of Massachusetts and was excelling in his college education. Yet, he withdrew from college for about one year to work steadfastly with me to sustain the Church on the Hill.

From 1997 through 2002, I experienced another breaking point. I was filled with grief because of Andy's death. Yet I was determined to do God's will. I was disillusioned over Andy's death, since I felt I did not have anyone to talk to about family issues.

Although Andy and I were divorced, besides God's divine intervention, I thought of him as the glue that held our family together.

At times he could be as stubborn as a mule; but I missed him terribly. We had first met in the COG in Paris at the Colombes home; yet, our struggles to be cult-free were successful. We had both become members of a local church, we were emotionally healthy, and we had accomplished our financial goals.

Most of time, I felt as though I was in a daze. Battling with bouts of grief and loss, I reminisced about times Andy and I discussed appropriate parental support for Rafael. Although I was proud that Rafael was excelling in college, I grieved over Andy's death.

Yet it was my duty to continue on. After all, I reasoned, Rafael still had one living parent. It was imperative that I pull myself together and provide the comfort Rafael needed during this time.

* * *

Mr. Jonathan Jones was a strong comforter for me during the difficult years after Andy's death. He has been a successful entrepreneur since 1957. He has retired as CEO of Jones & Sons Inc., a prominent heating and air conditioning firm based in Capitol Heights, Maryland. As our platinum sponsor and board member emeritus from 1997 until 2004, Mr. Jones vowed to financially support the Church on the Hill. I was thankful for his support and his mentorship.

In turn, through our business development seminars on Capitol Hill, we worked persistently with him as he experienced hardship and struggled to keep his firm open. Because of his endurance and his impressive work ethic, The Washington Post featured Jones & Sons, Inc., in an impressive article in the February 12, 2001 issue. The company had successfully installed the air conditioning system of the National Cathedral in Washington, D.C. By 2001, the firm had more than one hundred employees and annual sales of about twenty-five million dollars.

Women and Violent Deaths

On December 19, 2004, The Washington Post ran a front cover story, with the headline "Many New or Expectant Mothers Die Violent Deaths." The article depicted the plight of hundreds of pregnant women and new mothers who have been slain. All of the women were pregnant and had futures that seemed sure to unfold over many years. Compounding the problem is the growing number of women who have been carjacked, robbed, and kidnapped in broad daylight. These deaths have reached epidemic proportions, yet their stories have been hidden amongst the other homicide cases plaguing our nation.

Also in December 2004, the prosecution convicted Scott Petersen in the double murder trial that shocked America. He was convicted of the murder of his wife and unborn child. Amber Frye, his girlfriend, cooperated with the police to bring Scott to justice. Ultimately, his conviction provided some solace to the families of the women in this country who had lost their lives to violence. The verdict in this trial proved that justice can be served.

Women and Domestic Violence

I was deeply disturbed by the October 10, 2005, tragedy of Yvonne Johnson, who was doused with gasoline and set on fire by her estranged husband, Lester Thorn. He committed the crime at the cell phone store where she worked in Prince George's County, Maryland.

Former State's Attorney Glenn Ivey, Prince George's County, Maryland, stepped in and convicted Lester Thorn to life imprisonment in April, 2006 for this heinous crime. According to the Examiner (Wednesday, April 29 and 30, 2006), "A Prince George's County man was convicted Friday of trying to kill his estranged wife, who was set on fire last year at the cell phone store where she worked. The case was 'rooted in rage, propelled by malice and executed without mercy,' Prince George's County State's Attorney Glenn Ivey said."

The question is why did Lester Thorn do it? Were there alternatives available to him that could assist him to cope with his anger against his estranged wife?

To answer these questions, we need to examine the role of women in American society. With the advent of the Women's Liberation Movement and the influx of women entering the work force and now the political arena, women are taking their rightful place in society.

On Thursday, October 20, 2005, the Church on the Hill continued its focus on women's rights by hosting its second Women's Empowerment Rally on Capitol Hill at the Rayburn House Office Building. Former Congressman Albert R. Wynn (D-MD) was our sponsor. Former Deputy State's Attorney Pat Smoot (Prince George's County), from the office of the State's Attorney spoke out against domestic violence at the Rally. She managed the Domestic Violence unit at the Office of the State's Attorney.

Two of the tactics that the unit employs to assist women who become victims of domestic violence are: 1) providing a safety plan for couples who experience ongoing arguments and fighting at home, and 2) preventing the cycle of violence in the home through family counseling.

Programs for Ex-Offenders

The Domestic Violence Unit at the Office of the State's Attorney (Prince George's County, Maryland), has various programs to aid the ex-offender, such as counseling support, assistance to find employment, and programs that teach entrepreneurship.

As the judicial system copes with domestic violence, former Deputy Smoot declared that officers, lawyers, and judges should be better trained not to demean victims who become "prisoners in their own homes."

Also, too often, church leaders demean the vulnerable victims and do not believe the wife when she tells them that she is being abused. Most tragic are the cases where the abusive spouse is a law enforcement staff person. Often, fear keeps the abused wife from letting his superiors know about the abuse.

Most importantly, when violence enters a marriage, the bond is broken. Every effort should be made to assist families to grapple with this problem. Tragically, when children constantly witness violent acts against their mother, the cycle of abuse continues. Often these children become "batterers" in their adult lives.

In her book *Living History*, former First Lady Hillary Clinton writes a chapter called "Women's Rights are Human Rights," in which she clearly outlines the plight of many women in America and around the world. She states:

"I believe that on the eve of a new millennium, it is time to break our silence. It is time for us to say here in Beijing, and the world to hear, that it is no longer acceptable to discuss women's rights as separate from human rights. For too long, the history of women has been a history of silence. Even today, there are those who are trying to silence our words.

The voices of this conference and of the women at Huairou must be heard loud and clear: It is a violation of human rights when babies are denied food, or drowned, or suffocated, or their spines broken, simply because they are born girls. It is a violation of human rights when women and girls are sold into the slavery of prostitution. It is a violation of human rights when women are doused with gasoline, set on fire and burned to death because their marriage dowries are deemed too small. It is a violation of human rights when women are raped in their own communities and when thousands of women are subjected to rape as a tactic or prize of war. It is a violation of human rights when a leading cause of death worldwide among women ages fourteen to forty-four is the violence they are subjected to in their own homes by their own relatives. It is a violation of human rights when young girls are brutalized by the painful and degrading practice of genital mutilation. It is a violation of human rights when women are denied the right to plan their own families, and that includes being forced to have abortions or being sterilized against their will. If there is one message that echoes forth from this conference, let it be that human rights are women's rights and women's rights are human rights, once and for all."1

Ms. Justine Lloyd, sister of Yvonne Johnson, attended the Church on the Hill's August 2006, potluck prayer breakfast in downtown Silver Spring, Maryland. She confessed that Yvonne had been making great progress.

Through phone conversations and e-mail, the former Public Relations Chairperson of our National Network (NNCMW), Mr. Larry Michaels, offered spiritual support to the family. This was necessary during the family's time of recuperation from the violent act against Yvonne.

Also, the family asked the Church on the Hill for prayer support as they strived to set up a foundation. Such an effort would facilitate the proper handling of the contributions that the community was sending in to assist the family with Yvonne's care.

* * *

On Saturday, October 20, 2007, the Church on the Hill continued our work on behalf of women by conducting our Women's Empowerment Rally in PG County, Maryland. Former State's Attorney Glenn Ivey (Prince Georges County) was our special guest panelist during the panel discussion on "Domestic Violence." Also, I presented a business seminar on "The Road to Entrepreneurship." Attorney Sandra Townsend (Prince Georges County, Maryland) was also a guest panelist.

* * *

Eventually, after pre-marital counseling, I married Mr. Leroy Ramara in November, 1989. I worked hard to make this second marriage successful. Leroy was very kind to me during the two years that we courted. He even agreed to support me as I pursued my master's degree at Wesley Seminary. There were no signs of any kind of violent behavior.

To my surprise, then, over the first two years as a student at Wesley, Leroy began falsely accusing me of an affair with one of the students, Minister Gary Gaines at Wesley, who was a neighbor. His anger escalated when he visited the campus and saw me speaking with this person.

One morning, he became very angry, stating that I had purposely asked Minister Gaines to provide a ride home for me with the intention of seeking to have an affair with him. The anger intensified, and he began violently hitting me. We were in the kitchen of our new townhouse in Mitchellville, Maryland. With several blows to the right side of my head, Leroy almost knocked me unconscious. Thankfully, the screen door was ajar; and I escaped his violent abuse, which could have been fatal. I ran out onto the deck praying that I would survive the attack.

This was not the first time Leroy had hit me. It started with a slap in the face during the first year of our marriage. He was angry because I had forgotten to take an article of his clothing to the dry cleaners. The violence at the Lake Arbor townhouse escalated as he suddenly became angry and threw objects down the long stairwell.

To my dismay, the physical abuse I suffered from Leroy heightened until the violence became noticeable to my son, Rafael. Because he witnessed Leroy physically abusing me, Rafael's fear of him became evident. Rafael's grades at school started to drop significantly because of the domestic violence that he witnessed at our home.

* * *

I first requested marriage counseling at the United Methodist Church, Washington, D.C., where we attended. Leroy had been a faithful member. He had attended Bible study and was active as an usher. Pastor Roger Lanes had left the church by this time. Therefore, we had marital counseling with the new pastor, Dr. Roger Hines.

During our counseling sessions, Dr. Hines on several occasions questioned the domestic violence reports that I had made. Also, over the years, Leroy had provided significant financial support to his church. Therefore, Leroy's flagrant denial of any wife beatings caused my fear and anxiety to escalate. I often felt as if I was in a crowded room, screaming, with no one supporting me.

Thankfully, it appeared that only the female staff member at the church, Minister Barbara Stuart, believed me when I shared with her that I was suffering from domestic violence at our home. Minister Stuart had marital counseling with Leroy and me on several occasions in her office at the church. She tried to assist Leroy to find the cause for his violent temper. She made it clear to him that wife beating was not the way to get control of the marriage. She explained to us that talking about our difficulties and working on a plan to resolve our issues would be in our best interest.

During our counseling sessions, it was clear to me that Leroy had decided that he did not want me to continue my education at Wesley Seminary. He said that I had too much contact with men on the campus. Also, he insisted that we could not afford to have me attend school any longer. Finally, he demanded that I quit school and go back to work.

There was a major problem with Leroy's request. I was on a full scholarship, which required me to go to school full-time. If I withdrew from full-time study, I would lose my scholarship.

I did bring in some income through my Shaklee vitamin business. Because of our training at Wesley Seminary about proper nutrition, many of the students purchased vitamins from me. Also, while attending seminary, I still worked part-time at a law firm as a contract litigation secretary.

I admitted to Leroy that I knew that my attending Wesley Seminary was a financial sacrifice for us, but that the long-term results would be rewarding. Furthermore, I tried to explain to Leroy that my attending Wesley was a calling. I was certain that I had had a call on my life for the ministry since I had left the COG.

Although Leroy stated that he was interested in supporting me in ministry, his actions almost destroyed my reputation at Wesley and caused me unnecessary emotional pain. When I could no longer stand the fear and isolation of being constantly physically abused with limited support from the church, I then spoke with my advisor at Wesley and requested professional marriage counseling. Coming to my aid, the seminary staff members insisted that we have marital counseling. Also, the New York Ave. Presbyterian Church, where I was an intern, offered financial assistance.

When Leroy and I were I finally matched with a pastoral counselor, I felt we were justifiably getting the support we needed. We attended about five sessions of intense marital therapy. Finally, Leroy admitted his foul temper and apologized for his behavior. Yet, when the pastoral counselor referred him to a licensed psychiatrist, he refused to make an appointment. His reason: he did not want to receive counseling from a woman.

Furthermore, Leroy made it very clear that the only way to have peace at home was for me to quit attending Wesley Seminary. Consequently, for fear of my personal safety while pursuing my theological studies at Wesley, Leroy and I were separated in April, 1994.

* * *

Around the time of our separation, an unexpected phone call at our Lake Arbor townhouse startled me. A relative called to inform me that my sister Jessica had been fatally shot in the head. My world had now become a nightmare.

I called my sister Josephine in Brooklyn, and we began making plans to go to Macon, Georgia. It was important that we get to Georgia immediately. This was a major family crisis. I arranged to take one week of leave from Wesley Seminary. Since I was to graduate in May, taking time off from school at this time was a threat to my pending graduation.

* * *

When my family and I arrived in Macon, we worked assiduously to assure Jessica had an appropriate funeral.

Not only was I losing my second husband, but my favorite sister, Jessica, had been suddenly taken away from me. It was then that the Lord reminded me of the scripture, "No temptation has overtaken you except such as is common to man; but God is faithful, who will not allow you to be tempted beyond what you are able, but with the temptation you will also make the way of escape, that we may be able to bear it." (*1Cor.10:13.*)

* * *

What tools are required to prevent domestic violence?

1. A woman should recognize the signs of a violent husband:
    - occasional slaps across the face as punishment for your faults or something you have done wrong
    - throwing objects when angry, especially during an argument
    - prevention from having friends, or not being allowed to leave the house freely
    - excessive jealousy resulting in the husband's intention to control your every move
2. Seek professional counseling
3. Have a consistent professional counselor who is willing to

work with you and your spouse at least once a week for a minimum of an hour.

What advice can I give to those presently in a domestic violence situation?

1. Have a safety plan when the spouse who is accused of domestic violence threatens that he will "get you" when you get home. This includes a way of escape in the event of a violent incident.
2. If you are physically abused, have someone take pictures of your injuries and keep them in a safe place.
3. Open your own bank account. Keep extra money for pay phones, a pre-paid calling card, and a charged cell phone with you at all times.
4. Keep copies of your important (and your children's) papers in a metal box. You may need to take the box with you should a domestic violence incident occur.

Keep the following numbers in a safe place:

1. 1-800-MD-HELPS--Statewide Domestic Violence Helpline
2. 1-800-799-SAFE --National Domestic Violence Helpline

* * *

After Leroy and I were separated for a number of years, there had been several threats of violence. Also, he refused to support me in ministry.

After pastoral counseling with a prominent Christian counseling center in Largo, MD, I decided to divorce Leroy. This would assure my safety and my ability to continue in the ministry.

I filed for the divorce pro se. Eventually, I received a letter from the office of Court Clerk Sandra L. Johnson. I was granted an absolute divorce from Leroy Ramara by the Circuit Court of Prince George's County, Maryland, on July 22, 2002.

Women and Education

From 2002-2004, I was a full-time teacher in the D.C. Public Schools. I participated in the D.C. Teaching Fellows educational initiative. Former First Lady Laura Bush and former First Lady Hillary

Clinton assisted with launching this excellent program. Also, former Mayor Anthony Williams and former Superintendent Paul Vance (Montgomery County) participated in the design and implementation of this educational initiative.

One of the purposes of the D.C. Teaching Fellows program was to recruit second career professionals and encourage them to teach in the D.C. Public School system. The former leaders of the program, in conjunction with the "No Child Left Behind" initiative, wanted to ascertain what was amiss with the District's school system. Also, the program was implemented in an effort to "close the achievement gap."

The leaders of the D.C. Teaching Fellows program also aimed at reconstructing the methods to be used by principals in the system. Some had refused to make the necessary changes to improve the academic performance of the students.

Furthermore, they wanted to know how to repair the damage caused by corruption of some of its high level staff members. For example, during the time I worked for the school system, Barbara A. Bullock, former president of the teacher's union, was convicted and sent to prison for stealing money from the teacher's union.

Because of the work of the D.C. Teaching Fellows program, the D.C. Public School system is now led by the mayor (instead of the school board). Since that time, the school chancellors (and superintendents) have worked diligently on restructuring the school system by providing extra academic support for teachers and principals who needed to enhance their skills. This was an effort to improve the school system and bring the standards up to competitive national standards.

During the time that I worked full-time (2002-2004) for D.C. Public Schools, I also attended American University in the N.W. Washington, D.C, two nights a week. I matriculated in the graduate school of education from June 2002-December 2003.

I obtained the necessary credit hours to fulfill the course requirement of the D.C. Teaching Fellows program. As a result, in 2004, I was issued a provisional teacher's license. Currently, I am a bilingual (Spanish) substitute teacher for Montgomery County, MD public school system.

Women and Entrepreneurship

As we focus on "women's rights" in the U.S., we are compelled to provide a model that is a paradigm shift from the way women have been perceived throughout history. Women today, as a result of the Women's Liberation Movement, are thought of as more than just homemakers.

Strong female leadership in churches and on Capitol Hill and other political arenas throughout the country have now swayed the antiquated opinions of American citizens. Women today are finally being publicly recognized as effective leaders and role models!

In his 2005 Inaugural Speech, former President George Bush included the following key points:

"1) There should be no acts of humiliation and servitude toward women; 2) there should be economic independence rather than dependence; 3) the nation should abandon racism and bigotry and history has a visible direction."

On Thursday June 26 and Friday, June 27, 2008, former President George W. Bush conducted the Conference on Faith-Based and Community Initiatives at the Omni Sheraton Hotel in Washington. I attended the conference and was ecstatic about the program. Key congressional/political leaders were present to provide their testimony of how the Faith-Based and Community Initiative was positively affecting the country.

There were testimonies from many whose lives had been changed with assistance from a variety of national Faith-Based Initiative outreach programs. How encouraging to know that the whole course of the nation had changed since the Faith-Based Initiative had been launched.

Former President Bush spoke on Thursday, June 26, at the luncheon. He encouraged the Faith-Based Initiative churches and organizations to plunge ahead to take advantage of federal/state and local grants, which he had made available through the various agencies. The availability of these grants was enlightening to me. After the conference, I felt encouraged to continue in the ministry.

* * *

A major concern of women is promoting equal opportunity in the higher levels of the corporate structure. In addition, women should be afforded the same rights as their male counterparts when we compete for business loans to strengthen enterprises.

As women make significant progress in our businesses, we will compel higher government to introduce legislation that will assist us through low interest loans and grants. Continued support should be provided to those women who show that they have the necessary tools to be successful entrepreneurs.

In American society, it appears that the system is not designed for the common worker to get ahead. It is formulated so that we make just enough money through a job to return to work the next week. Some of you can identify with working "from paycheck to paycheck."

Although America's free enterprise system allows women to use creative measures to make a living, women still have part-time jobs in addition to a full-time career. Most single women live on a closely monitored budget to prevent overspending or to make sure their paychecks cover all of their monthly expenses. This includes rent, utility bills, and other living costs.

Mrs. Dee Jepsen served on President Ronald Reagan's Task Force as Special Assistant to the President (as liaison between women's organizations and the White House) from 1982-1983. She was also the special guest speaker at the Tuesday, December 12, 1995, National Network (NNCMW) Business Meeting at the Rayburn HOB. She is he wife of former Senator Roger Jepsen.

In her book *Women Beyond Equal Rights*, Dee Jepsen, writes: "Women are primarily responsible for passing on our culture, passing on our values and for shaping and molding the young lives of the leaders of tomorrow. We women have often been taken for granted, and seldom taken seriously by many in our society. What is needed now is healing, not more hostility. Hostility is not a solution, but a new problem."2

In spite of current conditions, we can combat homelessness, poverty, unemployment, and underemployment through our aggressive program to assist women to be successful in business. Since most women earn much less than their male counterparts, entrepreneurship is the key to assist us as we strive toward financial independence. Women and entrepreneurship will be a topic for further exploration as the Church on the Hill plans our annual events.

* * *

Too often, divorce or the loss of a job causes the financial collapse of many women. In cases of divorce, she is often penalized when a husband walks out on her or she has to leave the home for her own safety. Compounding the problem is the need to remain financially stable, especially if children are involved. Her inability to meet the mortgage payments or provide adequate childcare for her children so that she can pursue a career, often leads a single woman to become homeless. Or, if she has not been in the job market for many years, she may find herself among the "working poor," who have minimum wage jobs and are unable to keep up with an increasingly changing economic system.

Women and Politics

With the rising popularity of Secretary of State Hillary Clinton, America must now seriously consider women as viable candidates for the office of President of the United States. While she served as First Lady of the United States, Mrs. Clinton was a member of Foundry United Methodist Church. I visited the church upon an invitation from Minister Monique Jones. She was a fellow classmate from September 1991 to May 1994, at Wesley Seminary. Also, she was Youth Minister for the Clintons' daughter, Chelsea, while she completed her internship at the church.

During my visit at Foundry UMC, Minister Jones asked me to continue in prayer for the Clintons, after she had graduated from Wesley. Minister Jones had taken an offer from the United Methodist Church to pastor a church out of the Washington metropolitan area.

I have been impressed with Secretary of State Hillary Clinton. She has shown strong faith as a devout United Methodist. I have always admired how she faithfully stood by her husband, former President Bill Clinton, during one of their most turbulent times - the affair with a White House intern. The Christian community has continued to show tremendous support and forgiveness for the Clintons.

Another successful woman, former Alaska Gov. Sarah Palin, electrified the nation when she agreed to run on the Republican ticket as a candidate for Vice President of the United States. I was impressed with her forthrightness and energetic approach to confronting the array of economic and moral traumas of our nation.

Both of these women have made history as they embarked on changing the attitude of our country about the role of women in politics. The question is when will we have a woman president? To accomplish this goal as a nation, we have to continue affirming that women can perform successfully in the political arena.

Domestic Violence and Landlords

On Friday, April 18, 2007, I was wrongfully escorted off the premises of a downtown Silver Spring home where I was renting the second floor level of a three-story, single-family home. I was trying to save money by dividing household expenses while I worked as a bilingual substitute teacher for the Montgomery County public schools.

The owner of the home, Mr. Sanchez, informed me that he would consider assisting me with a Church on the Hill worship service. We had invited the Senate Chaplain, the Rev. Dr. Barry Black to join us for a March 11, 2007, worship service at the Southern Asian Seventh Day Adventist Church in Silver Spring, Maryland. This would be our first Church on the Hill Silver Spring service. Therefore, it would be a dedicatory service, which could spear head our expansion into the Silver Spring metropolitan area. Rev. John Frost of the Forcey Memorial Church, Silver Spring, Maryland, assisted with preparing for the service.

To my dismay, Mr. Sanchez became angry one April evening over a disagreement about major repairs that needed to be done to the house. When visiting the second floor unit, he began throwing my clothes around and slamming doors, causing a ruckus. I was frightened by this incident. He was about six feet, four inches tall and weighed about three hundred pounds. I called the police since this was not the first time that he had shown emotional outbursts. I could not endure the landlord's violent temper any longer.

The needed repairs at the home, which Mr. Sanchez refused to address, resulted in a breach in the lease agreement. Also, his negligence interrupted my work and often prevented me from working consistently.

I decided to move out of the second floor unit. Unfortunately, the tenant in the basement apartment, Mr. Linden, began harassing me. One day, he forcibly snatched a handcart out of my hand while I was attempting to move my personal belongings off the property. Since I was concerned about my personal safety, I visited the Domestic Violence department at the courthouse and filed for a protective order against Mr. Linden.

I later found out during a peace order hearing at the courthouse that Mr. Sanchez had filed false charges against me. He alleged that I harassed and shoved him. To the contrary, Mr. Sanchez had done the following to me: given me a thirty-day notice to vacate the second floor unit, after which he proceeded to lock me out from the aforementioned premises with nowhere to go.

In Montgomery County, there are programs for women who are married and fleeing their spouses for fear of domestic violence and other repeated emotional attacks on them. But there was no housing available when a landlord was being violent. This type of domestic violence is the most emotionally disturbing since the landlord had threatened eviction by locking me out of the property. However, I had refused to be mentally and verbally abused by him.

According to Angela Brown in her book *When the Doors Close, Look to Windows*:

"All the usual doors were shut. I needed a key. Then the sunlight shone through the windows, and I knew that with a great deal of effort, I could work and care for my son. Sometimes when things seem most bleak and we feel all doors are locked, we can get a sign from our higher power that we can achieve what we once only dared to think about. This is how it happened to me, and many people whose stories I've heard have also found that after all seemed hopeless, something happened that opened a locked door or allowed the sun to enter through the windows."3

It was about one month (June 1, 2007) before any normalcy occurred again in my life. Miraculously, I was able to get a new lease from a landlord in the Silver Spring metropolitan area. I had known about the house for a little over a year.

Mr. Fred Lawrence, the owner of the home had been building a new three bedroom townhouse onto his current house for rental. The stunning white house, with a red door, is quaintly nestled on a small hill surrounded by about one-half acre of land. The other part of the house has five bedrooms where the landlord's family resided.

It behooves me as I reflect on the blessings of God, that in all things He is able to do "exceedingly, abundantly above all that we ask or think." (*Eph. 3:20.*). Our God is indeed a miracle worker!

After discussion with Mr. Lawrence about renting the townhouse, I decided to sign a one-year lease agreement (February 2007-2008).

To my credit, as a faithful member of the family of God, several Christian agencies, like Community Ministry of Montgomery County, were faithful in their support of me. Also included was strong support from the Baptist Church and Catholic Charities. They came to my rescue and assisted me as I made the move. Most importantly, I am deeply grateful for prayers of faith community who offered their staunch support during my time of testing. I will be forever appreciative of their support!

* * *

I have a fond memory of a picturesque sermon I heard one bright Sunday morning in June, 2007, at a prominent Baptist Church in Rockville, Maryland called "Who Owns the Snake?" The message was a vivid reminder by a prominent Baptist teaching pastor, the Rev. Terry Thompson. He confirmed that the devil is only allowed to keep us during a specific time of testing.

Quietly seated next to Ms. Nancy Cooper, who was a premier

deacon of the church, the pastor reminded the congregation that our trials - mine had lasted approximately twenty-five days - were sanctioned by God. During the visit to this place, God showed me what steps I needed to take to restore my dignity in the clergy community. Ultimately, God is still faithful, even though we remain faithless.

It became evident to me then that I still had something to live for. I believe that the Lord, our God, is able to prevent us from falling and can heal us physically, emotionally, and spiritually by the wave of His mighty hand. God is indeed even able to deliver us from the hands of the enemy in order that we might fulfill His divine destiny for our lives!

I am forever grateful to Pre-Paid Legal Services, Inc., (now Legal Shield) and the other faithful private attorneys, who assisted me during my time of crisis.

Women and Polygamous Sects

According to the June 3, 2008,Washington Post, "More than 440 children of an insular west Texas polygamist group began returning to their parents and their homes on Monday after two months in state custody where they were exposed for the first time to a larger world that included bicycles, pepperoni pizza and news of moon landings."

In the article, it states that the police had also opened criminal investigation. They began a search for DNA samples from the sect's prophet, Warren Jeffs. Currently, he is in prison for the crimes he committed against innocent children and women when he reigned as prophet for the FLDS. The FLDS is not affiliated with the mainstream Church of Jesus Christ of Latter-day Saints.

* * *

The fundamentalist Church of Jesus Christ of Latter-day Saints (FLDS) compound was raided on April 3, 2008, by state officials, who were looking for evidence that underage girls were married to and having children with much older men. Although Texas authorities had begun to return the children to their parents, they were adamant that they would press ahead with their child abuse investigation. Thankfully, the judge's ruling included a provision that child-protection officials could visit at any time.

The children were taken because of the constant denial from the mothers that their children were being sexually or physically abused. Also, they stated that women are free to leave the ranch any time they wished. Therefore, they asserted that the phone call from a sixteen-year-old mother alleging abuse was a hoax from outside the compound.

Carolyn Jessup, in her book *ESCAPE*, reveals the startling details of her life as she grew up in the polygamist sect. By age 18 she was forced to marry a 45-year-old man. This resulted in the birth of eight children.

Deborah Davis and Carolyn Jessup

Like Deborah Davis, as related in her book, *The Children of God: The Inside Story,* Carolyn Jessop had eight children. Even though Carolyn did not want to marry Merril or sleep with him, she was forced to comply with the strict code of submission to her husband.

As in the COG, no form of birth control was acceptable, resulting in the birth of multiple children. This would increase the chances of a woman being dependent on the cult.

In Carolyn Jessup's story, it was shocking to learn that her fifth child was life threatening to her. She had severe illness and vomiting. Only fifty percent of her placenta was functioning, because it was "abrupted" and continued to leak blood into her uterus. Subsequently, this produced cramping that would potentially tear more of the placenta away. Therefore, Carolyn was commanded to spend the last month of her pregnancy in bed.

Distraught by the news, she wondered who would care for her other four children if she was confined to bed. She was certain that the other three wives wouldn't bring meals to her in bed or see that her children got enough food. Also, she had become attached to her children in her second-grade classroom.

However, her constant hemorrhaging prompted her to take her nurse's and her husband Merril's advice. She decided to confine herself to bed. She writes: "in a follow-up visit, I talked to Shirley about my fears of getting pregnant again. She said I didn't meet any of the risk factors for another abruption and assured me it would never happen again. She was wrong. I had three more life-threatening pregnancies."

"My pregnancy with Andrew changed my sense of security in the world. I had five healthy, beautiful children whom I cherished, but I was terrified of becoming pregnant again. I wanted birth control but had no access to it. The FLDS believed that if a woman used birth control to keep life from coming into the world, she would pay for it in her next life by being a childless servant to her husband's other wives throughout eternity."4

Jessup also tells us that she witnessed cruel treatment--physical and emotional abuse - toward women, men, and children in the FLDS. With forthrightness, she reveals the riveting and shocking details of her fifteen-year personal experience of being pregnant and emotionally abused at the hand of the FLDS.

When she decided to "escape" with her eight children, she drove out of the compound with barely enough gas in a van. Her brother said she had taken the children of one of the most powerful men in the FLDS. Yet, by His sovereignty, God protected her. With the support of ex-FLDS members, family members, and devoted colleagues, she managed to safely escape from the sect.

Using careful judgment and wisdom, as well as the advice of Dan, an ex-FLDS member, Carolyn contacted the attorney general's office. A colleague, Jolene, had assisted her to file for an emergency protective order. Also, she was instrumental in making sure word was passed to someone in the FLDS community that the attorney general's office was now involved.

Carolyn knew that her husband, Merril, would be hunting for her and the children. However, she knew that if Merril tried to take one of the children, he would have to answer to the law.

* * *

Dan encouraged Carolyn to tell the attorney general everything she knew about Merril's and Prophet Warren Jeffs's crimes. As she explains: "A judge could rule on the evidence in my case rather than condemn me as an immoral woman. I could tell a courtroom about Merril's abuse instead of having to talk to Warren Jeffs, another perpetrator. I was thirty-five years old and had never been in a fair fight or had anyone on my side. This was going to take some getting used to. But I was not going to back down. That was one of the few things about my life I did know."5

* * *

Miraculously, with the strong support of Lisa Jones, a former judge, Carolyn Jessup did eventually win a court case for custody of her eight children.

Though at first her husband had been allowed to travel to Colorado City with her children, she eventually won a court case to have Merril's visitation rights restricted to Salt Lake City because of his abuse of the children. In *ESCAPE,* she expresses her satisfaction:

"My heart stopped. I'd won. We were safe. I knew Merril would never put the effort into coming up to Salt Lake City. The fight was over. It was a huge win. I had proven that it was not in my children's interests ever to be in Colorado City. We were finally and truly free.

This was a groundbreaking case at many levels. If I could get my children out of the cult, any woman with enough determination could, too. The absolute power the FLDS had over women had been cracked. I had proved that a woman could not only flee and live on her own but also win custody of her children. It was a proud day."6

* * *

In this book, I have exposed the spiritual delusion that was caused by my two year journey as a Children of God disciple. Also, I have enlightened the readers that there are other destructive cults, wayward religious groups, and other sects who threaten the moral fiber of our society. Unfortunately, cults seek to lead young people astray during their most vulnerable times (i.e., when they are away from their parents at college).

These groups beguile their members by camouflaging their main purpose - to kill the self-will of an individual and to bring him or her under complete mind control. The lives of cult members center around expanding the goals and objectives of the organization, rather than focusing on winning souls into the kingdom of God.

I trust this book will provide greater insights into the realm of the spiritual. May you BEWARE of destructive cults and the hypocrisy of some religious groups that will eventually lead you astray.

Most importantly, keep your eyes focused on God's perfect will for your life. Ultimately, may you always be found faithful in the Master's service.

Appendix

Chapter 1: Madrid

1.	"A que precio?" he asked.	At what price?
2.	“Barato," I replied in Spanish.	Cheap.
3.	"Como se llama?" he asked.	What is your name?
4.	“Me llamo Faye," I replied.	My name is Faye.
5.	"Espero que te pasas un buen tiempo a Madrid," he replied.	I hope you have a good time in Madrid.
6.	"Gracias!"	Thanks.
7.	"Buenos tardes, señoritas," said the landlord who greeted us at the stairs.	Good afternoon.
8.	"Con mucho gusto.”	Nice meeting you.
9.	"Hasta luego. Tengo que ir al bano."	Good-bye. I have to go to the bathroom.
10.	"huevos revueltos"	scrambled eggs
11.	“pasteleria”	Spanish bakery

Chapter 2: The Encounter

1.	Spanish *sangria*: popular Spanish beverage.	Most cafés in Spain serve it with meals.
2.	*Como estas*?" I replied.	How are you?
3.	"*Muy bueno*," he said.	Very good.
4.	“*Hola, mi nombre es Brian*,” he said in a casual voice.	Hi, my name is Brian.
5.	"Quien es?"	Who is'this?
6.	"Soy Faye. Esta Daniel?" I asked.	This is Faye. Is Daniel there?
7.	"Si, espera un momentito."	Yes, wait a moment.

8.	When Daniel came to the phone he said, "*Hola, soy Daniel.*"	Hi Faye, this is Daniel.
9.	"*Si*," he replied.	Yes.

Chapter 3: 'Los Ninos de Dios" (*The Children of God*)

1.	"Puedo tener sopa para el bano?"	Can I have soup for the bathroom?
2.	"*Oh, tu quieres jabon para el bano*,"Señora Martinez answered.	Oh, you want soap for the bathroom.
3.	"*Yo no se*," she replied bashfully.	I don't know.
4.	"*Espero que si*," I said as we walked briskly out of the front door of the apartment building.	I hope so.
5.	"Faye, *su amigo esta aqui*," Señora Martinez said.	Faye, your friend is here.
6.	"Por favor."	Please.

Chapter 4: Paris

1.	Waking, I heard a voice shouting, "*Nous sommes arrivé*!"	We have arrived.
2.	"*Como estas*?" I asked.	How are you?
3.	"*Estoy bien*," he answered.	I am fine.
4.	"*Me encanta con Paris*," I said.	I am enchanted with Paris.
5.	"*Esta bien*," I said as we took off.	That's good.
6.	We call ourselves "*Les Enfants de Dieu*."	The Children of God.

Endnotes

Introduction

1. Roberts, Richard. *The God of a Second Chance.*(Richard Roberts, 1985), p. 11

Chapter 6: Rambuteau

1 "Die Daily," ML 182, pars. 4-5

2 "Fighters," ML 551

Chapter 8 – The Struggle Within

1. Harrison, Buddy, *Dr. Doyle Hear, See, Do.* (Tulsa, Oklahoma: Harrison House Inc., 1985), p. 53
2. Hagin, Kenneth. *How You Can Be Led by The Spirit of God.* (Kenneth Hagin Ministries, 1986), p.23
3. Harrison, Buddy. (1985, 45)
4. Davis, Deborah. *The Children of God: The Inside Story.* (Grand Rapids, MI: Zondervan 1984), p. 189-190
5. Ibid. p. 191
6. Brogan, Frankie Fonde. *The Snare of the Fowler.* (Lincoln, Virginia: Chosen Books, 1982), p. 6-7
7. Hagin, Kenneth. (1986, 25)
8. Ibid. p. 121
9. Ibid. p. 122

Chapter 9: The Tender Years

1. Copeland, Gloria, *God's Will for You.* (Fort Worth, TX: Kenneth Copeland Publications, 1972), p. 16
2. Ibid., p. 19
3. Ibid., p. 21
4. Ibid. p. 22

Chapter 16: Not My Kid

1. Davis, Deborah. (1984, 144)
2. Ibid., p. 101
3. Hagin, Kenneth. (1986, 121)
4. Davis, Deborah. (1984, 99)
5. Ibid. p. 146

Chapter 17: The Cult Influence

1. Davis, Deborah. (1984, p. 14)
2. Ibid, p. 123
3. Love, James Dr. *The Gathering Place.* (Grand Rapids, MI: Zondervan, 2002), p. 41
4. Davis, Deborah. (1984, 202-203)
5. Enroth, Ronald and Melton, J. Gordon. *Why Cults Succeed Where The Church Fails*. (Elgin, Illinois: Brethren Press, 1985), p. 47
6. Ibid. p 54
7. Davis, Deborah. (1984, 127)
8. Ibid. p. 197
9. Warren, Rick. *The Purpose Driven Life*. (Grand Rapids, MI: Zondervan, 2002), p. 79
10. Ibid. p. 201

Chapter 19: There is Life After the Cult

1. Enroth, Ronald M. and Melton, J. Gordon. (1985, 53)
2. Ibid. p. 53
3. Ibid. p. 54
4. Ibid. p. 54
5. Davis, Deborah. (1984, 127)
6. Ibid. p. 139

Chapter 20: Politics and the Church

1. Meeks, M. Douglas. *God the Economist.* (Minneapolis: Fortress Press, 1989), p. 77
2. MacNutt, Francis. *Healing.* (Notre Dame, IN: Ave Maria Press, 1974), p.133-134

3. Meeks, M. Douglas. (1989, 77)
4. Black, Barry. *From the Hood to the Hill.* (Nashville, TN: Thomas Nelson, Inc., 2006), p. 19-21

Chapter 21: When God Calls

1. Leonce, Peter Dr. *Prayer Will Knock it Down, But Praise Will* Knock *it Out.* (Arima, Trinidad: Karen Boyce, 2003), p. 52
2. Ibid. p. 30
3. Hill, Napoleon. *Think and Grow Rich.* (New York: Fawcett, 1988), p.21
4. Hill, Napoleon. (1988, 208)
5. Ibid. 229

Chapter 22: Women and the Twenty-First Century

1. Clinton, Hillary Rodham. *Living History.* New York: (Simon & Schuster, 2003), p. 305
2. Jepsen, Dee. *Women Beyond Equal Rights.* (Texas: Crescendo Corporation, 1984), p. 32
3. Brown, Angela. *When All the Doors Close, Look to the Windows.* (Pennsylvania: Dorrance Publishing Company, 1996), p. 29-30
4. Jessup, Carolyn. *ESCAPE.* (New York: Broadway Books, 2007), pg. 214-215
5. Ibid. pg. 347
6. Ibid. pg. 385

CPSIA information can be obtained at www.ICGtesting.com
Printed in the USA
LVOW07s2200260515

440025LV00001B/156/P